"... AND THE HITS JUST KEEP ON COMIN'"

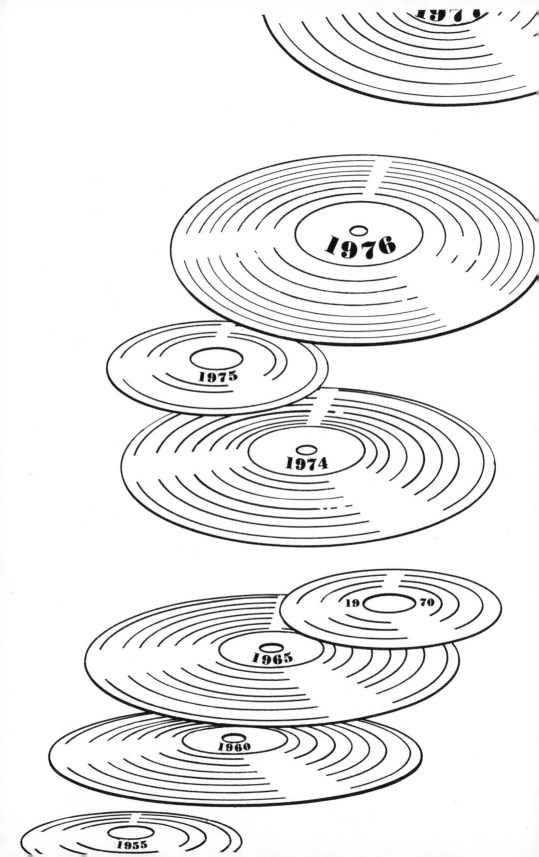

"...AND THE HITS JUST KEEP ON COMIN'"

PETER E. BERRY
("The Flying Dutchman")

SYRACUSE UNIVERSITY PRESS   1977

Copyright © 1977 by Syracuse University Press
Syracuse, New York 13210

All Rights Reserved
First Edition

Library of Congress Cataloging in Publication Data

Berry, Peter E
    ". . . and the hits just keep on comin' ".

    Discography: p.
    1. Music, Popular (Songs, etc.)–United States–
Discography. 2. Music, Popular (Songs, etc.)–United
States–Chronology. I. Title.
ML156.4.P6B47   784'.0973   76-48921
ISBN 0-8156-0134-4
ISBN 0-8156-0135-2 pkb.

Manufactured in the United States of America

To Betty, who lost her kitchen table for almost six months.

CONTENTS

FOREWORD

Strange! I opened the mail this morning, and—lo and behold—there is a manuscript, bound in black. Unusual? No. Shall I look at it? It's probably the sweat and toil of some eager songwriter hoping I can get his efforts on to wax. Might as well! There could be another "Stardust" in here.

I'll be damned, it's from Dutch. Since when is he writing songs? Jokes, maybe; songs, no!

That's the way it was about a week ago, when, amid a very busy week that would take me from Philly to New York on one of those "record offers" that either materialize or vaporize, I sat on the Metroliner digging the doings of the Flying Dutchman. ". . . And the Hits Just Keep On Coming' " made that ninety-odd-mile journey a trip into the very guts of my past. Dutch—if you call him Pete, he rarely turns around—has stuffed twenty-two years of "pop culture" into a book that I hope eventually gets into pocket-size so I can keep it handy for those musical arguments that always develop in Philly taverns.

I first met Pete Berry in 1965, when my manager Alan White—a former DJ, and today a discotheque innovator—dragged me into the hinterlands of North Carolina for a rock show in Winston-Salem, where we stayed at one of those look-alike Quality Inns and, in a three-day "cram session," taught some local musicians the arrangements to my "vast" repertoire, managed to find all the local "brown bag" joints, and found out what the Flying Dutchman was all about. Honestly? Okay. He was the most opinionated individual I ever met. This radio "music director" could tell me the release date of my first Decca disk, and then, in the next breath, inform me that unfortunately my "timing" was lousy. He was right, sure, but who needed that from an absolute stranger.

Well, the Flying Dutchman isn't a stranger anymore. It's been more than a decade since our first meeting—me, the quiet kid from Philly, and Dutch, the loud kid from almost everywhere. No wonder he knows so much about records; he played them in at least a dozen different states. I can't keep track of the cities, towns, and burgs—Milwaukee, Richmond, New Haven, Memphis, Baltimore, Syracuse, Pittsfield, Providence, Denver—and those are the ones I know about.

The Flying Dutchman and Len Barry go together like peas in a pod, but don't get the idea we're related. Oh, we do relate. In the fifties, I was a kid singing on the streets of South Philly and Dutch was giving away DJ sample records on the streets of Albany, New York. And we were both crazy about the Platters! By the sixties, I was losing a "Grammy" award by inches while Dutch was losing the Billboard "Disc Jockey of the Year" award by the centimeters of an audition tape. In the seventies, as I sat down and wrote a barrelful of songs, Dutch was writing one hell of a good book on the subject that has made both of our lives fun—music. That's our common denominator, baby, MUSIC.

If you want the facts, if you want the background, if you want some opinions that go somewhere, along with some laughs and heartbreaks, start reading.

Len Barry

(Len Barry, today a writer-producer living in Philadelphia, was the well-known lead singer of The Dovells, a "Grammy Award" nominee for his self-penned smash "1-2-3," and writer-producer of the Electric Indian's 1969 top ten recording of "Keem-O-Sabe.")

INTRODUCTION

My wife claims that my massive interest in statistics is influenced by the "stars"—the fact that I am a "Virgo" indicates to her that I am critically and analytically possessed by perfectionist traits. I sincerely doubt this, not being moved to superstition; but, I admit, something has compelled me to keep stacks of trivial data in neat files throughout the years.

My first awareness of the immense enjoyment one receives from the keeping of statistical records was in the late forties when, as a child, I watched my father create a wonderfully accurate, day-by-day journal of the batting averages of each member of the Boston Red Sox. At any given moment, Dad could render to a neighbor intriguing "stats" about Ted Williams, Johnny Pesky, and Bobby Doerr, baseball giants of their day. It wasn't long before my father's hobby influenced me.

During the bitter Korean conflict, I scanned the daily Boston newspapers for tidbits of national security—American-Chinese troop strengths, tank supremacies, and comparative airplane power. In a purple scrapbook I cataloged this treasury of information and became—or at least considered myself—an expert on the relative merits of the Russian "T-34" tank as opposed to our less-maneuverable Patton tank. When President Eisenhower administered the truce negotiations at Panmunjom, my interests rapidly switched to a new subject, one that has held my interest for the past twenty-five years—popular music.

By 1954—greatly influenced by television's "Hit Parade," Martin Bloch's radio show "The Make-Believe Ballroom," and other radio programs that I picked up late at night on my tube-filled Philco portable—I approached my hometown radio station, WGAW in Gardner, Massachusetts, and convinced the program director that he should allow me to broadcast the ten most popular songs at our local high school. Every Saturday morning for the next two years, with a voice that reminded listeners of a cricket, I programmed the results of my teen survey. I remember weeks when songs like Mario Lanza's "Drink, Drink, Drink" were number one, and weeks when the emerging rock songs like "Ain't That a Shame" by Pat Boone were survey winners.

By 1956, with few credentials, I entered commercial radio on a full-time basis, and for the next twenty years I conducted a love affair with the popular music scene, weekly subscribing to the well-known trade magazines—*Billboard, Cashbox, Radio and Records,* and *Record World.* Each year, as New Year's Eve approached, I calculated year-end "top fifty" charts, composed of the year's biggest hit songs. These, unchanged, are what you will find at the end of each chapter of this book. Each is a blending of facts gathered from the abovementioned trades, year-end reports issued by the music newsletters—George Lorenz's "Behind The Scenes," Bill Gavin's "The Gavin Report," Dick Reuss' "Southern Music Survey," and Bob Hamilton's "The Hamilton Report," the individual playlists and weekly top-forty charts released by the radio stations where I was employed, and from the others that would share their "wealth."

Compiling a music survey is a subjective activity, since there can be no totally accurate poll of public taste. Trade magazine surveys are a combination of various information gleaned from record shops, wholesalers, discotheques, radio stations, and, in some cases, juke-box operators. Newsletters are greatly influenced by self-serving factors: their editors spend their days making telephone calls to record promotion people who tend to overestimate the influence of their own products. Radio station playlists are compiled in various manners involving the record sales in local shops, requests received weekly from listeners, and, all too often, the "gut feelings" of overzealous music directors. By investigating all these sources at year's end, one paints a fairly accurate portrait of the music landscape, but the end product is still extremely subjective.

Examples of discrepancies in music surveys indicate how difficult it is to make a definitive decision. In 1965 the "trades" announced different number-one songs for that year, from Sam the Sham's "Wooly Bully" to the Supremes' "Back in My Arms Again"; my own painstaking compilation of numerous sources resulted in "I Can't Help Myself" by the Four Tops emerging as the year's most popular song, yet there is room for conjecture. Other years, like 1962, find statisticians in total agreement, indicating Chubby Checker's "The Twist" the universally accepted winner.

In 1975, as program director of radio station WNDR in Syracuse, New York, I set out to construct—from scratch—a Golden Oldie Library comprising the major hits of past years. Out came my well-preserved surveys of years gone by, and created was the germ of an idea that has become this book.

Realizing that I required a list of number-one songs for every week of the past twenty-two years, I began my research and quickly learned how difficult and expensive it can be to trace this kind of information. Eventually, from the Research Department of *Billboard Magazine,* came the information that allowed me to complete the listings that can be found in each of the following chapters.

What fun it is to scan these chart toppers! Memories of "lost" incidents flash across the conscious mind as one peruses this history of one thousand, one hundred and thirty-three weeks, through October 15, 1976. For instance, when Elvis' "Heartbreak Hotel" was number one in the nation in 1956, I can fondly remember holding hands with Judy Donovan, rendering quarters into a jukebox at the Woodland Spa; when "Heartaches by the Number" by Guy Mitchell was "numero uno" for two weeks in late 1959, I can recall hitch-hiking from Albany, New York, to Los Angeles, California, on a short-but-eventful vacation; and when the BoxTops' "The Letter" achieved number one for four weeks in 1967, I remember winning a contract dispute with a Winston-Salem, North Carolina, radio station. You can do the same sort of reminiscing, my friend—glance at this parade of number-one hits and conjure up some great memories: "I remember when that was a hit, I was . . ."; it's that easy.

Each of the accompanying chapters contains an inventory of the top-five most influential artists of the year. These are of my choosing; the results, once again, are subjective. The awards are based on how many hits these individuals and groups issued, how many total records they sold, and how much response they garnered from my radio audiences. Regional influences are evident as my gypsy-like career carried me to: WGAW, Gardner, Massachusetts (1954); WBRU and WHIM, Providence, Rhode Island (1955-56); WCAT, Athol, Massachusetts (1956); WBRK, Pittsfield, Massachusetts (1957); WABY, Albany, New York (1957-63); WPET, Greensboro, North Carolina, and WBLK, Buffalo, New York (1964), WTOB, Winston-Salem, North Carolina (1965-68), WLEE, Richmond, Virginia, and WAVZ, New Haven, Connecticut (1969); WRIT, Milwaukee, Wisconsin, and WMPS, Memphis, Tennessee (1970); WFBR, Baltimore, Maryland (1971-73), WNDR, Syracuse, New York (1974-76); and KLZ, Denver, Colorado (1976). During this mobile twenty-two year period, I was a music director six times and a program director four times. I also managed to produce, or be involved in the release of, eight records—all notable failures. They varied from folk songs like "Thirty Eight Slug" to Elvis imitations like "Blue Suede Shoes" to hard-rock items like "Pain" by the Novas Nine—the last of these songs had the distinction of reaching the "very bottom" of a trade magazine popularity survey for one week in 1968. During this same period, I had two brief "tide-me-over" jobs, laboring for two record distributors, the ill-fated Atlas Company in Albany and the highly-regarded Rosen's in Philadelphia. No doubt about it, I loved popular music and still do.

As the format of this book developed, I discovered that such important proclamations as Oscar winners and Grammy winners were difficult to trace. Most almanacs tabulate the yearly Oscar recipients in the well-known acting departments but rarely register the "song of the year." A long-distance call to the Academy of Motion Picture Arts and Sciences on the West Coast, and a delightful conversation with a cooperative receptionist, gave me this information for publication. The Grammys were initiated in 1958, but the periodicals which chronicle the results are now out of print. A diligent search through the microfilm section of the Syracuse Public Library gave me only a partial list of these award winners; thus, another call to the National Academy of Recording Arts and Sciences brought me an information-packed booklet in the mail, from which I present the three major category winners of each year.

All the preceding intelligence is bathed in that subjectivity that I have mentioned. Year-end surveys are compiled from numerous conflicting sources; leading artists of each year are personally selected; weekly number-one songs are attained from so many different sources that they vary from publication to publication; Academy Award winning tunes are selected by peer groups, as are the Grammy winners. The only accurate barometer of a song's value is its commercial merit—that is why I have included in the discography of this book the "audited" Gold Records, certified by the Recording Industry Association of America (RIAA). A three-day weekend in New York City led me to this gold mine of informational wealth. The RIAA started awarding "gold" certification in 1958, so many earlier recordings did not receive official "gold" status. In the first ten years of RIAA endeavor, they were cautious in giving their stamp of approval—most awards went to long-established labels. By the late sixties, they became reasonably representative of the entire music industry—the exceptions are the Detroit Motown—Tamla labels, never audited. Prior to that, record companies ballyhooed their own "gold" achievements. In fact, RCA Victor has claimed over seventy million sellers for Elvis Presley; RIAA has awarded him only twenty-eight million, placing him behind the Beatles.

I pondered many weeks before attempting the gargantuan chore of adding a large discography to the end of this volume. I decided that it was a must. How many times in my career I have wished I might recall when a particular composition achieved its greatest success, and have been unable to do so. When it comes to the chronology of a song, if you ask three people, you will get three different answers. Some tunes are released more than once ("Louie, Louie," "The Twist," and "Nights in White Satin" are examples); some songs gain popularity one year and sustain their acceptance in the next year ("I

Feel Fine," "That's the Way I Like It"); some releases are immensely popular in one region of the country but wait months, or even years, to acquire hit stature in other regions ("Sweet Pea"); and other songs are released one year, become hits in the next, and pass the million mark at a much later period ("Battle Of New Orleans").

Adding to this statisticians' nightmare some disks which sell a million copies never make it to the national top ten, because most surveys are based on weekly trends and not the over-all sales figures. Some songs are what disk jockeys call "turntable hits," album selections that are not released as singles until a later date ("Smoke On the Water")—some never become singles ("Stairway to Heaven").

My discography attempts to index alphabetically the leading hits and "gold" LPs of the major artists and orient them to the calendar of man—the selections are based on my own landscape-view of the music scene. Your own personal favorite may be missing, but I had to draw a bottom-line somewhere, or things would get completely out of hand. As I traced the chronology of various hits, if I possessed a reliable record chart indicating a song's period of immense popularity, I cataloged that release and the date of its greatest achievement; if I didn't locate it on a chart and felt that it still needed listing, I noted the year of its greatest popularity; and in the case of those that defy annotation, I turned to the "majority opinion" of those people—numerous as they are—that assisted me in tracing each song's history. These nostalgia buffs ran the gamut from radio announcer to record company personnel, and they are listed at the end of this book. In a small percentage of cases, I have avoided dating selections because I realized that "no date" is better than one that will invariably cause argument ("Rudolph, the Red-Nosed Reindeer").

In the discography I have not posted the record labels of any artist; most "oldies" and standards have been rereleased under new banners. To stipulate any specific company is useless to the consumer in most instances. Sometimes, these recordings have been discontinued or are out of print—the latest label information, and availability, can be discerned in most record shops by referring to the cumbersome and swollen pages of the ever-changing "Phono-Log," a publication that is updated every month or so.

Finally, the text of this book is a compilation of the trends, fads, and directions through which the "pop" music industry has journeyed in the past two decades. From Bill Haley's pioneering efforts in the mid-fifties to the emergence of "disco" in the mid-seventies, here are the personal reflections of a disc jockey who has been a voyeur of the marvelous and mysterious events that have rapidly transpired. I once said that I loved all forms of music, from "opera" to "pop," with one noted exception—the polka. The recording "In Heaven There Is No Beer" changed my mind; I even like a good "Polish-prance." Music is fun. You can talk and argue about it for hours.

The popular idiom reflects society's deepest conflicts: from love to politics, from the blue to the joyous, from the ridiculous to the sublime. "Pop" music—top forty, if you like— is the folk song of the fleeting moment.

The first ditty I remember singing as a child is "Don't Sit Under the Apple Tree"; it began my romantic involvement with music. Just yesterday, I fell head-over-heels in love with the lanky Emmy Lou Harris and her recordings in the field of "progressive country." Between these two puppy loves I have experienced a period of much happiness, attained from my own personal response to "pop" music. It has been a marriage that can never end in "D-I-V-O-R-C-E," so help me, Tammy Wynette.

Denver, Colorado   Peter E. Berry

Fall 1976   ("The Flying Dutchman")

"... AND THE HITS JUST KEEP ON COMIN'"

The Rimshot Heard 'Round The World 1955

The roots of rock & roll music reach back to the late forties and early fifties when two musical impulses, country & western and rhythm & blues, collided. In those formative years we knew them popularly as "hillbilly" and "race" music; in one corner Hank Williams, Jimmy Rodgers, and the Carter Family and their Nashville brethren made inroads into the pop scene when innumerable top artists recorded their material, and in the other, Amos Milburn, Fats Domino, Johnny Otis, and dozens of comrades hammered out a new beat that caught the fancy of scores of avid youngsters. Here was the fuel to power a new vehicle, and the mass of American youth needed but one spark to ignite their enthusiasm.

In 1952, a vocal-instrumental group that combined the simplicity of c&w and the throb of r&b, Bill Haley's Saddlemen, created that initial spark. Almost immediately changing their name to Bill Haley and the Comets, they signed a contract with the small but innovative Essex label. Some of the Comets' early treasures included "We're Going To Rock This Joint Tonight," "Rock-A-Beatin' Boogie," and "Crazy, Man, Crazy." By 1954, these hard-driving efforts received some radio airplay, as did other white groups' recordings, like the Crewcuts cover version of the Chord's "Sh-Boom," instilling a new rhythm to pop music and sneaking almost unnoticed on to the trade magazines' music charts.

Amid these early outings, Alan Freed, a Cleveland disc jockey and leading exponent of the new sound, seized upon a lyric line from a Bill Haley record and coined the phrase "rock & roll." Al-

1

though "Tin Pan Alley" didn't grasp what was happening, other disc jockeys in the larger cities filled the evening ether with the vibrations of this infectious beat. A change was imminent in popular music, and the first cannonade was about to be fired.

Meanwhile, the popular hits of 1955 appeared similar to the pap of the preceding years as the Chordettes harmonized "Mr. Sandman" to number-one in the nation, Bill Hayes and Fess Parker extolled the virtues of frontier existence in "The Ballad Of Davy Crockett," and Perez Prado scored a Latin victory with his "Cherry Pink And Apple Blossom White." The Fontane Sisters borrowed from an r&b group, the Charms, and "Hearts of Stone" reached the top position on television's "Hit Parade," but, despite this, the "real thing" remained in the wings.

Decca Records signed Bill Haley and the Comets in 1954, and two of their releases sold relatively well in the record shops: "Shake, Rattle & Roll" and "Rock Around the Clock." The record company promotion men realized that coast-to-coast exposure was needed for the Comets' product, and the breakthrough came in the early summer of '55. Caught up in the new awareness trend in motion pictures, tides of teenagers stood in line for hours to view Glenn Ford, representing the establishment, and Sidney Poitier, allied with delinquency, collide head-to-head in the controversial "Blackboard Jungle."

The opening scene of this movie changed the American music landscape for the next twenty-odd years. Glenn Ford, starring as a new-wave teacher in a New York City school, confronted his class of ill-bred students in their initial combat. Stepping off a bus and walking through a depressing schoolyard of mingling and angry teens, he entered a new world, and with him, rock & roll came to class that day. With a reverberating rimshot and "One o'clock, two o'clock, three o'clock rock," the musical wave of the future came to life.

American youth had heard its first rock commercial song, in a movie, no less; thousands of teens left their local movie houses that day with all intentions to purchase the record "Rock Around the Clock" or to request it on their favorite radio station. Around the nation, radio station music directors dusted off copies of the record that were a year old, some copies imprinted on the already defunct 78 rpm disc.

2

"Rock Around the Clock's" unique opening rimshot and elementary lyrics are paltry by today's standards, but these simple ingredients, blended by mere chance in some recording studio, soon became the national anthem of young America. "Rock Around the Clock" eventually became the best-selling popular song of all-time, surpassed only by a holiday classic, Bing Crosby's "White Christmas." Though the unofficial figures may be slightly inflated, "Rock Around the Clock" has sold over twenty-five million vinyl copies. This rock & roll "standard" has been celebrated in three movies: "Blackboard Jungle," launching its success; "Rock Around the Clock," inspired by the song; and "American Graffiti," dedicated to the kids who bought the record in the first place. By the late sixties, the English would revive the song again, and it soared to number-one on the charts; and again, in the seventies, "Rock Around the Clock" discovered new life as the first theme song for the television show, "Happy Days."

Bill Haley's opening rimshot exploded round the world and is still echoing, paving the way for Elvis, the Beatles, and hundreds of other aspiring artists who make rock & roll music one of America's leading exports to the peoples of the world, for better or for worse.

1. "Rock Around the Clock," Bill Haley & The Comets
2. "Ballad Of Davy Crockett," Bill Hayes
3. "Cherry Pink & Apple Blossom White," Perez Prado
4. "Melody Of Love," Billy Vaughn
5. "Yellow Rose of Texas," Mitch Miller
6. "Ain't That a Shame," Pat Boone
7. "Sincerely," McGuire Sisters
8. "Unchained Melody," Al Hibbler/Les Baxter
9. "Crazy Otto Medley," Johnny Maddox
10. "Mr. Sandman," Chordettes
11. "Cry Me a River," Julie London
12. "Tweedle Dee," Georgia Gibbs
13. "I Hear You Knockin'," Gale Storm
14. "Only You," The Platters
15. "Learnin' The Blues," Frank Sinatra
16. "Hearts of Stone," Fontane Sisters
17. "Teach Me Tonight," DeCastro Sisters
18. "Tutti Fruiti," Pat Boone
19. "Sixteen Tons," Tennessee Ernie Ford
20. "Moments To Remember," Four Lads
21. "Earth Angel," Penguins
22. "Love Is a Many-Splendored Thing," Four Aces
23. "Autumn Leaves," Roger Williams
24. "Pledging My Love," Johnny Ace
25. "Dungaree Doll," Eddie Fisher
26. "No Not Much," Four Lads
27. "It's Almost Tomorrow," Dream Weavers
28. "Dance with Me Henry," Georgia Gibbs
29. "It's a Sin To Tell a Lie," Something Smith & Redheads
30. "Let Me Go, Lover," Joan Weber
31. "Darling Je Vous Aime Beaucoup," Nat King Cole
32. "How Important Can It Be," Joni James
33. "Shifting Whispering Sands," Billy Vaughn

34. "Bo Diddley," Bo Diddley
35. "Go On with the Wedding," Patti Page
36. "Heart," Four Aces
37. "Story Untold," Nutmegs
38. "Ko Ko Mo," Perry Como
39. "Black Denim Trousers," Cheers
40. "Maybellene," Chuck Berry
41. "Wake the Town & Tell the People," Les Baxter
42. "Close Your Eyes," Five Keys
43. "Most Of All," Don Cornell
44. "I've Got A Woman," Ray Charles
45. "Love & Marriage," Dinah Shore
46. "When You Dance," Turbans
47. "Seventeen," Boyd Bennett
48. "I Want You to Be My Baby," Lillian Briggs
49. "Speedo," Cadillacs
50. "That's All I Want from You," Jaye P. Morgan

Number-One Songs of '55 *(Cashbox)*

"Mr. Sandman" (3), Chordettes
"Let Me Go Lover" (2), Joan Weber
"Hearts of Stone" (1), Fontane Sisters
"Sincerely" (6), McGuire Sisters
"Ballad Of Davy Crockett" (5), Bill Hayes
"Cherry Pink & Apple Blossom White" (10), Perez Prado
"Rock Around the Clock" (8), Bill Haley & The Comets
"Yellow Rose Of Texas" (6), Mitch Miller
"Love Is a Many-Splendored Thing" (2), Four Aces
"Autumn Leaves" (4), Roger Williams
"Sixteen Tons" (7), Tennessee Ernie Ford

Most Significant Artists of '55

Bill Haley & The Comets
Pat Boone
Perez Prado
Four Aces
Platters

Academy Award (Oscar) Winner of '55

"Love Is A Many-Splendored Thing"
   from *Love Is A Many-Splendored Thing*
Major recording: Four Aces

Thank You, Dorsey Brothers! 1956

The awe-inspiring notables linked to Elvis Presley are numerous, but, invariably, the credit for his discovery is lodged posthumously in the tomb of Ed Sullivan. Indeed, Ed was the driving force that catapulted the hip-shaking talents of the lad from Mississippi into a national Sunday night viewing habit, an occurence that ofttimes split family loyalties asunder. While son and daughter raved about the multi-talents of the minstrel with the crooked lip, Mom and Dad decried the immorality of his pumping pelvis. Sullivan aided and abetted this confrontation to such an extent that he is forever distinguished with the unearthing of Elvis. Not true!

Sadly, the real entrepreneurs and treasure seekers are given a backseat. It was Sam Phillips of Sun Records who took a former truck driver and converted his country-oriented singing into the then-popular Carl Perkins-style of "Blue Suede Shoes." A promotional genius, Colonel Parker, who spotted writing before it was on the wall, guaranteed that the infant prince of rock & roll received the adulation, and accompanying remuneration, that he deserved. Concert promoters, from Winston-Salem, North Carolina, to Hartford, Connecticut, risked the smirks of their colleagues and booked this then-unknown into theaters and stadiums. Executives at RCA Victor made a "random study" decision to table the universally accepted talents of Eddie Fisher and collectively placed their eggs in one basket. Elvis Presley joined Victor in 1956, and his career mushroomed to yet-unheard of proportions.

Elvis' road to a "pot of gold" lay ahead in the relatively

young world of television. In the late spring of 1956, and on into the summer months, Jackie Gleason's summer replacements, the Dorsey Brothers, showcased the pulsating rhythms of the unknown tornado from the yet-unheralded Memphis, Tennessee.

The first time I caught Elvis in action was during a final-exam break at Brown University, a sedate Ivy League school in Providence, Rhode Island. Faunce House, the recreation center of the school, housed a movie theater and student lounge, with pool tables, snack bar, and television set. One Saturday evening, depressed by the tedium of a three-hour Spanish final exam, I draped my youthful, but weary bones on a leather lounger to watch the tube.

"And now, by popular demand, the Dorsey Brothers present the new, nationwide rage, for his second straight week, Elvis Presley!"

Elvis Presley? Who the hell and what the hell was an "Elvis"? (SFX: general derision and cat calls.)

"Well, it's one for the money and two for the show, Three to get ready, and four to go!"

Good Lord! The place went insane. (SFX: pandemonium.)

"I got a woman, sweet as she can be . . ."

Whatever this character on television was doing, I was sure of one thing: it relieved fatigue faster than three back-to-back "Road Runner" cartoons; the tensions of scholasticism melted into the night.

"Well, it's Saturday night and I just got paid . . ."

The adulation created by Elvis that evening would not subside for another decade, until a similar performance by four British lads in 1964. From the leather-jacketed motorcycle set to the fraternal order of Ivy Leaguers, we had chosen a national representative that night. Elvis beat the hell out of Jimmy Dean and his "look-alike" peers; this greasy-haired kid not only pouted and sneered, but, to boot, he cocked his right leg and fired from a jolting hip!

And to everyone's amazement, it was all coming down with the Dorsey Brothers. Was this the same Tommy Dorsey that had taken a relatively unpolished Frank Sinatra from the Harry James gang in the forties and shaped him into the future bobby soxers' delight? Once was magnificent; twice was sheer genius. Tragically, before 1956 ended, Tommy Dorsey passed away, but not before he bonded his name with the coming storm. Indeed, Ed Sullivan saturated the nation's living rooms with the sights and sounds of Elvis in the fall of 1956, but he could never claim he created this ''musical giant'', as he would not create the initial excitement and mania over the latterday Liverpudlians. Ed Sullivan would just count the change and watch his Trendex rise.

Thank you, Dorsey Brothers; you made a congress of teens ecstatic and a bevy of record dealers rich.

1. "Don't Be Cruel"/"Hound Dog," Elvis Presley
2. "The Great Pretender," Platters
3. "Heartbreak Hotel," Elvis Presley
4. "My Prayer," Platters
5. "The Wayward Wind," Gogi Grant
6. "Whatever Will Be, Will Be," Doris Day
7. "Lisbon Antigua," Nelson Riddle
8. "Canadian Sunset," Hugo Winterhalter
9. "Honky Tonk Part II," Bill Doggett
10. "Canadian Sunset," Andy Williams
11. "Moonglow & the Theme From *Picnic*," Morris Stoloff
12. "Poor People of Paris," Les Baxter
13. "Rock & Roll Waltz," Kay Starr
14. "In the Still of the Night," Five Satins
15. "Hot Digitty," Perry Como
16. "Blue Suede Shoes," Carl Perkins/Elvis Presley
17. "I Want You, I Need You, I Love You," Elvis Presley
18. "I'm In Love Again," Fats Domino
19. "Why Do Fools Fall in Love," Frankie Lymon & The Teenagers
20. "I Almost Lost My Mind," Pat Boone
21. "Tonight You Belong to Me," Patience & Prudence
22. "Green Door," Jim Lowe
23. "Blue Monday," Fats Domino
24. "Allegheny Moon," Patti Page
25. "Ivory Tower," Cathy Carr
26. "Just Walking in the Rain," Johnnie Ray
27. "Love Me Tender," Elvis Presley
28. "See You Later Alligator," Bill Haley & The Comets
29. "Band Of Gold," Don Cherry
30. "True Love," Bing Crosby & Grace Kelly
31. "Standing on the Corner," Four Lads
32. "The Magic Touch," Platters
33. "Blueberry Hill," Fats Domino

10

34. "I'll Be Home," Pat Boone
35. "A Tear Fell," Teresa Brewer
36. "The Flying Saucer," Buchanan & Goodman
37. "The Fool," Sanford Clark
38. "Song For *A Summer's Night*," Mitch Miller
39. "Friendly Persuasion," Pat Boone
40. "Singing the Blues," Guy Mitchell
41. "On the Street Where You Live," Vic Damone
42. "Eddie My Love," Teen Queens
43. "More," Perry Como
44. "Memories Are Made of This," Dean Martin
45. "After the Lights Go Down Low," Al Hibbler
46. "A Rose & a Baby Ruth," George Hamilton IV
47. "Since I Met You Baby," Ivory Joe Hunter
48. "Roll Over Beethoven," Chuck Berry
49. "Jamaica Farewell," Harry Belafonte
50. "Love Is Strange," Mickey & Sylvia

Number-One Songs of '56 *(Cashbox)*

"Sixteen Tons" (1), Tennessee Ernie Ford
"Memories Are Made of This" (5), Dean Martin
"Rock & Roll Waltz" (1), Kay Starr
"Lisbon Antigua" (4), Nelson Riddle
"Poor People of Paris" (4), Les Baxter
"Heartbreak Hotel" (7), Elvis Presley
"Wayward Wind" (6), Gogi Grant
"I Want You, I Need You, I Love You" (1), Elvis Presley
"My Prayer" (2), Platters
"Don't Be Cruel"/"Hound Dog" (11), Elvis Presley
"Love Me Tender" (5), Elvis Presley
"Singing The Blues" (4), Guy Mitchell

Most Significant Artists of '56

Elvis Presley
Platters
Fats Domino
Pat Boone
Chuck Berry

Academy Award (Oscar) Winner of '56

"Whatever Will Be, Will Be"
    from *The Man Who Knew Too Much*

Major recording: Doris Day

A Standard is Set—Buddy Holly, 1936–59

1957

Never was a more unlikely candidate for stardom unearthed than the "late and great" Buddy Holly. Born in Lubbock, Texas, Buddy was raised on a diet of Hank Williams' ballads and the other country stock of the day. His early vocal efforts, magnified by his lackluster appearance and his "scholarly" pair of hornrimmed glasses, showed little if any promise. His ability to imitate indicated a strong reverential regard for Elvis and an obvious respect for the stylings of Bill Haley and The Comets. Yet, a rock & roll first, Buddy's unique "uh-uh-oh," dominated his vocals and was the distinction that made him immensely popular.

Holly did not bound on to the rock scene as had many of his contemporaries like Jerry Lee Lewis and Chuck Berry; he was an integral part of the widely acclaimed group, the Crickets. In essence, he was the Crickets. Their first national hit, "That'll Be the Day," became a number-one song for a single week in the summer of 1957. (He would never again top the charts in his abbreviated career.) Decca Records assigned the Crickets to their rock & roll label, Brunswick; and, because of prior contract commitments to Buddy, they would assign him to their monetarily successful subsidiary, Coral, famous for artists like the McGuire Sisters, Teresa Brewer, and Alan Dale. Buddy's first solo effort to reach the top forty was "Peggy Sue," in which his "hiccuping" phraseology prevailed.

Why then, if Buddy Holly was never an extraordinary teenage idol or even a consistently chart-topping artist, has his name been associated with the rock & roll legend? Three things: (1) he proved conclusively that almost any kid off the street with guitar, talent, and desire could attain recognition in the new mode of music that had swept the country; (2) his musical presentation was simplicity itself, with little or no gimmicky augmentation that saturated the music industry in the late fifties and early sixties; and (3), ironically, he died at the height of his career.

Near the town of Mason City, Iowa, Buddy, Ritchie Valens, and J. P. Richardson (the Big Bopper), plummeted to earth in a private plane, rented to fly them to a rock concert. It was February 3, 1959. Singer Don McClean later eulogized that tragic date as "the day the music died"; and, with some governmental assistance, early rock & roll did die within a year.

By 1960, Congress investigated the entire structure of the music industry; broadcast titans like Alan Freed, Dick Clark, and Peter Tripp were alleged to have received "payola" for their early efforts in airing rock records. No longer could one individual, on a shoestring budget, create a record company and sell a million copies of a recording by an unknown artist. (Example: Wilbert Harrison's "Kansas City"). The Federal Communications Commission knelled a death-blow to one-man record operations, and radio stations defensively assumed control of every musical piece broadcast by their personalities. Anything with a rock & roll beat was especially suspect; and, in the early sixties, with a new conservatism, the record industry would integrate the purity of rock with strings and gimmicks in the releases of Elvis, Brenda Lee, Frankie Avalon, and their peers.

A sign of the times, Buddy Holly's final record to attain hit stature, "I Guess It Doesn't Matter Anymore," was influenced by the coming trend of lushness. Previously, Buddy set a musical standard that would not be forgotten in the impending dark ages of rock & roll. By 1964, and the arrival of the Beatle craze, the new British groups, who idolized Buddy and his efforts, re-created his fundamental rock style. The Beatles named their group in honor of Buddy's Crickets; the Hollies blatantly offered tribute to his name; and a whole new generation recorded his material and eagerly listened to collections of his unreleased tapes, attempting to regenerate his magic.

To his legion of fans, Buddy Holly's battles with the greats

14

were legendary. The Crickets competed with Bobby Darin's one-time "group," the Rinky Dinks, in an outing called "Early In The Morning;" another major clash, followed with avarice by the record collector, pitted Holly against Elvis in the simultaneous releases of "You're So Square, Baby, I Don't Care." These Holly recordings and his later, more sophisticated and pioneer efforts, became the inspirational catalog for the new industry hopefuls, Bobby Vee, Tommy James, Bobby Fuller, and even Bob Dylan.

Today, as one scans the am & fm radio spectrums, Buddy Holly's vocal style stands out, as if punctuated by some mystical and supernatural return from the grave. Henry Gross, Dr. Hook, Eric Clapton, and Aerosmith, all owe their prosperity to a skinny, unpretentious star of the late fifties. He had a style that had to be copied.

1. "Tammy," Debbie Reynolds
2. "Love Letters in the Sand," Pat Boone
3. "It's Not For Me to Say," Johnny Mathis
4. "Young Love," Tab Hunter
5. "Little Darlin'," Diamonds
6. "All Shook Up," Elvis Presley
7. "Chances Are"/"Twelfth Of Never," Johnny Mathis
8. "Bye Bye Love," Everly Brothers
9. "Round & Round," Perry Como
10. "Jailhouse Rock," Elvis Presley
11. "Diana," Paul Anka
12. "So Rare," Jimmy Dorsey
13. "Wake Up Little Susie," Everly Brothers
14. "Honeycomb," Jimmie Rodgers
15. "Come Go with Me," Del-Vikings
16. "Teddy Bear," Elvis Presley
17. "Don't Forbid Me," Pat Boone
18. "I'm Gonna Sit Right Down & Write Myself a Letter," Billy Williams
19. "Silhouettes," Rays
20. "You Send Me," Sam Cooke
21. "That'll Be the Day," Buddy Holly & Crickets
22. "Party Doll," Buddy Knox
23. "Butterfly," Andy Williams/Charlie Gracie
24. "Banana Boat (Day-O)," Harry Belafonte
25. "Too Much," Elvis Presley
26. "Fascination," Jane Morgan
27. "A White Sport Coat," Marty Robbins
28. "I'm Walkin'," Fats Domino
29. "Banana Boat Song," Tarriers
30. "Teenage Crush," Tommy Sands
31. "Rock & Roll Music," Chuck Berry
32. "Peggy Sue," Buddy Holly
33. "Dark Moon," Gale Storm
34. "Marianne," Terry Gilkyson & Easyriders
35. "Searchin' "/"Young Blood," Coasters

16

36. "Gone," Ferlin Husky
37. "Whole Lotta Shakin' Goin' On," Jerry Lee Lewis
38. "April Love," Pat Boone
39. "My Special Angel," Bobby Helms
40. "School Day," Chuck Berry
41. "Be Bop Baby," Rick Nelson
42. "Melodie D'Amour," Ames Brothers
43. "White Silver Sands," Don Rondo
44. "Send For Me," Nat King Cole
45. "Old Cape Cod," Patti Page
46. "Little Bitty Pretty One," Thurston Harris
47. "Happy Birthday Baby," Tune Weavers
48. "Raunchy," Bill Justis
49. "Mr. Lee," Bobbettes
50. "Rainbow," Russ Hamilton

Number-One Songs of '57 *(Cashbox)*

"Singing The Blues" (5), Guy Mitchell
"Too Much" (3), Elvis Presley
"Young Love" (4), Tab Hunter
"Party Doll" (1), Buddy Knox
"Round & Round" (1), Perry Como
"All Shook Up" (8), Elvis Presley
"Love Letters In the Sand" (5), Pat Boone
"Teddy Bear" (7), Elvis Presley
"Tammy" (3), Debbie Reynolds
"Diana" (1), Paul Anka
"That'll Be the Day" (1), Buddy Holly & Crickets
"Honeycomb" (2), Jimmie Rodgers
"Wake Up Little Susie" (1), Everly Brothers
"Jailhouse Rock"/"Treat Me Nice" (7), Elvis Presley
"You Send Me" (2), Sam Cooke
"April Love" (2), Pat Boone

17

Most Significant Artists of '57

Elvis Presley
Johnny Mathis
Everly Brothers
Paul Anka
Pat Boone

Academy Award (Oscar) Winner of '57

"All The Way"
 from *The Joker Is Wild*
Major recording: Frank Sinatra

18

I Hear Tiny Voices   1958

"Come on-a my house, my house-a come on . . ."

Some discographers propose that Rosemary Clooney's "Come on-a My House" was a pioneer in the field of rhythm back in 1951 and opened the door for the coming rock & roll era. Ross Bagdasarian, who wrote that number one song, came into his own in 1956 as David Seville and recorded the instrumental hit, "Armen's Theme." If it had not been for his "mechanically" creative juices, David undoubtedly would have been a success as an artist and repertoire man at Liberty Records and joined the ranks of Mitch Miller, Nelson Riddle, and Don Costa; but in 1958 gimmicks had a preponderance in popular music, and David accidentally stumbled upon the "ultimate" commercial weapon.

By recording an instrumental track at one tape speed, slowing it down, and singing along with the reduced speed, David achieved an eerie effect. Returning the tape to normal speed, he possessed the original instrumental, and, in addition, an over-dubbing of tiny voices that could easily be mistaken for the chants of little men from outer space. David quickly composed a song to pit against his new technique, and the result was a hit recording, "Witch Doctor," that attained number one in the trade magazines in the late spring and was the precursor of a bevy of imitators. Within weeks, an established country & western artist, Sheb Wooley, entered the top-forty field with a novelty tune extolling the horrific capabilities of "The Purple People Eater," "one eyed, one horned" with a "walla walla bing bang." Sheb gained the number-one distinction, also.

19

From the Jack Paar television show came Betty Johnson, distinctively assisted by another little bitty voice. Her plight was overwhelming; "The Little Blue Man" haunted her every move.

The "little voice" fad was with us, but the connoisseurs of such fine madness were well aware that the industry had created an identity problem. Witch doctors, purple people eaters, and little blue men couldn't all communicate identically. David Seville, father of the movement, returned to the drawing board and gave birth to three definitive "little voices" who garnered so much national acceptance and recognition at Christmas, they temporarily surpassed Elvis in popularity.

Enter Alvin and the Chipmunks. A boisterous family clan of human tiny tots were incapable of paralleling their vocal machinations. The Chipmunks' able-bodied leader, Alvin, was an anti-social, tenacious renegade, unrelentless in his efforts to "screw up" the everyday, normal chipmunk existence. Truly, Alvin distinguished himself as the first recording artist to do his "own thing." "The Chipmunk Song" sold millions during the Christmas rush of 1958, and sales lingered long into January 1959.

David Seville's dedication to insanity not only rewarded him financially but made him a national hero of questionable merit. He inspired every youngster with a two-speed tape machine to "give it a go." What creative young derelict, armed with taperecorder, has not called some innocent victim at three in the morning with the plaintive and prerecorded, "Hi, this is Alvin the Chipmunk. Can I speak to your old lady?"

The Chipmunks remained with us in varying degrees of popularity, sensationally with the sub-teens, until 1972, when David Seville passed on to the land of multitrack recording studios. Alvin and his compatriots acquired a plethora of competition, including the Nutty Squirrels; but who adores old, grey squirrels when he can break bread with a bronze-colored, teenie weenie, cuddly chipmunk? In 1959, the Coasters gave us "Charlie Brown," replete with a chorus of little voice cohorts. Alas, they were only human!

No doubt, someday a creative talent will reverse the David Seville technique and ignite another musical rage—the ultimate, a deep-throated dragon. Time will tell.

1. "Nel Blu Dipinto Di Blu (Volare)," Domenico Modugno
2. "It's All in the Game," Tommy Edwards
3. "All I Have To Do is Dream," Everly Brothers
4. "Patricia," Perez Prado
5. "Little Star," Elegants
6. "At The Hop," Danny & the Juniors
7. "Bird Dog," Everly Brothers
8. "Twilight Time," Platters
9. "Catch a Falling Star," Perry Como
10. "Witch Doctor," David Seville
11. "Return to Me," Dean Martin
12. "Tequila," Champs
13. "Poor Little Fool," Ricky Nelson
14. "Purple People Eater," Sheb Wooley
15. "Get a Job," Silhouettes
16. "He's Got the Whole World in His Hands," Laurie London
17. "Yakety Yak," Coasters
18. "It's Only Make Believe," Conway Twitty
19. "Tea For Two Cha Cha," Warren Covington & Tommy
      Dorsey Orchestra
20. "Tom Dooley," Kingston Trio
21. "Rockin' Robin," Bobby Day
22. "Sail Along Silvery Moon," Billy Vaughn
23. "Splish Splash," Bobby Darin
24. "Who's Sorry Now," Connie Francis
25. "Topsy Part II," Cozy Cole
26. "Tears on My Pillow," Little Anthony & Imperials
27. "The Stroll," The Diamonds
28. "Secretly," Jimmie Rodgers
29. "Just a Dream," Jimmy Clanton
30. "Wear My Ring around Your Neck," Elvis Presley
31. "You Cheated," Shields
32. "Don't"/"I Beg Of You," Elvis Presley
33. "Chantilly Lace," Big Bopper
34. "When," Kalin Twins
35. "Susie Darlin'," Robin Luke

36. "Everybody Loves a Lover," Doris Day
37. "Sweet Little Sixteen," Chuck Berry
38. "Good Golly Miss Molly," Little Richard
39. "Hard Headed Woman," Elvis Presley
40. "Fever," Peggy Lee
41. "Chanson D'Amour," Art & Dotty Todd
42. "Do You Wanna Dance," Bobby Freeman
43. "Sugartime," McGuire Sisters
44. "To Know Him Is to Love Him," Teddy Bears
45. "Try Me," James Brown
46. "My True Love," Jack Scott
47. "Oh Julie," Crescendos
48. "Chipmunk Song," David Seville & Chipmunks
49. "Rebel Rouser," Duane Eddy
50. "The End," Earl Grant

Number-One Songs of '58 *(Cashbox)*

"At The Hop" (5), Danny & the Juniors
"Don't"/"I Beg Of You" (5), Elvis Presley
"Tequila" (5), Champs
"Twilight Time" (1), Platters
"Witch Doctor" (2), David Seville
"All I Have To Do is Dream" (4), Everly Brothers
"Purple People Eater" (6), Sheb Wooley
"Hard Headed Woman" (2), Elvis Presley
"Poor Little Fool" (2), Ricky Nelson
"Nel Blu Dipinto Di Blu" (5), Domenico Modugno
"Little Star" (1), Elegants
"It's All in the Game" (6), Tommy Edwards
"It's Only Make Believe" (1), Conway Twitty
"Tom Dooley" (2), Kingston Trio
"To Know Him Is to Love Him" (3), Teddy Bears
"Chipmunk Song" (2), David Seville & Chipmunks

Most Significant Artists of '58

Everly Brothers
Buddy Holly
Elvis Presley
David Seville
Ricky Nelson

Academy Award (Oscar) Winner of '58

"Gigi"
> from *Gigi*

Major recording: Maurice Chevalier

NARAS (Grammy) Major Category Winners of '58

Record of the Year:
> "Nel Blu Dipinto Di Blu," Domenico Modugno

Album of the Year:
> "The Music From *Peter Gunn*," Henry Mancini

Song of the Year:
> "Nel Blu Dipinto Di Blu," Domenico Modugno

We Love You, Dick. Yes, We Do! 1959

The story of "American Bandstand" and its meteoric rise from local acclaim in Philadelphia to the best-known, best-loved source of popular music in the nation, has been spun innumerable times. It is a tale of success that transcends the sagas of Elvis Presley and the Beatles. Dick Clark's "American Bandstand" was the vehicle that taxied superstars to their ultimate destinations and bussed an astronomical amount of "seven day wonders" to oblivion. If one were an aspiring rock star, Dick could make or break you. Chubby Checker, Dee Dee Sharp, Annette Funicello, Bobby Rydell, and Freddy Cannon were a few that skyrocketed to teenage acclaim. Meanwhile, Fabian, the Quaker City Boys, and the Playboys surfaced momentarily in a flash of fleeting glory only to have their lights snuffed.

Dick Clark turned Philadelphia into the mecca for unknown, undiscovered singers. In the fifties, rumor had it that a brief vacation in Philly was so beneficial to one's health that a sixteen-year-old ingenue might sprout highly sensitized vocal chords and, within weeks, undergo a metamorphosis, transforming her into another Lesley Gore. In fact, to many ascending warblers, "American Bandstand" was comparable to the Vatican; if they came to worship the "Pope of Pop," they might be blessed. Of course, some refused to make the crusade to Eastern Pennsylvania, including Elvis; historically, kings and pontiffs have had disregard for each other.

Yet, most young mistrels desired this expedition "in hopes

that Saint Nicholas soon would be there." It little mattered if a group of bandstanders gave a potential hit one of those typical 40 percent ratings; that, in itself, denoted recognition of extraordinary value. Philadelphia ballooned with successful recording studios, manufacturers, and distributors; to them, Clark was the "goose that laid the golden egg," and vinyl embryos sometimes matured into prolific longplaying records.

In the halcyon days of television, the question was raised: how can the industry graphically present phonograph records on a small screen and appeal to a large segment of the home audience? The premise was preposterous. No one in their right mind would pan a TV camera on a spinning disc for an extended period of time and expect public acclaim. Dick Clark licked that. The answer: a studio of rippin', rockin', and boppin' teenagers begging the attention of the viewer with a house full of his own rippin', rockin', and boppin' teenagers. Overnight, Dick Clark became the nation's leading "teeny bopper" sitter, the forerunner of "Sesame Street" and current reruns of "Mod Squad."

Dick was so damned clean and pretty, and in such sartorial splendor, parents knew they could trust their daughter to his care. And, among his various responsibilities, he resolved one of puberty's major calamities. At age thirteen, a teenage girl is socially gregarious; the average teenage boy is not. Clark, with his radiant smile, condoned young females dancing and cavorting together in the seclusion of their own homes, if not publicly. There are no graphs or statistics, but I'll wager the delinquincy rate in America plummeted in the afternoon hours. Here was a new permissiveness and idolatry; even Mom adored Dick Clark, emulating her children by learning the twist and eventually dragging Dad to the local nitery and coercing him to endeavor one of the most primitive gyrations of any generation.

We can pan Dick Clark all we want. The fact remains, despite the innuendos of sinister "under the table payments" from record companies, he altered the face of the American music establishment, and he did it cosmetically. Any personality who was fortunate enough to exhibit his wares on a local or regional "bandstand-type" program, blesses Mr. Clark. Even today, broadcasters, with tongue in cheek and indications of envy, speculate his good looks will diminish. Don't hold your breath!

26

1. "Mack The Knife," Bobby Darin
2. "Battle of New Orleans," Johnny Horton
3. "Venus," Frankie Avalon
4. "There Goes My Baby," Drifters
5. "Lonely Boy," Paul Anka
6. "Personality," Lloyd Price
7. "Sleepwalk," Santo & Johnny
8. "Put Your Head on My Shoulder," Paul Anka
9. "Dream Lover," Bobby Darin
10. "Kansas City," Wilbert Harrison
11. "Come Softly to Me," Fleetwoods
12. "Three Bells," Browns
13. "Smoke Gets in Your Eyes," Platters
14. "Charlie Brown," Coasters
15. "A Fool Such as I"/"I Need Your Love Tonight," Elvis Presley
16. "Just a Matter of Time," Brook Benton
17. "Stagger Lee," Lloyd Price
18. "Mr. Blue," Fleetwoods
19. "Sea of Love," Phil Phillips
20. "Don't You Know," Della Reese
21. "Lipstick on Your Collar," Connie Francis
22. "A Big Hunk of Love," Elvis Presley
23. "Quiet Village," Martin Denny
24. "Primrose Lane," Jerry Wallace
25. "Deck of Cards," Wink Martindale
26. "What a Difference a Day Makes," Dinah Washington
27. "Pink Shoelaces," Dodie Stevens
28. "I Only Have Eyes for You," Flamingos
29. "A Teenager in Love," Dion & Belmonts
30. "Kookie Kookie, Lend Me Your Comb," Ed Byrnes
31. "Sorry (I Ran All The Way Home)," Impalas
32. "The Happy Organ," Dave Baby Cortez
33. "Seven Little Girls, in the Back Seat," Paul Evans
34. " 'Til I Kissed You," Everly Brothers
35. "Since I Don't Have You," Skyliners
36. "Lavender Blue," Sammy Turner

37. "Dedicated to the One I Love," Shirelles
38. "Sixteen Candles," Crests
39. "My Heart Is an Open Book," Carl Dobkins, Jr.
40. "Donna," Ritchie Valens
41. "Hawaiian Wedding Song," Andy Williams
42. "Teen Beat," Sandy Nelson
43. "Heartaches by the Number," Guy Mitchell
44. "Why," Frankie Avalon
45. "Waterloo," Stonewall Jackson
46. "Red River Rock," Johnny & Hurricanes
47. "Broken Hearted Melody," Sarah Vaughn
48. "Gotta Travel On," Billy Grammer
49. "Frankie," Connie Francis
50. "Shimmy Shimmy Ko Ko Bop," Little Anthony & Imperials

Number-One Songs of '59 *(Billboard)*

"Chipmunk Song" (2), David Seville & Chipmunks
"Smoke Gets in Your Eyes" (3), Platters
"Stagger Lee" (4), Lloyd Price
"Venus" (5), Frankie Avalon
"Come Softly To Me" (4), Fleetwoods
"The Happy Organ" (1), Dave Baby Cortez
"Kansas City" (2), Wilbert Harrison
"The Battle of New Orleans" (6), Johnny Horton
"Lonely Boy" (4), Paul Anka
"A Big Hunk of Love" (2), Elvis Presley
"The Three Bells" (4), Browns
"Sleepwalk" (2), Santo & Johnny
"Mack the Knife" (9), Bobby Darin
"Mr. Blue" (1), Fleetwoods
"Heartaches by the Number" (2), Guy Mitchell
"Why" (1), Frankie Avalon

Most Significant Artists of '59

Bobby Darin
Buddy Holly
Johnny Horton
Frankie Avalon
Lloyd Price

Academy Award (Oscar) Winner of '59

"High Hopes"
    from *A Hole In The Head*

Major recording: Frank Sinatra

NARAS (Grammy) Major Category Winners of '59

Record of the Year:
    "Mack The Knife," Bobby Darin

Album of the Year:
    "Come Dance with Me," Frank Sinatra

Song of the Year:
    "The Battle Of New Orleans," Jimmy Driftwood

hot pursuit, devoted his final words from his bullet-ridden body to his Mexican beloved. Johnny Preston's "Running Bear" risked life and limb to rendezvous with his Indian princess on the far side of a swirling vortex. The Everly Brothers spent a harrowing night at the airport terminal only to receive word at dawn's early light that "Ebony Eyes" would arrive by hearse. Larry Verne's Indian fighter met his just reward, no thanks to "Mr. Custer" or his red-skinned opponents.

As 1960 depressingly advanced, it was obvious that something should be done to rid us of this banality; a proponent for the living was demanded or the nation would not have anyone left to sing or be sung about. From the wilderness of country & western creativity arrived Bob Luman with a ready solution, "Let's Think About Living." None of this "death trip" for Bob; his hue and cry was for life and its innumerable advantages. Almost immediately heeded, Bob terminated death in the music industry, and, by 1964, fairytale fatalities in popular music waned rapidly. J. Frank Wilson would beg one "Last Kiss" in an Indy-style crash; Dicky Lee's "Patches" would depart face down in the river, psychologically depredated by the ill-will of her waspish father; and Jan and Dean would hazard "Dead Man's Curve." But with a new positivism, the Beatles came to life and so did music. We learned it was more fun to advertise "I Want To Hold Your Hand" and live to tell about it.

The Great Adventure and its Financial Reward

In early rock & roll songs, two subjects dominated, requ
unrequited love. It is difficult to determine which was t
popular. A wild and unsubstantiated guess places the ur
lovers far ahead of their opposing number. The record (
charmed the consumer with heartbroken laments of so:
gal or guy spurned by his or her lost love and their atte
overcome the sordid situation. Country singers succeed
mizing the adulterous conduct of countless young love
ing an art form previously taboo in the forties and fifti
decades were musically tame, and one could but hint a
ings and detriments of "hanky panky." Once in awhile
an exception; Bill Haley managed to slip by the censor
"one-eyed cat peeping in a seafood store," merely an (
the part of a naive record company executive.

By 1960 America's youth craved more than a trc
moaning his loss in "Oh, Carol." MGM Records and a !
artist, Mark Dinning, coined the monetarily successful
that enjoyed catholic popularity at the beginning of t
"death" and all its heartbreaking implications. "Teen
a tribute to the insurmountable, a sweetheart lost for
infinite unknown. This pioneer tearjerker set the stag
less parade of tragic love affairs whose reward was hu
Ray Peterson, gasping his final breath from the drivei
twisted wreck, asked us to "Tell Laura I Love Her." !
bins, in a paradox of good and evil ("El Paso"), with

1. "Theme From *A Summer Place*," Percy Faith
2. "Save the Last Dance for Me," Drifters
3. "It's Now or Never," Elvis Presley
4. "The Twist," Chubby Checker
5. "Itsy Bitsy Teeny Weeny Yellow Polka Dot Bikini," Brian Hyland
6. "He'll Have to Go," Jim Reeves
7. "Cathy's Clown," Everly Brothers
8. "I'm Sorry," Brenda Lee
9. "Walk Don't Run," Ventures
10. "Running Bear," Johnny Preston
11. "Stuck on You," Elvis Presley
12. "Everybody's Somebody's Fool," Connie Francis
13. "Teen Angel," Mark Dinning
14. "Handy Man," Jimmy Jones
15. "Only the Lonely," Roy Orbison
16. "My Heart Has a Mind of Its Own," Connie Francis
17. "Greenfields," Brothers Four
18. "Please Help Me, I'm Falling," Hank Locklin
19. "El Paso," Marty Robbins
20. "Alley Oop," Hollywood Argyles
21. "Kiddio," Brook Benton
22. "Night," Jackie Wilson
23. "Chain Gang," Sam Cooke
24. "Good Timin'," Jimmy Jones
25. "Wild One," Bobby Rydell
26. "Theme From *The Apartment*," Ferrante & Teicher
27. "Baby You Got What It Takes," Brook Benton & Dinah Washington
28. "Mr. Custer," Larry Verne
29. "He Will Break Your Heart," Jerry Butler
30. "Puppy Love," Paul Anka
31. "Sink the Bismarck," Johnny Horton
32. "Sweet Nothin's," Brenda Lee
33. "Devil or Angel," Bobby Vee
34. "I Want To Be Wanted," Brenda Lee

35. "Because They're Young," Duane Eddy
36. "Paper Roses," Anita Bryant
37. "The Big Hurt," Toni Fisher
38. "Way Down Yonder in New Orleans," Freddy Cannon
39. "You Talk Too Much," Joe Jones
40. "White Silver Sands," Bill Black Combo
41. "Finger Poppin' Time," Hank Ballard
42. "Where or When," Dion & Belmonts
43. "Volare," Bobby Rydell
44. "Burning Bridges," Jack Scott
45. "This Magic Moment," Drifters
46. "You Got What It Takes," Marv Johnson
47. "Harbor Lights," Platters
48. "I'm Hurtin'," Roy Orbison
49. "A Rockin' Good Way," Brook Benton & Dinah Washington
50. "What in the World's Come Over You," Jack Scott

Number-One Songs of '60 *(Billboard)*

"El Paso" (2), Marty Robbins
"Running Bear" (3), Johnny Preston
"Teen Angel" (2), Mark Dinning
"Theme From *A Summer Place*" (9), Percy Faith
"Stuck on You" (4), Elvis Presley
"Cathy's Clown" (5), Everly Brothers
"Everybody's Somebody's Fool" (2), Connie Francis
"Alley Oop" (1), Hollywood Argyles
"I'm Sorry" (3), Brenda Lee
"Itsy Bitsy Teenie Weeny Yellow Polka Dot Bikini" (1), Brian
    Hyland
"It's Now or Never" (5), Elvis Presley
"The Twist" (1), Chubby Checker
"My Heart Has a Mind of Its Own" (2), Connie Francis
"Mr. Custer" (1), Larry Verne
"Save the Last Dance for Me" (3), Drifters

34

"I Want To Be Wanted" (1), Brenda Lee
"Georgia on My Mind" (1), Ray Charles
"Stay" (1), Maurice Williams & Zodiacs
"Are You Lonesome Tonight" (6), Elvis Presley

Most Significant Artists of '60

Brenda Lee
Elvis Presley
Drifters
Roy Orbison
Connie Francis

Academy Award (Oscar) Winner of '60

"Never On Sunday"
    from *Never On Sunday*

Major recording: Don Costa

NARAS (Grammy) Major Category Winners of '60

Record of the Year:
    "Theme From *A Summer Place*," Percy Faith

Album of the Year:
    "Button Down Mind," Bob Newhart

Song of the Year:
    "Theme From *Exodus*," Ernest Gold

"I've Got This Incredible Recording and a Stack of Twenties . . ."

The *Random House Unabridged Dictionary* defines *payola* as "a secret or private payment in return for the promotion of a product, service, and so on, through the abuse of one's position, influence, or facilities." We could end this piece with that interpretation and neglect Congress' monumental efforts of 1960 and 1961, but such an example of mass hysteria deserves greater background.

In 1958, the press dazed the nation with its exposé of Sherman Adams, an aide to President Dwight D. Eisenhower, and his acceptance of a freezer from a Boston industrialist. This, accompanied by Richard Nixon's fabled public denial of influence in his renowned "Checkers" speech and television's crimson flush from the quiz show scandal, sent the investigative reporter on his rounds questing the next lucrative revelation. The recording manufacturers and their distributors, pipelines to America's disc jockeys, fell victim to the stampede, joined, en route, by soul-searching politicians, looking for bleach to erase their own stains.

With a McCarthy penchant for assumed numbers, in 1960 a House of Representatives subcommittee reported that at least two hundred and seven well-known radio personalities had received "under the rug" payments from record company promotion men. For these self-serving efforts, a New York City grand jury indicted eleven jocks; Alan Freed, Dick Clark, and Peter Tripp, to name a few, would receive the widest public attention for their wheeling and dealing. The results were devastating to the infant, rock & roll.

Within months, in most cases, the individual radio announcer ceased to select his own music for broadcast; radio executives and "democratic" committees determined those records to be aired. Washington's bureaucracy perpetrated an amazingly diabolical process: discs that demonstrated activity on the trade magazines' charts obtained more radio exposure, while the same trades checked identical radio outlets to see which hits they were cultivating. It was a closed ring, a vicious circle, and, with the exception of a few daring broadcasters, the sources for exposure of new product virtually dried up. Of course, payola still ran rampant, but with payments disbursed to a higher caste. The number of general managers and program directors that subsequently vacationed in the Bahamas and the twenty-five count boxes of "freebie" LPs dealt out is not on record.

The influence of the congressional investigation, and later allegations by Jack Anderson and team, are still felt. A weekly audit of *Billboard*'s "Hot 100" will demonstrate the influence of the industry giants who found small reason to slip a dollar here and there and the systematic destruction of the small record firm who could not afford nationwide advertising to ballyhoo its releases. Today, Columbia, and subsidiaries; the Kinney Corporation, a conglomerate of Warner Brothers, Atlantic, Elektra, and more; RCA, with coast-to-coast omnipotence; and their brethren, the other monsters, dominate the popular music scene. Hit singles are now spawned from albums, instead of the ancient tradition of albums arising from hit singles. The Cameos, the Swans, the Imperials, the Alladins, etc., have declined in numbers, bit the dust, or become part of a massive corporate cluster.

There is no ethical or moral justification for any form of payola, but the facts testify to its existence in every walk of commercial life. This sort of compensation is an illegal method of breaching the goliaths' stranglehold on what should be a creative edifice. The large and prestigious record company is not abominable and, by all means, is essential, but so are the small, singular organizations operating from dusty warehouses. Payola brought them to fruition in the fifties and, with the assassination of the secret payment, the bantams found no equivalent replacement but big corporate distribution of their output.

Congress solved one problem, and, in the effort, created another, substantially more detrimental. Gone are the radio titans

38

like Alan Freed, George Lorenz (the "Hound Dog"), and Norm
Prescott, who sincerely motivated their audiences to prize the
world of popular music; born, instead, are the new breed, Don
Imus, Dan Ingram, and Larry Lujack, who survive on their personalities and humor with a dash of repetitious top-forty monotony
as their mainstay.

1. "Tossin' & Turnin'," Bobby Lewis
2. "Calcutta," Lawrence Welk
3. "Runaway," Del Shannon
4. "Will You Love Me Tomorrow," Shirelles
5. "Are You Lonesome Tonight," Elvis Presley
6. "Last Date," Floyd Cramer
7. "Theme from *Exodus*," Ferrante & Teicher
8. "Travelin' Man," Ricky Nelson
9. "Wonderland by Night," Bert Kaempfert
10. "Mother-In-Law," Ernie K-Doe
11. "Michael," Highwaymen
12. "Boll Weevil Song," Brooke Benton
13. "Raindrops," Dee Clark
14. "Blue Moon," Marcels
15. "Quarter to Three," Gary U.S. Bonds
16. "Running Scared," Roy Orbison
17. "Pony Time," Chubby Checker
18. "New Orleans," Gary U.S. Bonds
19. "Runaround Sue," Dion
20. "Where the Boys Are," Connie Francis
21. "Daddy's Home," Shep & The Limelights
22. "North to Alaska," Johnny Horton
23. "One Hundred Pounds of Clay," Gene McDaniels
24. "A Thousand Stars," Kathy Young
25. "Take Good Care of My Baby," Bobby Vee
26. "The Mountain's High," Dick & Dee Dee
27. "Wooden Heart," Joe Dowell
28. "Shop Around," Miracles
29. "Angel Baby," Rosie & The Originals
30. "Stand by Me," Ben E. King
31. "Wheels," Billy Vaughn
32. "Surrender," Elvis Presley
33. "Crying," Roy Orbison
34. "Last Night," Mar-Keys
35. "I Like It Like That," Chris Kenner
36. "Stay," Maurice Williams & Zodiacs

37. "Poetry in Motion," Johnny Tillotson
38. "Apache," Jorgen Ingmann
39. "I've Told Every Little Star," Linda Scott
40. "Don't Worry," Marty Robbins
41. "Calendar Girl," Neil Sedaka
42. "You're Sixteen," Johnny Burnette
43. "Rubber Ball," Bobby Vee
44. "Hats Off to Larry," Del Shannon
45. "Moody River," Pat Boone
46. "Dum Dum," Brenda Lee
47. "You Can Have Her," Roy Hamilton
48. "Happy Birthday Sweet Sixteen," Neil Sedaka
49. "Hello Walls," Faron Young
50. "Hit The Road, Jack," Ray Charles

Number-One Songs of '61 *(Billboard)*

"Wonderland By Night" (3), Bert Kaempfert
"Will You Love Me Tomorrow" (2), Shirelles
"Calcutta" (2), Lawrence Welk
"Pony Time" (3), Chubby Checker
"Surrender" (2), Elvis Presley
"Blue Moon" (3), Marcels
"Runaway" (4), Del Shannon
"Mother-In-Law" (1), Ernie K-Doe
"Travelin' Man" (2), Ricky Nelson
"Running Scared" (1), Roy Orbison
"Moody River" (1), Pat Boone
"Quarter to Three" (2), Gary U.S. Bonds
"Tossin' & Turnin' " (7), Bobby Lewis
"Wooden Heart" (1), Joe Dowell
"Michael" (2), Highwaymen
"Take Good Care of My Baby" (3), Bobby Vee
"Hit The Road, Jack" (2), Ray Charles
"Runaround Sue" (2), Dion

"Big Bad John" (5), Jimmy Dean
"Please Mr. Postman" (1), Marvelettes
"The Lion Sleeps Tonight" (2), Tokens

Most Significant Artists of '61

Roy Orbison
Dion
Del Shannon
Neil Sedaka
Gary U.S. Bonds

Academy Award (Oscar) Winner of '61

"Moon River"
    from *Breakfast At Tiffany's*
Major recordings: Henry Mancini, Andy Williams

NARAS (Grammy) Major Category Winners of '61

Record of the Year:
    "Moon River," Henry Mancini
Album of the Year:
    "Judy At Carnegie Hall," Judy Garland
Song of the Year:
    "Moon River," Henry Mancini, Johnny Mercer

Let's Dance, Boog-idy Boog-idy Shoop 1962

In 1962 a watered-down rock & roll leaped the generation gap and down came the age barriers, once and for all. Mom and Dad put on their boogie shoes and jumped with a terpsichorean delight alongside junior at places like the Peppermint Lounge, a synthetic national monument and musical tribute to its era. Dancing and popular music, perpetually, have gone hand in hand through the ages, the pre-rock days dominated by various folk ballets including the "Hokey Pokey," the "Bunny Hop," and the staple, the "Lindy," a high-step motivated by most any up-tempo hit record. With the advent of the teen-rock colossus and the gyrations of the early Dick Clark advocates, dancers experimented with brief fads such as the "Stroll," particularly easy to engage in with most Fats Domino records; the "Cha-lypso," a variation of the cha-cha, allowing male and female to surrender their basic instinct to touch; the "Slop," a contortion related to the instrumentals of Noble "Thin Man" Watts, Duane Eddy, and Bill Doggett; and the old standby, the "Jitterbug," a purely anachronistic designation, better placed in the thirties and forties.

The fifties spawned Hank Ballard's recording of "The Twist," inaugurating a new dance that gained little attention at the time and certainly not the ascendancy it would soon acquire. A relatively unknown singer from Philadelphia, Chubby Checker, covered Hank's recording in 1960, exhibited it on the "American Bandstand" afternoon outing, and—WOW! The teens of America transformed it into an overnight sensation, but the adults instinc-

43

tively remained true to their fox trots, waltzes, and mambos, at least for the time being. This decade-opening year saw the birth of several other youth-oriented dance favorites including the Dovell's "Bristol Stomp."

By 1962, the whole movement became a full-blown national rage. On dance floors of small nightclubs, from the now-immortal Peppermint Lounge, to dives like the University Palace in Albany, New York, where I personally ministered early discotheque to a chain gang of outrageous, but merry, drunks, the dance was the thing. Chubby's "The Twist" returned to the charts and was unanimously proclaimed the number-one song of the year; Joey Dee and the Starlighters' "The Peppermint Twist" finished number two in popularity; and Dee Dee Sharp's "Mashed Potato Time" rounded out the top five. What a year for a hop, skip, and jump! Dick Clark scouted South Street in Philadelphia for any fledgling who chirped and/or hatched an innovative dance step, and, by year's end, Berry Gordy in Detroit mastered two of the biggest dance-oriented discs of all-time.

Back in the city of brotherly love, Little Eva suggested a "big boss line" for "The Loco-Motion," Len Barry and his Dovells extended their hit streak with "Bristol Twistin' Annie," and Chubby Checker was crowned "the dance king," presenting his court "The Poneytime," "The Fly," and the back-breaking "Limbo Rock." From the motor city came those two dynamite dance classics, the Contours' "Do You Love Me" and the Marvelettes' "Please, Mr. Postman." The moppets of the Northeast chose to design their own dance, they called the "Bitch," though on the air, we mellowed that apt description to the "Big-B." This kind of young originality eventually ended the reign of the twist, and a rash of self-contrived dance steps became provincial favorites. The year 1963 saw a Memphis radio talent, Rufus Thomas, show us "The Dog" and how to "walk" it; Bent Fabric donated a gentle beat to the cause, "The Alley Cat"; and in Baltimore, local chorines improvised an inane frolic to celebrate Boots Randolph's "Yakety Sax." Record company A & R men, headstrong to dictate their own choreography, added a touch of Latin, and Eydie Gorme proclaimed "Blame It On the Bossa Nova," an enigma that no one attempted except Arthur and Katherine Murray. Sam Cooke tried to add excitement to the death throes of the twist with "Twistin'

44

The Night Away," and the Isley Brothers chimed in with their "Twist And Shout," a song that would receive an honest burial by the Beatles in 1964.

By the time the English groups recaptured the colonies in 1964, the dance fad was waning. A few hardcore enthusiasts endeavored steps like "The Twine Time" by Alvin Cash, but, for all intents and purposes, the hully gully, the Madison, and the daddy of them all, the twist, vanished until the arrival of the nostalgia craze in the seventies.

1. "The Twist," Chubby Checker
2. "Peppermint Twist," Joey Dee & The Starlighters
3. "Moon River," Henry Mancini
4. "Mashed Potato Time," Dee Dee Sharp
5. "Stranger on the Shore," Mr. Acker Bilk
6. "I Can't Stop Loving You," Ray Charles
7. "The Lion Sleeps Tonight," Tokens
8. "Johnny Angel," Shelly Fabares
9. "The Stripper," David Rose
10. "The Wanderer," Dion
11. "Duke of Earl," Gene Chandler
12. "The One Who Really Loves You," Mary Wells
13. "Roses Are Red," Bobby Vinton
14. "Big Bad John," Jimmy Dean
15. "You'll Lose a Good Thing," Barbara Lynn
16. "Hey Baby," Bruce Channel
17. "Ramblin Rose," Nat King Cole
18. "Monster Mash," Bobby Pickett
19. "Do You Love Me," Contours
20. "Loco-Motion," Little Eva
21. "Soldier Boy," Shirelles
22. "Green Onions," Booker T. & The MG's
23. "Sherry," Four Seasons
24. "Midnight in Moscow," Kenny Ball
25. "Palisades Park," Freddy Cannon
26. "Can't Help Falling in Love," Elvis Presley
27. "Walk on By," Leroy Van Dyke
28. "I Know," Barbara George
29. "It Keeps Right On A-Hurtin'," Johnny Tillotson
30. "Twist & Shout," Isley Brothers
31. "Breaking Up is Hard to Do," Neil Sedaka
32. "Town Without Pity," Gene Pitney
33. "Wolverton Mountain," Claude King
34. "Let Me In," Sensations
35. "Surfin' Safari," Beachboys
36. "Party Lights," Claudine Clark

46

37. "Run To Him," Bobby Vee
38. "Twistin' the Night Away," Sam Cooke
39. "Good Luck Charm," Elvis Presley
40. "Love Letters," Ketty Lester
41. "Please Mr. Postman," Marvelettes
42. "Alley Cat," Bent Fabric
43. "Patches," Dickey Lee
44. "Sheila," Tommy Roe
45. "He's a Rebel," Crystals
46. "Sealed With a Kiss," Brian Hyland
47. "Goodbye Cruel World," James Darren
48. "Norman," Sue Thompson
49. "Don't Break the Heart That Loves You," Connie Francis
50. "You Better Move On," Arthur Alexander

Number-One Songs of '62 *(Billboard)*

"The Lion Sleeps Tonight" (1), Tokens
"The Twist" (2), Chubby Checker
"Peppermint Twist" (3), Joey Dee & The Starlighters
"Duke of Earl" (3), Gene Chandler
"Hey Baby" (3), Bruce Channel
"Don't Break the Heart That Loves You" (1), Connie Francis
"Johnny Angel" (2), Shelley Fabares
"Good Luck Charm" (2), Elvis Presley
"Soldier Boy" (3), Shirelles
"Stranger on the Shore" (1), Mr. Acker Bilk
"I Can't Stop Loving You" (5), Ray Charles
"The Stripper" (1), David Rose
"Roses Are Red" (4), Bobby Vinton
"Breaking Up Is Hard to Do" (2), Neil Sedaka
"Loco-Motion" (1), Little Eva
"Sheila" (2), Tommy Roe
"Sherry" (5), Four Seasons
"Monster Mash" (2), Bobby Pickett

"He's a Rebel" (2), Crystals
"Big Girls Don't Cry" (5), Four Seasons
"Telstar" (2), Tornadoes

Most Significant Artists of '62

Chubby Checker
Ray Charles
Gene Pitney
Joey Dee & The Starlighters
Four Seasons

Academy Award (Oscar) Winner of '62

"Days Of Wine & Roses"
    from *The Days Of Wine & Roses*

Major recordings: Henry Mancini, Andy Williams

NARAS (Grammy) Major Category Winners of '62

Record of the Year:
    "I Left My Heart In San Francisco," Tony Bennett

Album of the Year:
    "The First Family," Vaughn Meader

Song of the Year:
    "What Kind Of Fool Am I," Leslie Bricusse, Anthony Newley

Surfin' the USA

1963

Every spring, as the last flake of snow vanishes, as nature awakes its hibernating multitudes, and as the bloom of youth responds to its primordial desires, disc jockeys christen this season of rebirth by exhuming those fantastically happy and universally loved summer songs of yesteryear. When one hears a Beach Boys' oldie, beach parties and beer blasts can't be too far behind, and one can envision their constituents—the ever-present transistor radio propped in the sand, the scantily clad bikini beach baby, and, drawn magnetically to this spectacle, a deeply tanned young man aware that it is "summertime and the living is easy."

That was the plaintive musical statement of Sam Cooke in 1957 in his recording of George Gershwin's "Summertime," an avant-garde indicator of the rituals to come. As the late fifties advanced, the redundancy of the Jamies' "Summertime, Summertime" extolled the virtues of the summer vacation, Eddie Cochran expostulated "The Summertime Blues," Jerry Keller jubilantly exclaimed "Here Comes Summer," and in 1960, Brian Hyland generated an overnight summer smash with "Itsy Bitsy Teenie Weenie Yellow Polka Dot Bikini," ingenuously describing a marvelous piece of apparel that had arrived triumphantly from France and its Mediterranean beaches. The hedonistic philosophy that would dominate summer music in the future was revealed in 1961—the movie *Where the Boys Are*, and Connie Francis' rendition of the title song described the antics of the new rock & roll generation who would swarm the beaches of Florida, South Carolina, and

Eastern Maryland, every Easter weekend in endless procession.

The yearly craze for the pulsations of the summer were now an American institution and the esprit de corps went on unabated in any great measure until 1965. The stimulus was the great sport of surfing, initiated in Hawaii and brought east via Southern California. In January 1962, the Beach Boys, with new words like *wipeout,* launched a record entitled "Surfin' " on an obscure label, and it became a local hit in the warmer climes of the West Coast. By summer Capitol Records signed Brian Wilson and his colleagues to a long contract and "Surfin' Safari" was an instant national hit, triggering the numerous "beach songs" of the next two summers. Connie Francis, inspired by her previous format and the new demand, spelled out the intoxication of summer in "V-A-C-A-T-I-O-N."

Even as city officials barricaded the beaches at season's end, a spinoff, "hot rod" records, the same rhythmic music with a change of lyrics, filled in the dreary winter months. The Beach Boys gunned their accelerators and burned rubber in a "409."

The banner year for anyone cataloging this new musical phenomena was 1963. Connie Francis was consistently on the make as she mused her fantasies to "Follow The Boys"; the Beach Boys once again were "Surfin' U.S.A.," hot on the heels of a sensual delight, anonymously named "Surfer Girl"; Jan and Dean joined the Chamber of Commerce public relations team and invited epicurean teens to unite in "Surf City," a number-one song for two weeks; and the Trashmen, in a most bizarre and disquieting parody, chanted "papa oom mow mow" and assaulted the world with their "Surfin' Bird." The open road, saturated with custom conveyances, was applauded again when the Beach Boys were entangled in a "Shut Down" in "A Little Deuce Coupe," and the Ripchords exclaimed, "Hey, Little Cobra" on their way to Jan and Dean's "Drag City."

This string of hits celebrated the new mobility of American youth who, for the first time, possessed the plentiful dollars and the high-speed chariots to propel them to those places in the sun. Rock & roll music chronicled the whole story of the "endless summer" and the latter-day Mongolian hordes who roamed the recreation areas of the United States in search of self-gratification with little, if any, appreciation of the natural beauty surrounding them. After all, this was "Where the Action Is."

The "Beatlemania" of 1964 would slow this musical race with the times, as the English monopolized the charts and devastated the Beach Boys' tuneful monument to lust and ambrosia. A foreboding of impending disaster was admonished as "Daddy took her T-Bird away" in Brian Wilson's classic, "Fun, Fun, Fun," and Jan and Dean found it cumbersome and hair-raising on "Dead Man's Curve"—the forerunner of Sears's Baja experiments. The mass appeal of surfing, drag racing, and their shared pratfalls, were waning in the fickle microcosm of popular music. Clearly prognosticated by the Drifters, there was more provocative action to be had "Under the Boardwalk"!

1. "Sugar Shack," Jimmy Gilmer & The Fireballs
2. "Go Away Little Girl," Steve Lawrence
3. "Limbo Rock," Chubby Checker
4. "Blue Velvet," Bobby Vinton
5. "Telstar," Tornadoes
6. "End of the World," Skeeter Davis
7. "I Will Follow Him," Little Peggy March
8. "Can't Get Used to Losing You," Andy Williams
9. "Fingertips Part II," Little Stevie Wonder
10. "Return to Sender," Elvis Presley
11. "Up on the Roof," Drifters
12. "Rhythm of the Rain," Cascades
13. "Big Girls Don't Cry," Four Seasons
14. "In My Room"/"Be True to Your School," Beach Boys
15. "Hey Paula," Paul & Paula
16. "He's So Fine," Chiffons
17. "Surfin' USA"/"Shut Down," Beach Boys
18. "So Much in Love," Tymes
19. "Walk Like a Man," Four Seasons
20. "Puff the Magic Dragon," Peter Paul & Mary
21. "Walk Right In," Roof Top Singers
22. "My Boyfriend's Back," Angels
23. "Easier Said Than Done," Essex
24. "Our Day Will Come," Ruby & Romantics
25. "Mockingbird," Inezz Foxx
26. "If You Wanna Be Happy," Jimmy Soul
27. "Ruby Baby," Dion
28. "Surf City," Jan & Dean
29. "Sukiyaki," Kyu Sakamoto
30. "It's My Party," Lesley Gore
31. "Blame it on the Bossa Nova," Eydie Gorme
32. "I Love You Because," Al Martino
33. "Pipeline," Chantays
34. "Hello Stranger," Barbara Lewis
35. "Be My Baby," Ronettes
36. "Wipe Out," Surfaris

37. "Two Faces Have I," Lou Christie
38. "Blowing in the Wind," Peter Paul & Mary
39. "Wild Weekend," Rockin' Rebels
40. "You're the Reason I'm Living," Bobby Darin
41. "You Can't Sit Down," Dovells
42. "Candy Girl," Four Seasons
43. "Heat Wave," Martha & The Vandellas
44. "If I Had a Hammer," Trini Lopez
45. "Surfer Girl," Beach Boys
46. "Bobby's Girl," Marcie Blaine
47. "From a Jack to a King," Ned Miller
48. "You've Really Got a Hold on Me," Miracles
49. "Hello Muddah, Hello Faddah," Alan Sherman
50. "Lonely Bull," Tijuana Brass

Number-One Songs of '63 *(Billboard)*

"Telstar" (1), Tornadoes
"Go Away Little Girl" (2), Steve Lawrence
"Walk Right In" (2), Rooftop Singers
"Hey Paula" (3), Paul & Paula
"Walk Like a Man" (3), Four Seasons
"Our Day Will Come" (1), Ruby & Romantics
"He's So Fine" (4), Chiffons
"I Will Follow Him" (3), Little Peggy March
"If You Wanna Be Happy" (2), Jimmy Soul
"It's My Party" (2), Lesley Gore
"Sukiyaki" (3), Kyo Sakamoto
"Easier Said Than Done" (2), Essex
"Surf City" (2), Jan & Dean
"So Much in Love," (1), Tymes
"Fingertips Part II" (3), Little Stevie Wonder
"My Boyfriend's Back" (3), Angels
"Blue Velvet" (3), Bobby Vinton
"Sugar Shack" (5), Jimmy Gilmer & The Fireballs

"Deep Purple" (1), Nino Tempo & April Stevens
"I'm Leaving it up to You" (2), Dale & Grace
"Dominique" (4), Singing Nun

Most Significant Artists of '63

Beach Boys
Four Seasons
Lesley Gore
Bobby Vinton
Peter Paul & Mary

Academy Award (Oscar) Winner of '63

"Call Me Irresponsible"
from *Papa's Delicate Condition*
Major recording: Frank Sinatra

NARAS (Grammy) Major Category Winners of '63

Record of the Year:
"The Days Of Wine & Roses," Henry Mancini

Album of the Year:
"The Barbra Streisand Album," Barbra Streisand

Song of the Year:
"The Days Of Wine & Roses," Henry Mancini, Johnny Mercer

"I'm Doing this Study of Al Martino's Potential . . ."

Nineteen hundred and sixty-four was the year of mass hysteria and teenage eruption, as preconceived icons came tumbling down and established methodology ground to a halt in the record industry. Suddenly, the previously dominant Beach Boys produced little clamor and excitement; the Four Seasons, tremendous favorites, settled for mild adulation; the Righteous Brothers, thought to be on their way to instantaneous stardom, took a respite and waited a year; and dozens of other American groups, waiting in the wings, did just that.

It began in 1963 when an English group, represented in this country on the Swan label, crawled lazily on to the national pop-indicator charts, barely survived a week in the high nineties, and again had lackluster results on the Vee-Jay label, despite the fact Great Britain was in the throes of hysteria, initiated by this group's "Mersey-beat," their satirical and ambivalent attitude toward their work, and their pre-Victorian moplike hair. An American news program presented a short insert depicting these Liverpudlians' meteoric rise in conservative Europe, which, in turn, encouraged Jack Paar to telecast a lengthy film clip of what could only be described as "riot time" at one of their many, cacaphonic performances. Most of us in the top-forty field of radio viewed that Paar presentation and concluded that something was about to explode, as did the staff of the "Ed Sullivan Show" and several astute executives in Hollywood at the Capitol Tower.

Soothsayers of the public's purchasing habits, especially in the record industry, acutely recalled that Bing Crosby had monopolized the thirties, Frank Sinatra had unraveled "bobby soxers" in the forties, and Elvis Presley had cornered the vinyl market of the fifties. There was no doubt about it—a new rage was imminent. The sixties had yet to produce an American deity, with the exception of Fabian, who, in the end, proved that you can fool all the people only part of the time. Over-all sagging record sales indicated that the music business was approaching the dregs of rock bottom, and the prophets willingly sought a messiah—or messiahs. Their arrival became legendary and their immediate ascendancy would be myth if the sales charts, and resulting commissions, didn't prove otherwise.

Murray "the K" gave these four lads from Liverpool the key to New York and they unlocked and unleashed a tempest. Ed Sullivan—it seemed like history repeating itself—unveiled their mixed bag of tricks and explosive talent from coast to coast. Shea Stadium, the monolithic edifice, became their stage for an incredible night of pandemonium that can be compared with the future "Woodstock." City after city packed their auditoriums and stadiums to capacity, while newscasters exploited the furor and presented hourly diatribes analyzing their every move, from cuisine preferences to potty habits. Countless thousands of teens combed their own tresses with expediency in hopes that their hair would grow prolifically. National music charts became the personal property and kingdom of this one, unbelievably talented organization, and five record companies rushed out singles, both old and new, ranging from good to terrible.

Amid this madness, a lone Capitol record promoter set out in his automobile from his home in Connecticut, with his usual trunk-full of current singles and albums. His route took him to Hartford, north through Springfield, Massachusetts, and, finally, to Albany, New York, and a radio station WABY, where I was the late afternoon personality, the station iconoclast, and, more importantly, the music director.

Merv treated me to lunch that day and my record-hustling friend instigated one of the most brilliant and well coordinated pitches I had ever experienced. His lengthy commercial, laced with anecdotal pleasures, terminated with the curious display of an

56

ominous black portfolio that he had held firmly, since his arrival, with an obvious pride for its confidential contents.

"Dutch," he grasped my forearm with a serious intonation in his voice, "I'm going to share a well-kept secret with you. This black book is filled with facts, sales figures, projections, and much more; this is an extensive study that I've spent months on, and now, I'm sure about it. This is an aggregate study of Al Martino's potential with Capitol for 1964."

He paused and smiled.

"There's no doubt about it, this will be Al's finest year with our company!"

A moment of silence followed. As he leaned back in his chair, wiping his lips with a linen napkin, he reached down to a stack of promotional records on the floor beside him, and, as an afterthought, said, "Oh yeah. Incidentally, I've got a new LP and a single by some English group of kids that the Tower is really hot for. I don't know."

He sipped his drink.

"I think they're called the Beatles."

1. "I Want to Hold Your Hand," Beatles
2. "She Loves You," Beatles
3. "Oh Pretty Woman," Roy Orbison
4. "I Get Around," Beach Boys
5. "Hello Dolly," Louis Armstrong
6. "Louie Louie," Kingsmen
7. "Everybody Loves Somebody," Dean Martin
8. "My Guy," Mary Wells
9. "Dominique," Singing Nun
10. "Glad All Over," Dave Clark Five
11. "Where Did Our Love Go," Supremes
12. "There I've Said It Again," Bobby Vinton
13. "She's a Fool," Lesley Gore
14. "Love Me Do," Beatles
15. "People," Barbra Streisand
16. "Java," Al Hirt
17. "Forget Him," Bobby Rydell
18. "Kissin' Cousins," Elvis Presley
19. "A Hard Day's Night," Beatles
20. "I'm Leaving it up to You," Dale & Grace
21. "Washington Square," Village Stompers
22. "Under the Boardwalk," Drifters
23. "Ringo," Lorne Greene
24. "Fun Fun Fun," Beach Boys
25. "Dawn (Go Away)," Four Seasons
26. "Chapel of Love," Dixiecups
27. "A World Without Love," Peter & Gordon
28. "Love Me With All Your Heart," Ray Charles Singers
29. "Suspicion," Terry Stafford
30. "Little Children," Billy J. Kramer & Dakotas
31. "Since I Fell For You," Lenny Welch
32. "Leader of the Pack," Shangri-Las
33. "Rag Doll," Four Seasons
34. "Wishin' & Hopin'," Dusty Springfield
35. "Busted," Ray Charles
36. "Can I Get a Witness," Marvin Gaye

37. "It's All Right," Impressions
38. "Do Wah Diddy Diddy," Manfred Mann
39. "Fools Rush In," Ricky Nelson
40. "Walkin' the Dog," Rufus Thomas
41. "Please, Please Me," Beatles
42. "You Don't Own Me," Lesley Gore
43. "Baby Love," Supremes
44. "Can't Buy Me Love," Beatles
45. "Deep Purple," Nino Tempo & April Stevens
46. "Walk On By," Dionne Warwick
47. "Nitty Gritty," Shirley Ellis
48. "Don't Let the Rain Come Down," Serendipity Singers
49. "House of the Rising Sun," Animals
50. "Come a Little Bit Closer," Jay & The Americans

Number-One Songs of '64 *(Billboard)*

"There! I've Said It Again" (4), Bobby Vinton
"I Want To Hold Your Hand" (7), Beatles
"She Loves You" (2), Beatles
"Can't Buy Me Love" (5), Beatles
"Hello Dolly" (1), Louis Armstrong
"My Guy" (2), Mary Wells
"Love Me Do" (1), Beatles
"Chapel of Love" (3), Dixiecups
"A World Without Love," (1), Peter & Gordon
"I Get Around" (2), Beach Boys
"Rag Doll" (2), Four Seasons
"A Hard Day's Night" (2), Beatles
"Everybody Loves Somebody" (1), Dean Martin
"Where Did Our Love Go" (2), Supremes
"The House of the Rising Sun" (3), Animals
"Oh Pretty Woman" (3), Roy Orbison
"Do Wah Diddy Diddy" (2), Manfred Mann
"Baby Love" (4), Supremes

"Leader of the Pack" (1), Shangri-Las
"Ringo" (1), Lorne Greene
"Mr. Lonely" (1), Bobby Vinton
"Come See About Me" (1), Supremes
"I Feel Fine" (1), Beatles

Most Significant Artists of '64

Beatles
Beach Boys
Supremes
Four Seasons
Dave Clark Five

Academy Award (Oscar) Winner of '64

"Chim Chim Cher-ee"
    from *Mary Poppins*

Major recording: Julie Andrews & Dick Van Dyke

NARAS (Grammy) Major Category Winners of '64

Record of the Year:
    "The Girl From Ipanema," Stan Getz & Astrud Gilberto

Album of the Year:
    "Getz/Gilberto," Stan Getz & Joao Gilberto

Song of the Year:
    "Hello, Dolly!" Jerry Herman

60

A Tambourine on a Top Hat 1965

Ask any "nostalgiac" the famous artist who recorded "Reet Petite," and he'll probably answer, Jackie Wilson; ask him who wrote the tune, and he'll likely shake his head in dismay. Query the same person what Barrett Strong's only hit record was, and he may immediately reply, "Money"; yet ask him the significance of the disc, and, undoubtedly, he'll offer you a few moments of ominous silence. The prosperity of these two rock curios have a common denominator, Berry Gordy, Jr., the prodigy who founded and erected record companies in Detroit and fathered the most voluminous Horatio Alger tale in the history of the American music industry.

In 1957 Berry penned the Wilson hit, "Reet Petite," and with little optimistic response from the publishing people, continued his full-time occupation on the assembly lines of the Ford Motor Company. With the extra dollars earned from his part-time effort as a songwriter, he organized Anna Records and convinced a club singer, Barrett Strong, to record one of Gordy's songs, "Money." History notes its minor success.

With the knowledge that record wholesalers rarely discharge payments on an initial release or, at least, until a second hit is established, Berry Gordy embarked on a yellow brick road that would ultimately guide him to a kingdom of self-wizardry that sprawled from the Motor City to the City of Angels. With the Miracles, a group he had recorded two years earlier, he struck gold for the first time in 1960 with the million seller, "Shop Around."

61

The lead singer of the Miracles, Smokey Robinson, soon to be a producer-writer for Motown-Tamla enterprises, was one of the towering discoveries of rock & roll and the rhythm & blues genre.

Gordy soon unearthed three exciting larks, the Marvelettes, and his second chart-topper, "Please Mr. Postman," showered more revenue into the Motown coffers. To quote a radio aphorism of the period, "the hits just kept on comin' " with succeeding winners by the Contours ("Do You Love Me," 1962), Martha & the Vandellas ("Come And Get these Memories," 1963), Marvin Gaye ("Stubborn Kind Of Fellow," 1962), Mary Wells ("The One Who Really Loves You," 1962), Kim Weston ("Love Me All the Way," 1963), Stevie Wonder ("Fingertips," 1963), the Supremes ("When the Lovelight Starts Shining," 1964), the Temptations ("The Way You Do the Things You Do," 1964), Jr. Walker and the All-Stars ("Shotgun," 1964), the Isley Brothers ("This Old Heart Of Mine," 1966), and the Four Tops ("I Can't Help Myself," 1965). Add to this list other successes—Diana Ross (after exiting as lead of the Supremes), Tammi Terrell (a single but sometimes partner of Marvin Gaye), Rare Earth (Gordy's first group to enter the field of "hard rock"), Gladys Knight and the Pips (a group that made their first Detroit-based appearance on the charts in 1967), and the Spinners (who achieved moderate acclaim in Detroit, but attained greater stature with Atlantic Records).

Berry Gordy, Jr., built an empire of sophisticated "soul," and though many of his children left the sandbox, the castle has yet to crumble. Dissenting critics claim his product lacked originality, that his "soul" was overly commercial, and that his long string of hits was mired in one, unchanging beat. Many claimed he was an introspective tyrant, controlling every facet of his artists' lives, from stage to boudoir. Closer to fact, Gordy uncovered obscure acts and remodeled their styles until he had produced superstars; and he accomplished this from a third city, Detroit, far from the established studios of New York and Los Angeles. No doubt, the rhythm lines of his recordings, with their heavy emphasis on the bass, were shrouded in duplication, but it was never colorless. His music was always danceable, and that sold records. A musician friend of mine once pointed out that, invariably, Motown hits underlined the sound of a tambourine placed on a top hat, just another distinction that made Gordy millions.

From records Berry acceded to motion pictures; from Detroit, and Tamla-Motown-Soul, he moved part of his operation to the West Coast, opening a subsidiary, Mowest, and financed high-budget movies like *Lady Sings The Blues* and *Mahogany*, both starring his court favorite, Diana Ross. These financial investments followed a period of white backlash in the late sixties, when top-forty radio eschewed soul music as if it were a carrier of the plague. During this repressive epoch, Motown's product, to quote Eddie Kendricks, "kept on truckin'," little affected by Middle America's display of bigotry. With few exceptions—the Supremes' "Living in Shame" did contain the lyric line "my mother died while making homemade jam"—Gordy rarely produced stiffs; most of his records could have been top-ten songs. He produced such consistently good material, radio stations just couldn't find room or time to play it all.

Today, with the exodus of Mary Wells, the Four Tops, Gladys Knight and the Pips, the Isley Brothers, and the Spinners to competitive labels, critics have predicted that Berry Gordy's flame will diminish; but, out of the ashes, his new sparks include the Jackson Five, Eddie Kendricks, Willie Hutch, and Diana Ross with her 1976 million-dollar chart-topper "Love Hangover." He keeps churning out winner after winner, and with an established rank of artists like Smokey Robinson, the Miracles, Marvin Gaye, and a camp of solid hitmakers, he shows little sign or desire for abdication.

Berry Gordy, Jr., from the assembly line to the executive suite, is an inspiration for a business dominated by cartels, owned and operated by firms whose major assets include parking lots.

1. "I Can't Help Myself," Four Tops
2. "I Got You Babe," Sonny & Cher
3. "(I Can't Get No) Satisfaction," Rolling Stones
4. "Wooly Bully," Sam The Sham & The Pharoahs
5. "Downtown," Petula Clark
6. "You've Lost That Loving Feeling," Righteous Brothers
7. "Help!" Beatles
8. "My Girl," Temptations
9. "You Were On My Mind," We Five
10. "Can't You Hear My Heartbeat," Herman's Hermits
11. "King of the Road," Roger Miller
12. "The Birds & the Bees," Jewel Akins
13. "Help Me Rhonda," Beach Boys
14. "Mrs. Brown, You've Got a Lovely Daughter," Herman's Hermits
15. "Shot Gun," Jr. Walker & All Stars
16. "Hold Me, Thrill Me, Kiss Me," Mel Carter
17. "Crying in the Chapel," Elvis Presley
18. "This Diamond Ring," Gary Lewis & Playboys
19. "Stop! In the Name of Love," Supremes
20. "The 'In' Crowd," Ramsey Lewis Trio
21. "Silhouettes," Herman's Hermits
22. "I'll Never Find Another You," Seekers
23. "Mr. Tambourine Man," Byrds
24. "Cara Mia," Jay & the Americans
25. "Papa's Got a Brand New Bag," James Brown & Famous Flames
26. "Unchained Melody," Righteous Brothers
27. "Eve of Destruction," Barry McGuire
28. "Ticket to Ride," Beatles
29. "Yes I'm Ready," Barbara Mason
30. "Cast Your Fate to the Wind," Sounds Orchestral
31. "Game of Love," Mindbenders
32. "Hang On Sloopy," McCoys
33. "Come See About Me," Supremes
34. "Like a Rolling Stone," Bob Dylan

35. "The Name Game," Shirley Ellis
36. "Back In My Arms Again," Supremes
37. "Ferry Across The Mersey," Gerry & Pacemakers
38. "Go Now," Moody Blues
39. "I Know a Place," Petula Clark
40. "Baby I'm Yours," Barbara Lewis
41. "I'm Telling You Now," Freddy & Dreamers
42. "Eight Days a Week," Beatles
43. "I Feel Fine," Beatles
44. "A Walk in the Black Forest," Horst Jankowski
45. "I'm Henry VIII, I Am," Herman's Hermits
46. "Mr. Lonely," Bobby Vinton
47. "Down in the Boondocks," Billy Joe Royal
48. "I'll Be Doggone," Marvin Gaye
49. "I Hear a Symphony," Supremes
50. "Get Off My Cloud," Rolling Stones

Number-One Songs of '65 *(Billboard)*

"I Feel Fine" (2), Beatles
"Come See About Me" (1), Supremes
"Downtown" (2), Petula Clark
"You've Lost That Loving Feeling" (2), Righteous Brothers
"This Diamond Ring" (2), Gary Lewis & the Playboys
"My Girl" (1), Temptations
"Eight Days A Week" (2), Beatles
"Stop! In the Name of Love" (2), Supremes
"I'm Telling You Now" (2), Freddy & the Dreamers
"Game of Love" (1), Mindbenders
"Mrs. Brown, You've Got a Lovely Daughter" (3), Herman's
    Hermits
"Ticket to Ride" (1), Beatles
"Help Me Rhonda" (2), Beach Boys
"Back In My Arms Again" (1), Supremes
"I Can't Help Myself" (2), Four Tops

65

"Mr. Tambourine Man" (1), Byrds
"Satisfaction" (4), Rolling Stones
"I'm Henry VIII, I Am" (1), Herman's Hermits
"I Got You Babe" (3), Sonny & Cher
"Help!" (3), Beatles
"Eve of Destruction" (1), Barry McGuire
"Hang On Sloopy" (1), McCoys
"Yesterday" (4), Beatles
"Get Off My Cloud" (2), Rolling Stones
"I Hear a Symphony" (2), Supremes
"Turn Turn Turn" (3), Byrds
"Over & Over" (1), Dave Clark Five

Most Significant Artists of '65

Beatles
Supremes
Herman's Hermits
Righteous Brothers
Petula Clark

Academy Award (Oscar) Winner of '65

"Shadow Of Your Smile"
    from *The Sandpiper*
Major recording: Tony Bennett

Record of the Year:
   "A Taste Of Honey," Herb Alpert & Tijuana Brass

Album of the Year:
   "September Of My Years," Frank Sinatra

Song of the Year:
   "The Shadow Of Your Smile," Paul Webster & Johnny Mandel

Showers and Towers and Caravans **1966**

Whenever I inform my teenage son Paul that in 1957 I was a recipient of five hours of live, and in-person, rock & roll for less than four dollars, had dynamite seating, and viewed more than fifteen top acts, he just shakes his head and skulks away, on his way to the local auditorium to purchase a six dollar and fifty cent ticket to observe a solitary act, not always of superstar proportions. Well, it's true. In the winter of 1957, I paid three dollars and fifty cents to share space in the Providence Arena with the Platters, Little Richard, Bill Haley and the Comets, Shirley and Lee, Chuck Berry, Mickey and Sylvia, and a dozen other popular rock stars of the period. The show spanned a timeless duration, police breaking up intermittent fights between each and every proceeding. Sadly, those cavalcades have vanished now, but they prevailed for more than a decade.

Even in the sixties, when I was an enterprising morning personality at radio station WTOB, in Winston-Salem, North Carolina, a show casually observed by Tom Wolf in his "Electric Kool-Aid Acid Test," our management sponsored giant rock shows on a monthly subscription—the admission never exceeded five dollars at the door.

If I were not advertising a Dick Clark "Caravan," I was hawking a Gene Pitney "Shower Of Stars," and with the avarice, but not the gift, of P. T. Barnum, my partner Alan White and I were concocting our own contrivances: "Tower(s) Of Power." My first dabble in the art of ballyhoo came in the early sixties, when I pre-

vailed on the city fathers of Albany, New York, to rent me a high
school auditorium for the presentation of such luminaries as
Freddy Cannon, Tommy Roe, the Duprees, and several other minor performers. Despite the surprise guest appearance of hip-
shaking Curtis Lee, I took a monetary bath. Graciously, the
mayor's office neglected to charge me for the building—a bureau-
cratic foul-up—and I walked away unscathed.

In 1966, after a series of Dick Clark's traveling salvation
shows, featuring Paul Revere and the Raiders, Herman's Hermits,
the Monkees, the Animals, and lesser notables like Billy Joe Royal,
Round Robin, and Joe South, I was excitedly preparing a Flying
Dutchman Tuesday night special, irresistably entitled, "The Tower
Of Power." There was one minor, irritating problem: Tuesday
night in the Bible Belt of North Carolina can, and usually does,
digress into a placid evening. Despite the laborious efforts of Lou
Christie, Barbara Lewis, and the Toys, my partner and I barely
retrieved our investment and got out by the skin of our mutual
teeth.

It was more temperate to sponsor ready-made shows, and,
from that moment on, that's what we did. Today, in a world of
one-act appearances, I miss these milestones that were landmark
events to the populace of any moderately sized city. Without them,
I might never have beheld ten-thousand screaming fans greeting
the Animals' Eric Burdon at the airport and viewing, in awe, his
collapse in an inebriated state shortly after leaving his plane; I certainly would not have been part of B. J. Thomas' threat to pop
John Sebastion in the mouth, if John's younger brother, and road
manager for the Lovin' Spoonful, continued to prevent the Tri-
umphs from setting up their equipment on stage; I would not have
marveled at Lou Christie's private secretary and gypsy, who trav-
eled as his companion, compiling his daily horoscope; my wife
might have never been titillated by Davey Jones of the Monkees
racing around backstage in the buff; my son would not have sat on
Diana Ross's lap, a discredit to the rumor that she was unfriendly
while on tour; I might never have introduced the Yardbirds to a
screaming audience twenty minutes before their equipment was
ready; and I might never have transported Brian Hyland and Bobby
Goldsboro from Charlotte to Winston-Salem in the back seat of a
Ford, as they feigned being gay to my chagrin.

70

The composite rock shows had a spontaneity and the tense atmosphere made anything possible. I remember the night two radio time-salesmen harvested Peter Noone's profits for the night in a crap game. I recall the wild-eyed excitement when our station's announcing staff fetched twenty teenagers to a tea for the Monkees. I still cringe at the thought of my wife, Betty, telling a boisterous gentleman in the next row to shut up because she couldn't hear the performance of Blood, Sweat, and Tears, and his later introducing himself as José Feliciano. I panic at the mere mention of Steppenwolf, remembering their mischievious activities in one of New Haven's finest restaurants, dispersing Parker House rolls as missiles directed at any patron seemingly over thirty-five years of age. Most of all, I recollect four thousand teens packed like sardines into a gymnasium for a free dance featuring Len Barry, Joe South, Gene and Debbe, James and Bobby Purify, and Bobby Lewis—it was only after the show that we learned to our horror that all the fire doors had been firmly chained all evening!

By the seventies, one-act shows dominated and admission prices soared. An occasional "Rock and Roll Revival" strived to bring back the congenial atmosphere and the zaniness of those old rock "goliaths," but the uncontrived lunacy was gone. Mark Lindsay was not there playing "grabsy" with Paul Revere; the Lovin' Spoonful no longer did forty-five-minute tuneups on stage; Round Robin, three hundred pounds of bubbling personality, wasn't wandering around the dressing room in his jock strap; and Johnny Thunder was not threatening a disc jockey's life for his goosing Dionne Warwick.

If you still crave those hearty days gone by, scan *TV Guide* for reruns of the "Monterrey Pop Festival," the Stone's "Gimme Shelter," or the social experience at "Woodstock"; or you can wait until your local sheriff periodically condescends to a rock festival in a nearby pasture or football stadium. Till then, a toast to Gene Pitney, sitting backstage in his underwear, totaling the night's receipts on his portable adding machine.

1. "Cherish," Association
2. "(You Are My) Soul & Inspiration," Righteous Brothers
3. "Reach Out I'll Be There," Four Tops
4. "96 Tears," ? & Mysterians
5. "The Ballad of the Green Berets," SSgt. Barry Sadler
6. "Last Train to Clarksville," Monkees
7. "You Can't Hurry Love," Supremes
8. "California Dreamin'," Mammas & Papas
9. "Poor Side of Town," Johnny Rivers
10. "These Boots Were Made for Walkin'," Nancy Sinatra
11. "Monday, Monday," Mamas & Papas
12. "Born Free," Roger Williams
13. "We Can Work It Out," Beatles
14. "Summer in the City," Lovin' Spoonful
15. "Strangers in the Night," Frank Sinatra
16. "What Becomes of the Broken Hearted," Jimmy Ruffin
17. "Hanky Panky," Tommy James & Shondells
18. "Good Lovin'," Young Rascals
19. "Lightning Strikes," Lou Christie
20. "When a Man Loves a Woman," Percy Sledge
21. "Winchester Cathedral," New Vaudeville Band
22. "Kicks," Paul Revere & Raiders
23. "My Love," Petula Clark
24. "Wild Thing," Bobby Hebb
25. "Sunny," Bobby Hebb
26. "Good Vibrations," Beach Boys
27. "Paint It Black," Rolling Stones
28. "Paperback Writer," Beatles
29. "Sweet Pea," Tommy Roe
30. "Sunshine Superman," Donovan
31. "You Keep Me Hanging On," Supremes
32. "Turn Turn Turn," Byrds
33. "Sounds of Silence," Simon & Garfunkel
34. "Devil with a Blue Dress"/"Good Golly Miss Molly," Mitch Ryder
35. "Born a Woman," Sandy Posey

36. "Little Red Riding Hood," Sam The Sham & Pharoahs
37. "You Don't Have to Say You Love Me," Dusty Springfield
38. "Red Rubber Ball," Cyrkle
39. "A Groovy Kind of Love," Mindbenders
40. "I'm Your Puppet," James & Bobby Purify
41. "Ain't Too Proud To Beg," Temptations
42. "Cool Jerk," Capitols
43. "Walk Away Renee," Left Banke
44. "Day Dream," Lovin' Spoonful
45. "I Am a Rock," Simon & Garfunkel
46. "B-A-B-Y," Carla Thomas
47. "Time Won't Let Me," Outsiders
48. "Elusive Butterfly," Bob Lind
49. "Bus Stop," Hollies
50. "See You in September," Happenings

Number-One Songs of '66 *(Billboard)*

"Sounds of Silence" (2), Simon & Garfunkel
"We Can Work It Out" (3), Beatles
"My Love" (2), Petula Clark
"Lightning Strikes" (1), Lou Christie
"These Boots Are Made for Walking" (1), Nancy Sinatra
"The Ballad of the Green Berets" (5), Sgt. Barry Sadler
"(You Are My) Soul & Inspiration" (3), Righteous Brothers
"Good Lovin' " (1), Young Rascals
"Monday, Monday" (3), Mamas & Papas
"When a Man Loves a Woman" (2), Percy Sledge
"Paint It Black" (2), Rolling Stones
"Paperback Writer" (2), Beatles
"Strangers in the Night" (1), Frank Sinatra
"Hanky Panky" (2), Tommy James & Shondells
"Wild Thing" (2), Troggs
"Summer in the City" (3), Lovin' Spoonful
"Sunshine Superman" (1), Donovan

73

"You Can't Hurry Love" (2), Supremes
"Cherish" (3), Association
"Reach Out I'll Be There" (2), Four Tops
"96 Tears" (1), ? & Mysterians
"Last Train to Clarksville" (1), Monkees
"Poor Side of Town" (1), Johnny Rivers
"You Keep Me Hanging On" (2), Supremes
"Winchester Cathedral" (3), New Vaudeville Band
"Good Vibrations" (1), Beach Boys
"I'm a Believer" (1), Monkees

Most Significant Artists of '66

Mamas & Papas
Monkees
Beatles
Rolling Stones
Simon & Garfunkel

Academy Award (Oscar) Winner of '66

"Born Free"
        from *Born Free*

Major recording: Roger Williams

Record of the Year:
    "Strangers in the Night," Frank Sinatra

Album of the Year:
    "Sinatra—A Man & His Music," Frank Sinatra

Song of the Year:
    "Michelle," John Lennon, Paul McCartney

Blue Eyes in the Soul   1967

Influenced by the "super hit" philosophy of AM radio, 1967 was the last year any specific mode of popular music dominated the youth scene. That form, rhythm & blues, recently renamed "soul," did not totally capture the attention of the teen record buyer. Too many forms of rock surfaced that year, signaling the future wave of specialization. Bob Dylan, founder of a new cult of intelligentsia, created pop songs that were quasi-political statements, underlined with a new youth-bedeviled ideology. The Beatles, other English groups, and many of their American imitators scrapped their "Mersey beat" and entered a realm of new ideas stated explicitly in the pioneer "Rubber Soul" album of late 1965. Innovative instrumental techniques—the vanguard devoured the development of "controlled feedback," the new twists in amplification, and the commercially marketed gimmicks like Vox's "Wah-Wah"—were commerce for the Electric Prunes, the Yardbirds, and the Doors. The incredible popularity of Herman's Hermits and the Monkees spawned a new, financially rewarding mediocrity, aptly named "bubble gum"; the fifteen and under set eagerly followed the chants of the soon-to-be super talents of the 1910 Fruit Gum Company, the Cowsills, the Partridge Family, and, later, the Osmonds. Another part of pop music's new polarization was created by the broadcasters and called "easy listening," a euphemism for the old "middle of the road." Critics decided that "chicken rock" would be more apropos.

As the musical variants of the future were closing ranks,

Memphis, Tennessee, Muscle Shoals, Alabama, and a newly reno-
vated Philadelphia, delivered a bombardment of soul artists—Sam
and Dave ("Soul Man"), Eddie Floyd ("Knock on Wood"), Otis
Redding ("Try A Little Tenderness"), Cliff Nobles and Company
("The Horse"), Aretha Franklin ("Respect"), Arthur Conley
("Sweet Soul Music"), and, by his own ingenuity, James Brown
("Cold Sweat"). Individually, they failed to make big impressions
on the year end summary charts of 1967, but the abovenamed,
and dozens of others, had the over-all effect of making it the year
of "soul."

The greatest impact was in the white community, as "blue-
eyed soul" achieved its one-year spurt of glory. The Righteous
Brothers, for whom the genre was named, had shown an early impact, respectfully emulating black soul with their recordings of
"You've Lost That Loving Feeling" and "(You are) My Soul and
Inspiration." Other white groups followed suit, the chief propo-
nents being the Young Rascals with hits such as "Groovin' " and
"How Can I Be Sure" and the Boxtops—who claimed the number-
one song of 1967 with "The Letter" and the Music Explosion with
"A Little Bit Of Soul." One artist, Roy Head ("Treat Her Right"),
had been so convincing at the art of "blue-eyed soul," he was
booked on one of the all-black rock shows that criss-crossed the
country. Audiences were less than receptive.

The Stax Record firm in Memphis was the single most important impetus for the new black music boom. With a group of
studio musicians, hard to equal in any of the recording centers of
the nation, Stax releases were punctuated by a powerful rhythm,
uniquely evincing an originality and basic structure that demonstrated little of the Detroit or New York sophistication. Scores of
worshippers trekked to the "City Of Cotton" on the Mississippi to
master the prevailing wisdom, to share the knack God had given
producer-artists like Isaac Hayes, and to attain the freshest and
purest sound of the day. Even Elvis Presley made a late-sixties
comeback, utilizing the studios, the musicians, and the songwriters
of his hometown—and aided somewhat by television and live performances.

Soul, and its blue-eyed counterpart, had a short-lived span of
popularity on top-forty radio, for the long hot summer of 1967
signaled the arrival of the big city riots. Radio stations irrationally

related the ghetto uprisings to the music of the black envoys. Soul artists, soul-influenced white groups, and even hard-rock advocates like the Doors—"Light My Fire" had suspiciously provocative lyrics—were hauled off the air. Until the dawn of the mid-seventies' "disco" music, and the return of the black singers to the top-forty charts, Memphis studios fell on hard times. Companies like Stax, deprived of their impact, filed for bankruptcy, unable to support themselves in the black market alone.

1. "The Letter," Box Tops
2. "Ode to Billie Joe," Bobbie Gentry
3. "To Sir with Love," Lulu
4. "Light My Fire," Doors
5. "Windy," Association
6. "I'm a Believer," Monkees
7. "Groovin'," Rascals
8. "Happy Together," Turtles
9. "Can't Take My Eyes Off You," Frankie Valli
10. "Respect," Aretha Franklin
11. "Something Stupid," Nancy & Frank Sinatra
12. "Little Bit of Soul," Music Explosion
13. "I Think We're Alone Now," Tommy James & Shondells
14. "I Was Made to Love Her," Stevie Wonder
15. "Sweet Soul Music," Arthur Conley
16. "Expressway to Your Heart," Soul Survivors
17. "Comeback When You Grow Up," Bobby Vee
18. "Never My Love," Association
19. "Kind of a Drag," Buckinghams
20. "Soul Man," Sam & Dave
21. "Apples, Peaches, Pumpkin Pie," Jay & Techniques
22. "Ruby Tuesday," Rolling Stones
23. "It Must Be Him," Vicki Carr
24. "All You Need Is Love," Beatles
25. "Come On Down to My Boat, Baby," Every Mother's Son
26. "Incense & Peppermints," Strawberry Alarm Clock
27. "Gimme Little Sign," Brenton Wood
28. "For What It's Worth," Buffalo Springfield
29. "Brown Eyed Girl," Van Morrison
30. "Love Is Here (& Now You've Gone)," Supremes
31. "Release Me," Engelbert Humperdinck
32. "The Rain, the Park & Other Things," Cowsills
33. "The Happening," Supremes
34. "Get On Up," Esquires
35. "Somebody to Love," Jefferson Airplane
36. "A Whiter Shade of Pale," Procol Harum

37. "Then You Can Tell Me Goodbye," Casinos
38. "Jimmy Mack," Martha & Vandellas
39. "On a Carousel," Hollies
40. "I Got Rhythm," Happenings
41. "Please Love Me Forever," Bobby Vinton
42. "Up, Up & Away," Fifth Dimension
43. "Cold Sweat," James Brown
44. "The Beat Goes On," Sonny & Cher
45. "Daydream Believer," Monkees
46. "Reflections," Supremes
47. "Penny Lane," Beatles
48. "98.6," Keith
49. "Silence Is Golden," Tremeloes
50. "Higher & Higher," Jackie Wilson

Number-One Songs of '67 *(Billboard)*

"I'm A Believer" (6), Monkees
"Kind of a Drag" (2), Buckinghams
"Ruby Tuesday" (1), Rolling Stones
"Love Is Here (And Now You've Gone)" (1), Supremes
"Penny Lane" (1), Beatles
"Happy Together" (3), Turtles
"Somethin' Stupid" (4), Nancy & Frank Sinatra
"The Happening" (1), Supremes
"Groovin' " (4), Rascals
"Respect" (2), Aretha Franklin
"Windy" (4), Association
"Light My Fire" (3), Doors
"All You Need Is Love" (1), Beatles
"Ode to Billie Joe" (4), Bobbie Gentry
"The Letter" (4), Box Tops
"To Sir with Love" (5), Lulu
"Incense & Peppermints" (1), Strawberry Alarm Clock

"Daydream Believer" (4), Monkees
"Hello Goodbye" (1), Beatles

Most Significant Artists of '67

Tommy James & Shondells
Rascals
Aretha Franklin
Box Tops
Association

Academy Award (Oscar) Winner of '67

"Talk to the Animals"
    from *Dr. Doolittle*
Major recording: Bobby Darin

NARAS (Grammy) Major Category Winners of '67

Record of the Year:
    "Up, Up & Away," Fifth Dimension
Album of the Year:
    "Sgt. Pepper's Lonely Hearts Club Band," Beatles
Song of the Year:
    "Up, Up & Away," Jim Webb

"We're Not Sure About Puff..." 1968

This is a confession—a cowardly admission, after the fact, that for three years, I naively broadcast, enjoyed, and discerned nothing about a portion of the music I was airing for my audience's pleasure. From late 1965, until my precipitous awakening in 1968, I had not the slightest inkling that a large segment of my radio audience was "pulling the wool over my eyes." In retrospect, it is hard to believe that I dwelled in such an ignominious atmosphere without responding to a trace of what transpired.

When the Beatles purchased their "Ticket To Ride" and graphically described the dreamlike benefits of a "Day Tripper," I marveled, but was perplexed, at their festive fascination with a double-decker bus. The Electric Prunes' "I Had Too Much To Dream Last Night" seemed, on the surface, an innocent bout with heartburn, and I rationalized that an Alka-Seltzer tablet would cure their plight. Blindly (pardon the pun), I considered the Rolling Stones threat to "Get Off My Cloud" as a prejudiced and violent statement of male defensiveness and, with typical male chauvinism, let it go at that.

By 1966, I willingly conceded that several rock singers displayed ambiguities in their compositions; for instance, Bob Dylan had lost me completely in "Like a Rolling Stone," as had Donovan in "Mellow Yellow." My innocence, or should it be called clear conscience, relied on the tried and true fact that music was for lovers and, occasionally, for the cynic, who snickered in wild abandon at anyone spinning a double entendre. Surely, in the back of

83

my mind, I presumed that the current crop of enigmatic tunes had clandestine meaning, but I was too busy to worry about it. And besides, though I have always enjoyed music for its melody and rhythm, to me lyrics were only superficial space consumers. Not completely in the dark, I did fathom the satirical comments of the Kinks in "Dedicated Follower of Fashion," the perverted message in Nancy Sinatra's "These Boots Are Made For Walkin'," and the rebellious spirit of the Mamas and the Papas' "California Dreamin'." After all, these songs begged to be heard and their messages seemed above suspicion. Only an idiot misinterpreted the meaning of "Eve of Destruction" by Barry McGuire, but the subtleties of the Lovin' Spoonful's "Daydream" only grazed the conscious mind of most Americans—I was certainly one of them.

Oh yes, I wondered about the chortles emanating from a youngster when he requested "Good Vibrations" by the Beach Boys, but I usually dismissed this merriment as a lamentable problem of puberty.

By 1968 cognizant broadcasters were seriously contemplating the consequences and the causal effects perpetrated by the invasion of drug-oriented recordings, but, even then, we paid little attention to them. The Door's "Light My Fire" seemed to be a reflection of what was happening in the big city streets—an anthem to dissent—and not the conspicuous four-minute commercial on the benefits of marijuana that it really was. My indifference was that of the average adult listener; few of my on-the-air comrades reacted any differently.

"Incense and Peppermints" by the Strawberry Alarm Clock— what was that all about? "With A Little Help From My Friends" by the Beatles, where intelligible, seemed to contain a socially acceptable premise. Procol Harum's "Whiter Shade of Pale," told of death and drugs; it depressed me to hear it, so why listen to the message? The Yardbirds' "Shape Of Things" was a threat to the establishment; I missed the communication. The Fifth Dimension's "Stoned Soul Picnic"; gee, I wondered if they had enough potato salad for such a hearty looking group of vocalists. Cliff Noble's "The Horse" was an instrumental; the title didn't strike me as odd, and our station used it as a background drop for a racetrack commercial!

It was the Friends of Distinction's annexation of a lyric line

84

to Hugh Masakela's instrumental, "Grazing in the Grass" and the Fifth Dimension's "Up Up and Away" that finally prompted my awakening. Was I the last to grasp this realization? An immediate survey of friends indicated that I was still ahead of the norm in decoding the cryptic pop song of the day.

When one acquires explosive knowledge, one is quick to retrospectively root out the data he has overlooked and missed in the past. With a new appreciation, I perceived what Donovan's "Hurdy Gurdy Man" was up to; I was aghast at the Byrds' frequent trips "Eight Miles High"; and analyzing the Amboy Dukes' "Journey To The Center Of The Mind," I became a voyeur peeping through a window whose shades were no longer drawn. My suspicions triggered a pointed finger which I cast in every direction. Night after night, I paused to meditate what Simon and Garfunkel were doing on their way to "Scarborough Fair," what was coming down on "Penny Lane," what sort of recreational facilities made "Mac-Arthur Park" so attractive, and what were the Hollies "circulating" "On a Carousel"?

My sudden revelations led to new investigatory heights—why were Herman's Hermits "Leaning on the Lamp Post"? Had those three upstarts, Peter, Paul, and Mary, deluded me all these years, and did "Puff, the Magic Dragon" really live by the sea, and was "Stewball" really a race horse?

This was catastrophic—a little knowledge was harmful. I ceased to listen to all lyrics, and I was torn inside; all sorts of suspicions pervaded my conscious mind. Some things were best left alone. The day I questioned the integrity of middle-aged Al Martino, I knew my involvement had ended. If Al wanted to have a little "Mary in the Morning," let him!

1. "Hey Jude," The Beatles
2. "Honey," Bobby Goldsboro
3. "Sunshine of Your Love," Cream
4. "Love Is Blue," Paul Mauriat
5. "(Sittin' On) the Dock of the Bay," Otis Redding
6. "Mrs. Robinson," Simon & Garfunkel
7. "People Gotta Be Free," Rascals
8. "Harper Valley PTA," Jeannie C. Riley
9. "This Guy's in Love with You," Herb Alpert & Tijuana Brass
10. "Tighten Up," Archie Bell & Drells
11. "Little Green Apples," O. C. Smith
12. "The Good, the Bad & the Ugly," Hugo Montenegro
13. "Young Girl," Gary Puckett & Union Gap
14. "Hello I Love You," Doors
15. "Cry Like a Baby," Box Tops
16. "Dance to the Music," Sly & Family Stone
17. "Stoned Soul Picnic," Fifth Dimension
18. "Grazing in the Grass," Hugh Masakela
19. "The Horse," Cliff Nobles & Co.
20. "Midnight Confessions," Grass Roots
21. "La La Means I Love You," Delfonics
22. "Judy in Disguise (With Glasses)," John Fred & Playboy Band
23. "I Wish It Would Rain," Temptations
24. "Mony, Mony," Tommy James & Shondells
25. "Angel of the Morning," Merrilee Rush
26. "Born to Be Wild," Steppenwolf
27. "Turn Around, Look At Me," Vogues
28. "Spooky," Classics IV
29. "Love Child," Diana Ross & Supremes
30. "Playboy," Gene & Debbe
31. "Cowboys to Girls," Intruders
32. "Those Were the Days," Mary Hopkin
33. "Simon Says," 1910 Fruitgum Company
34. "A Beautiful Morning," Rascals
35. "Hold Me Tight," Johnny Nash

36. "Lady Willpower," Gary Puckett & Union Gap
37. "The Look of Love," Sergio Mendes & Brasil 66
38. "Ballad of Bonnie & Clyde," Georgie Fame
39. "Fire," Crazy World Of Arthur Brown
40. "Theme From *The Valley Of The Dolls*," Dionne Warwick
41. "Classical Gas," Mason Williams
42. "Girl Watcher," O'Kaysions
43. "Green Tambourine," Lemon Pipers
44. "Jumping Jack Flash," Rolling Stones
45. "Slip Away," Clarence Carter
46. "Since You've Been Gone," Aretha Franklin
47. "MacArthur Park," Richard Harris
48. "Hello Goodbye," Beatles
49. "Light My Fire," Jose Feliciano
50. "Love Is All Around," Troggs

Number-One Songs of '68 *(Billboard)*

"Hello Goodbye" (2), Beatles
"Judy in Disguise (With Glasses)" (2), John Fred & Playboy Band
"Green Tambourine" (1), Lemon Pipers
"Love Is Blue" (5), Paul Mauriat
"(Sittin' On) the Dock of the Bay" (4), Otis Redding
"Honey" (5), Bobby Goldsboro
"Tighten Up" (2), Archie Bell & Drells
"Mrs. Robinson" (3), Simon & Garfunkel
"This Guy's in Love with You" (4), Herb Alpert & Tijuana Brass
"Grazing in the Grass" (2), Hugh Masakela
"Hello I Love You" (2), Doors
"People Gotta Be Free" (5), Rascals
"Harper Valley PTA" (1), Jeannie C. Riley
"Hey Jude" (9), Beatles
"Love Child" (2), Diana Ross & Supremes
"I Heard It Through the Grapevine" (3), Marvin Gaye

Most Significant Artists of '68

Beatles
Rascals
Dionne Warwick
Otis Redding
Herb Alpert & Tijuana Brass

Academy Award (Oscar) Winning Song of '68

"Windmills Of Your Mind"
    from *The Thomas Crown Affair*

Major recording: Noel Harrison

NARAS (Grammy) Major Category Winners of '68

Record of the Year:
    "Mrs. Robinson," Simon & Garfunkel

Album of the Year:
    "By the Time I Get To Phoenix," Glen Campbell

Song of the Year:
    "Little Green Apples," Bobby Russell

The Tower of Babel 1969

It has been relatively easy to describe the multiple forms and variances of rock & roll that have transpired since 1955. Fact: Bill Haley and the Comets made it all marketable. Fact: in 1956 Elvis Presley took out the patent on rock music. Fact: Hank Ballard escaped stardom when Chubby Checker borrowed his "Twist" and grabbed the acclaim for launching the dance craze of the early sixties. Fact: the Beatles gave birth in 1964 to the English monopoly of popular music. Fact: halfway through the sixties, "soul" gained massive national recognition and was to influence popular music in various forms. That's where fact ends, lost in a limbo of diversity.

In the late sixties, as if the result of some galactic explosion, the popular idiom splintered and broke into so many components that a microscopic analysis of each is a difficult if not Herculean task. The cause of this diffusion can be traced to several sources. One was the rapid acceleration and increasing listenership to FM radio, whose alternative programming deviated from hard-rock to progressive country & western, from album cuts to singles, from lush strings to neo-jazz, and away from banal top-forty disc jockeys toward mellowed diplomats who were more influenced by orchestration than sensation. Another directly related source was the music industry's new avenues in LP design and production. Whereas in earlier days, albums were showcases of one hit song surrounded by eleven other stock arrangements rushed to the vinyl, by the terminal years of the sixties, groups like Blood, Sweat, and

Tears, the Beatles, and the Rolling Stones were attractively packaged in integrated albums that could—and often did—contain half-a-dozen compositions of hit potential. And finally, the wide variety of record buyers no longer purchased records because they were exposed on top-forty radio; there was a healthy interest in innumerable fields of pop endeavor—folk-rock, hard-rock, baroque-rock, jazz-rock, country-rock, psychedelics, "bubble gum," and a multitude of others.

The generic term for the new phenomenon was "the new rock," and obviously it required more than a singular definition. People were drawn to their favorite embodiment of the pop idiom, and, in many instances, an overlapping of categories was acceptable to most, displaying the divergence of individual taste. A public display of this harmonious discord, the "Monterrey Pop Festival" in 1967, drew large and persevering crowds and a film crew from disparate segments of the population; it was a molecular entity, united by such divergent artists as Jimmi Hendrix, Big Brother and the Holding Company, Ravi Shankar, and Canned Heat. Two years later, the greatest gathering in American music history took place at a six-hundred-acre farm near Woodstock, New York, to consummate the marriage of varied musical ideologies. Total attendance figures of nearly one-half million were poo-pooed by the press and other detractors, yet even the most conservative guesses minimized the results at no fewer than three-hundred thousand kindred spirits. For four days, American youth mingled in a connubial-like "élan vital," shared collective bedrolls, smoked record quantities of dope, and even bathed together in an open display of nudity.

Entertainers—including Joan Baez, Jimmi Hendrix, Arlo Guthrie, and Sly and the Family Stone—perpetuated a seemingly endless consortium of the counter-culture rock idiom. To those in attendance, rock & roll suddenly attained a stature of maturity— no longer was Don Kirschner in the driver's seat, promoting the Archies by telephone and receiving immediate response from a communications system that controlled its audiences. The "new rock" advocates—personified at Woodstock—were selective and demanding; they sought performing excellence, intelligent and meaningful lyrics, and a conspicious absence of commercialism.

The sale of singles declined rapidly in proportion to the LPs

90

purchased; only the massive volume of traffic in the record stores kept the 45 rpm disc viable in the marketplace. The variety, the selectivity, and the active acceptance of the "new rock" forms by the public projected lesser-known artists to eminence. Lester Flatt and Earl Scruggs brought blue grass to a movie soundtrack; jazz musicians returned to recording dates as sidemen; and blacks performed openly with their Caucasian counterparts—creating the "salt and pepper" acts.

To this day, no matter how untiring the enterprising promoter, it is doubtful he will regenerate the accomplishments of a Colonel Parker or Brian Epstein, masters of their trade. Miniature ripples, like nostalgia and "disco," vex the waters; they are not tides but small deviations in an entertainment ocean. The record industry hierarchy has its favorites yet welcomes the miscellaneous splinter groups into the field.

1. "Sugar, Sugar," Archies
2. "Aquarius"/"Let the Sunshine In," Fifth Dimension
3. "Honkey Tonk Women," Rolling Stones
4. "Everyday People," Sly & Family Stone
5. "I Can't Get Next to You," Temptations
6. "Dizzy," Tommy Roe
7. "Hot Fun in the Summertime," Sly & Family Stone
8. "Build Me Up Buttercup," Foundations
9. "Hair," Cowsills
10. "One," Three Dog Night
11. "Crimson & Clover," Tommy James & Shondells
12. "I'll Never Fall In Love Again," Tom Jones
13. "Get Together," Youngbloods
14. "Love Theme From *Romeo & Juliet,*" Henry Mancini
15. "Crystal Blue Persuasion," Tommy James & Shondells
16. "Suspicious Minds," Elvis Presley
17. "Too Busy Thinking 'Bout My Baby," Marvin Gaye
18. "Proud Mary," Creedence Clearwater Revival
19. "Grazing in the Grass," Friends Of Distinction
20. "Sweet Caroline," Neil Diamond
21. "It's Your Thing," Isley Brothers
22. "Jean," Oliver
23. "Get Back," Beatles (with Billy Preston)
24. "What Does it Take to Win Your Love," Jr. Walker & All Stars
25. "Bad Moon Rising," Creedence Clearwater Revival
26. "(In The Year) 2525," Zager & Evans
27. "Baby I Love You," Andy Kim
28. "A Boy Named Sue," Johnny Cash
29. "My Cherie Amour," Stevie Wonder
30. "Spinning Wheel," Blood, Sweat & Tears
31. "Na Na Hey Hey Kiss Him Goodbye," Steam
32. "Easy To Be Hard," Three Dog Night
33. "In the Ghetto," Elvis Presley
34. "Baby It's You," Smith
35. "Only the Strong Survive," Jerry Butler
36. "Good Morning Starshine," Oliver

37. "Time of the Season," Zombies
38. "Little Woman," Bobby Sherman
39. "Wedding Bell Blues," Fifth Dimension
40. "These Eyes," Guess Who
41. "Love (Can Make You Happy)," Mercy
42. "Lay Lady Lay," Bob Dylan
43. "I Heard it Through the Grapevine," Marvin Gaye
44. "You Made Me So Very Happy," Blood, Sweat & Tears
45. "Leaving on a Jet Plane," Peter, Paul & Mary
46. "Put a Little Love in Your Heart," Jackie DeShannon
47. "Something"/"Come Together," Beatles
48. "Traces," Dennis Yost & Classics IV
49. "Twenty-Five Miles," Edwin Starr
50. "Everybody's Talkin'," Nilsson

Number-One Songs of '69 *(Billboard)*

"I Heard It Through the Grapevine" (4), Marvin Gaye
"Crimson & Clover" (2), Tommy James & Shondells
"Everyday People" (4), Sly & Family Stone
"Dizzy" (4), Tommy Roe
"Aquarius"/"Let the Sunshine In" (6), Fifth Dimension
"Get Back" (5), Beatles with Billy Preston
"Love Theme From *Romeo & Juliet*" (2), Henry Mancini
"(In The Year) 2525" (6), Zager & Evans
"Honky Tonk Woman" (4), Rolling Stones
"Sugar, Sugar" (4), Archies
"I Can't Get Next to You" (2), Temptations
"Suspicious Minds" (1), Elvis Presley
"Wedding Bell Blues" (3), Fifth Dimension
"Something"/"Come Together" (1), Beatles
"Na Na Hey Hey Kiss Him Goodbye" (2), Steam
"Leaving on a Jet Plane" (1), Peter, Paul & Mary
"Someday We'll Be Together Again" (1), Diana Ross & Supremes

Most Significant Artists of '69

Blood, Sweat & Tears
Creedence Clearwater Revival
Sly & Family Stone
Tommy James & Shondells
Fifth Dimension

Academy Award (Oscar) Winning Song of '69

"Raindrops Keep Falling On My Head"
    from *Butch Cassidy & the Sundance Kid*
Major recording: B. J. Thomas

NARAS (Grammy) Major Category Winners of '69

Record of the Year:
    "Aquarius"/"Let The Sunshine In," Fifth Dimension

Album of the Year:
    "Blood, Sweat & Tears," Blood, Sweat & Tears

Song of the Year:
    "Games People Play," Joe South

You Need a Scorecard, Part One 1970

When I resolved to place an extensive discography at the end of this book, I decided not to identify the record labels of the innumerable artists. So many alterations have taken place over the years with the exchanging of loyalties, the posting of label credits would be a deception. By 1970 so many label switches and changes of group composition were commonplace that one required a scorecard to keep track.

An early and important label change sent Ricky Nelson from MGM's subsidiary, Verve, to Imperial in 1957; after "A Teenager's Romance" propelled him to public acclaim, Imperial signed Ricky and released an immediate winner, "Be Bop Baby." In 1960 the popular Everly Brothers left Archie Bleyer's Cadence label and joined the recently inaugurated Warner Brothers' organization, immediately achieving their biggest-selling record, "Cathy's Clown." Andy Williams, within a year, followed suit, bolted from Cadence to Columbia, and rendered the not-so-instantaneously successful "I Can't Get Used to Losing You."

The "majors" had a definite attraction for blooming recording stars; they offered a larger piece of the action and, in some cases, a promise of up-front money. In 1960 Dion Dimucci retired from the Belmonts, released a series of impressive hits as a solo ("Runaround Sue"), and, finally, left the Laurie label completely, fleeing to Columbia where a long run of uninspiring hits led to his eventual decline in popularity. Eight years later, Dion returned to Laurie and gained instant rejuvenation with his own composition,

95

one of the biggest hits of the year, "Abraham, Martin, and John." There was a lesson to be learned: some performers required the stabilizing influence of a particular producer who understood and grasped the individual's quirks and special abilities.

Most paid no heed and were to be less fortunate than Dion. Johnny Mathis departed Columbia, signed an attractive contract with Mercury, and never recorded another major hit. A decade later he returned to Columbia, caused some chart activity with "I'm Comin' Home," and today remains with that company, no longer a sensation. The year 1962 saw Bobby Darin leave the Atlantic security blanket; he joined Capitol for a string of less-than-formidable hits, and, after a succession of agreements with other companies—including his own enterprise—he returned to Atlantic to carol Tim Hardin's tune, "If I Were a Carpenter." Despite this brief comeback, until his death, Bobby never rejoined the ranks of leading hitmakers. In 1965 the Dovells' Len Barry abruptly said farewell to Bernie Lowe's Cameo-Parkway chain and joined Decca for several outings, including the "Grammy" nominee, "1-2-3." Since his exodus from Decca, Len has been affiliated with so many labels, I've lost count. Today he is a writer-producer in Philadelphia, dreaming of that next hit with his latest find, a group named "Isis."

Similarly, Mary Wells was the first Berry Gordy, Jr. discovery to quit the Detroit assembly line; with Twentieth Century Fox Records she never again approached a hit and fell to relative obscurity. It happened to the incredibly popular Roy Orbison—moving from Monument to MGM in 1965, he went hitless.

Many pages could be filled with the various trials and tribulations of rock & roll stars, hop-scotching headlong into the seventies. Some made it; others failed miserably. One of the more interesting examples of metamorphosis was the case of one Patti Labelle. Her career can be best described by citing her record credits. Humbly starting in 1962 as one of the Bluebelles, she was soon given recognition: "The Bluebelles with Patti Labelle." She then received gratification as "Patti Labelle and the Bluebelles," reached for greater status as "Patti Labelle" minus the Bluebelles, and, finally, attained superstar billing as "Labelle." If she rises any further, she may be billed as the "Big L."

Diana Ross broke ties with the Supremes in 1969. Remaining

with Motown, her career skyrocketed, while the Supremes slipped into that abyss of obscurity that often threatens the horizons of the recording artist. In 1976, the Supremes returned to the charts with a new popularity in the discotheques. Jerry Butler split from the Impressions in 1958 after they had shared one hit, and was immediately successful with "He Will Break Your Heart." The formidable Impressions continued to churn out a string of hits under the capable leadership of Curtis Mayfield; Curtis left the group in 1970 with his solo enterprise, "Freddie's Dead," another deflating blow to the hit-making power of the Impressions. Both Butler and Mayfield still record—Mayfield has become somewhat of a legend in the songwriting field.

Earlier, many groups had survived and sometimes benefited from changes in personnel. The Drifters lost Clyde McPhatter in 1954 to the draft; when he returned, it was on his own. With "Treasures of Love" and several other gems, he continued in vogue. He died in 1972. Johnny Moore would exit as front man for the Drifters in 1957 with little success; Bobby Hendricks left in 1958 with one lone achievement, "Itchy Twitchy Feeling"; and, in 1960, Ben E. King abandoned the quartet to record "Spanish Harlem"—he was still on the charts in 1975 when his "Supernatural Thing" became a disco favorite. The Drifters outlived their many personnel changes, and today you can find several "Drifter-groups" traveling in many nostalgia road-shows, especially lamented in the South.

The comings and goings of the lead singer is not unique to this country, as you will see in the next chapter. As Tony Williams broke from the Platters, as David Ruffin terminated relations with the Temptations, as David Gates sought his own Bread, the late sixties would find the English groups splintering in their own dubious directions.

1. "Bridge Over Troubled Water," Simon & Garfunkel
2. "(They Long to Be) Close to You," Carpenters
3. "Raindrops Keep Falling on My Head," B. J. Thomas
4. "American Woman," Guess Who
5. "War," Edwin Starr
6. "Let It Be," Beatles
7. "Ain't No Mountain High Enough," Diana Ross
8. "Get Ready," Rare Earth
9. "I'll Be There," Jackson Five
10. "Mama Told Me (Not To Come)," Three Dog Night
11. "Everything Is Beautiful," Ray Stevens
12. "Make It with You," Bread
13. "Band of Gold," Freda Payne
14. "Cracklin' Rosie," Neil Diamond
15. "A B C," Jackson Five
16. "Hitchin' A Ride," Vanity Fair
17. "Candida," Dawn
18. "The Love You Save," Jackson Five
19. "Spirit in the Sky," Norman Greenbaum
20. "Thank You (Falettin Me Be Mice Elf Again)," Sly & Family Stone
21. "Ooh Child," Five Stairsteps
22. "Ball of Confusion," Temptations
23. "Spill the Wine," Eric Burden & War
24. "Which Way You Going Billy," Poppy Family
25. "Julie, Do Ya Love Me," Bobby Sherman
26. "Signed, Sealed, & Delivered," Stevie Wonder
27. "Green Eyed Lady," Sugarloaf
28. "Venus," Shocking Blue
29. "Ride Captain Ride," Blues Image
30. "Patches," Clarence Carter
31. "Lookin' Out My Back Door," Creedence Clearwater Revival
32. "Long & Winding Road," Beatles
33. "Rainy Night in Georgia," Brook Benton
34. "I Think I Love You," Partridge Family
35. "Give Me Just a Little More Time," Chairmen Of The Board

36. "Snowbird," Anne Murray
37. "Love Grows (Where My Rosemary Goes)," Edison Lighthouse
38. "Hey There Lonely Girl," Eddie Holman
39. "Reflections of My Life," Marmalade
40. "The Rapper," Jaggerz
41. "Cecelia," Simon & Garfunkel
42. "He Ain't Heavy, He's My Brother," Hollies
43. "Tighter & Tighter," Alive & Kickin'
44. "Come & Get It," Bad Finger
45. "Tears of a Clown," Smokey Robinson & Miracles
46. "Arizona," Mark Lindsay
47. "Indiana Wants Me," R. Dean Taylor
48. "Lola," Kinks
49. "Someday We'll Be Together Again," Supremes
50. "Fire & Rain," James Taylor

Number-One Songs of '70 *(Billboard)*

"Raindrops Keep Fallin' On My Head" (4), B. J. Thomas
"I Want You Back" (1), Jackson Five
"Venus" (1), Shocking Blue
"Thank You (Falettin Me Be Mice Elf Again)" (2), Sly & Family Stone
"Bridge Over Troubled Water" (6), Simon & Garfunkel
"Let It Be" (2), Beatles
"A B C" (2), Jackson Five
"American Woman"/"No Sugar Tonight" (3), Guess Who
"Everything Is Beautiful" (2), Ray Stevens
"Long & Winding Road" (2), Beatles
"The Love You Save" (2), Jackson Five
"Mama Told Me (Not To Come)" (2), Three Dog Night
"(They Long to Be) Close to You" (4), Carpenters
"Make It with You" (1), Bread
"War" (3), Edwin Starr
"Ain't No Mountain High Enough" (3), Diana Ross

"Cracklin' Rosie" (1), Neil Diamond
"I'll Be There" (5), Jackson Five
"I Think I Love You" (3), Partridge Family
"The Tears of a Clown" (2), Smokey Robinson & Miracles
"My Sweet Lord"/"Isn't It a Pity" (1), George Harrison

Most Significant Artists of '70

Jackson Five
Carpenters
Neil Diamond
Simon & Garfunkel
Beatles

Academy Award (Oscar) Winning Song of '70

"For All We Know,"
    from *Lovers & Other Strangers*

Major recording: Carpenters

NARAS (Grammy) Major Category Winners of '70

Record of the Year:
    "Bridge Over Troubled Water," Simon & Garfunkel

Album of the Year:
    "Bridge Over Troubled Water," Simon & Garfunkel

Song of the Year:
    "Bridge Over Troubled Water," Paul Simon

You Need a Scorecard, Part Two 1971

The most celebrated breakup of the seventies was, and still is, the dissolution of the world's most famous corporation, the Beatles. Propelled by Paul McCartney's first solo album in 1970, tensions built within the shaky structure of the Beatle camp, Apple Records; and, heading down "The Long and Winding Road," the "family" split asunder. John Lennon, guided by his wife, Yoko Ono, released a series of controversial singles and albums, including "Give Peace a Chance." John and Yoko Ono separated and then re-cemented their relationship, and John, still pouring out frequent hits, sought financial asylum in the United States. Due to a previous drug "incident" in England, he was refused a permanent visa. Thoughtfully, the U.S. federal courts overthrew this ruling and America has its own "Beatle."

Paul McCartney, probably the most charismatic of the Beatles, has consistently produced significant results, assisted by his wife Linda and the instrumental backgrounds of Wings. Paul has given us gold records like "Live and Let Die" and the more recent "Silly Love Songs" and "Let 'em In." Surprisingly, George Harrison, hardly thought to be an internationally moving spirit, has released a succession of staples from the single "What Is Life" to the in-person album, "Concert for Bangladesh," from the public appearance that raised twenty million dollars for the hunger-stricken masses of that emerging third world nation. Ringo Starr, critically believed "the least likely to succeed," has proved, to the contrary, that uninspiring renditions of "It Don't Come Easy" and

101

"You're Sixteen" are profitable. Rumors that the Beatles will reunite in the near future are circulated on a regular basis. A Capitol records 1976 re-release of their best "rock" material lends credence to the reunion theory, but to date, outward signs indicate this to be unlikely. We can only hope.

As the seventies arrived, the advent of "rock pools" sent various artists in many different directions; it was difficult for anyone but a "grade A" groupy to keep track of the movements. One of the more interesting dispersals involved the Buffalo Springfield, whose 1966 political statement, "For What It's Worth," set in motion a global trek involving most of its original members. Stephen Stills and Neil Young, joined by David Crosby of the Byrds and Graham Nash of the Hollies, formed the team of Crosby, Stills, Nash, and Young—initially limited to Crosby, Stills, and Nash. Later, all four members, stripped of mutual attraction, pursued solo careers with surprising public acceptance. Meanwhile, the Springfield's Rick Furay and Jim Messina formed the group, Poco, whose country-rock sound set off a West Coast wave of the future, and led to a major footnote, Loggins and Messina.

In 1964 the English blues group, the Animals, scored an international hit with "The House of the Rising Sun." Organist Alan Price immediately bolted the team and organized the Alan Price Set, a combo that acquired some distinction with "I Put a Spell on You" and "The House That Jack Built." Enigmatic lead singer of the Animals, Eric Burdon, sought new avenues in 1967 and recorded "San Franciscan Nights," a sales disappointment. After several years of minor popularity, he became the impetus for War's significant hit in 1970, "Spill The Wine." Today, War, sans Eric, has a history of "socially oriented" smashes. Eric has semi-retired to ethereal indistinction, War continues the trail of hits, and one member, Lee Oskar, spun off as a solo in 1976.

An example of group deviation, in a destructive sense, is that of Blood, Sweat, and Tears. Al Kooper, founder of the Blues Project, guided BS&T through their first album and—with the addition of gruff-voiced David Clayton-Thomas—a second that is considered one of the most imaginative LPs of all time—an album that contained an inordinate amount of excellent single releases. Thomas left the group in the early seventies, mastered a half-dozen lackluster releases, and returned to the womb in 1975. The resulting

102

effort, "Got To Get You Out of My Life," wandered lazily up the charts but with little resplendence.

The termination of the Beatle era gave us a St. Vitus dance of activity. Janis Joplin left Big Brother and the Holding Company holding the bag, released her best-selling album on Columbia, immortalized Kris Kristofferson's "Me And Bobby McGee," and died from an overdose—all in less than a two-year period. Producer-writer-singer Todd Rundgren satirically offered us quasi-groups like Runt and Grin, and, as a loner, executed the classic, "Hello, It's Me," in 1974 and "Good Vibrations" in 1976. Johnny Fogerty, the "frog-throated" force behind Creedence Clearwater Revival, experimented with his one-man band, the Blue Ridge Rangers ("Jambalaya") in 1973; CCR made an unexpected comeback in 1976 when Fantasy re-released the pulsating "I Heard It Through the Grapevine"—an instant disco delight. At decade's end, David Gates departed Bread and accomplished little, but thrived as a songwriter of ballads.

In the English mainstream, Van Morrison, unheralded leader of the hard-rock aspirants Them, soared to solo recognition with his "Brown-Eyed Girl" in 1967 and "Domino" in 1971. Van continues to be in demand at numerous concert sights. The early British duo, Peter and Gordon, was cancelled for lack of interest, but Peter Asher turned to the lucrative art of production, conjuring up hits for Linda Ronstadt, a young renegade from the Stone Poneys. The granddaddies of "sensual rock," the Rolling Stones— for various reasons from egos to drug busts—lost portions of their original cast, but social director Mick Jagger solidified their position of pre-eminence, and they endure as one of the few reminders of the 1964 English epidemic.

With less bravado, the soul groups have undergone countless changes. The Temptations wished David Ruffin goodbye and both have sustained their followings, though David required several years to establish himself in the marketplace. Isaac Hayes and Harold Melvin, who both began anonymously as integral members of early rhythm & blues groups, are now tops in their field. The genius of Smokey Robinson is missed by the Miracles, but both knew prosperity in 1976. Sylvia Robinson, formerly of Mickey and Sylvia, returned to the radio alone in 1973 with her erotic "Pillow Talk"; and in 1974, Shirley Pixley, of Shirley and Lee, founded Shirley and Company and gave the world a disco interpretation of "Shame, Shame, Shame." Dionne Warwick, linked to the bright days of Burt Bacharach, joined the Spinners in 1974 for "Then Came You."

The personnel changes of twenty-two years of rock & roll have been astronomical in number, and the branches of the family trees of some perennial favorites are as widespread as those of the royal House of Windsor.

1. "Joy to the World," Three Dog Night
2. "Maggie May," Rod Stewart
3. "One Bad Apple," Osmonds
4. "It's Too Late"/"I Feel the Earth Move," Carol King
5. "Take Me Home, Country Roads," John Denver
6. "How Can You Mend a Broken Heart," Bee Gees
7. "Go Away Little Girl," Donny Osmond
8. "Knock Three Times," Dawn
9. "Indian Reservation," Raiders
10. "Me & Bobby McGee," Janis Joplin
11. "Just My Imagination (Running Away with Me)," Temptations
12. "Want Ads," Honey Cone
13. "Brown Sugar," Rolling Stones
14. "Smiling Faces Sometimes," Undisputed Truth
15. "You've Got a Friend," James Taylor
16. "Treat Her Like a Lady," Cornelius Brothers with Sister Rose
17. "Uncle Albert/Admiral Halsey," Paul & Linda McCartney
18. "Mr. Big Stuff," Jean Knight
19. "What's Goin' On," Marvin Gaye
20. "The Night They Drove Ol' Dixie Down," Joan Baez
21. "Ain't No Sunshine," Bill Withers
22. "She's a Lady," Tom Jones
23. "Signs," Five Man Electrical Band
24. "Do You Know What I Mean," Lee Michaels
25. "Superstar," Murray Head
26. "Amos Moses," Jerry Reed
27. "Temptation Eyes," Grass Roots
28. "My Sweet Lord," George Harrison
29. "I Found Someone On My Own," Free Movement
30. "If You Could Read My Mind," Gordon Lightfoot
31. "Put Your Hand in the Hand," Ocean
32. "For All We Know," Carpenters
33. "Help Me Make it Through the Night," Sammi Smith
34. "Chick-A-Boom," Daddy Dewdrop
35. "Rose Garden," Lynn Anderson
36. "It Don't Come Easy," Ringo Starr

37. "Rainy Days & Mondays," Carpenters
38. "Never Can Say Goodbye," Jackson Five
39. "Gypsys, Tramps, & Thieves," Cher
40. "Don't Pull Your Love," Hamilton, Joe Frank, & Reynolds
41. "Whatcha See Is Whatcha Get," Dramatics
42. "Theme From *Shaft*," Isaac Hayes
43. "Mr. Bojangles," Nitty Gritty Dirt Band
44. "If You Really Love Me," Stevie Wonder
45. "Family Affair," Sly & Family Stone
46. "Yo Yo," Osmonds
47. "Proud Mary," Ike & Tina Turner
48. "Another Day," Paul McCartney
49. "Sweet City Woman," Stampeders
50. "I Don't Know How To Love Him," Helen Reddy

Number-One Songs of '71 *(Billboard)*

"My Sweet Lord"/"Isn't it a Pity" (3), George Harrison
"Knock Three Times" (3), Dawn
"One Bad Apple" (5), Osmonds
"Me & Bobby McGee" (2), Janis Joplin
"Just My Imagination (Running Away With Me)" (2), Temptations
"Joy to the World" (6), Three Dog Night
"Brown Sugar" (2), Rolling Stones
"Want Ads" (1), Honey Cone
"It's Too Late"/"I Feel The Earth Move" (5), Carole King
"Indian Reservation" (1), Raiders
"You've Got a Friend" (1), James Taylor
"How Can You Mend a Broken Heart" (4), Bee Gees
"Uncle Albert"/"Admiral Halsey" (1), Paul & Linda McCartney
"Go Away Little Girl" (3), Donny Osmond
"Maggie May"/"Reason to Believe" (5), Rod Stewart
"Gypsys, Tramps, & Thieves" (2), Cher
"Theme from *Shaft*" (2), Isaac Hayes
"Family Affair" (3), Sly & Family Stone
"Brand New Key" (1), Melanie

106

Most Significant Artists of '71

Three Dog Night
Osmonds
Carol King
Rod Stewart
Carpenters

Academy Award (Oscar) Winning Song of '71

"Theme from *Shaft*,"
     from *Shaft*

Major recording: Isaac Hayes

NARAS (Grammy) Major Category Winners of '71

Record of the Year:
     "It's Too Late," Carole King

Album of the Year:
     "Tapestry," Carole King

Song of the Year:
     "You've Got a Friend," Carole King

Those "Nostalgic" Oldies but Goodies 1972

On October 18, 1969, Richard Nader, one-time—but little noted—disc jockey, improvised the "original" rock & roll revival and delighted an SRO crowd at Madison Square Garden's Felt Forum, thus officially beginning the nostalgia craze that had been smoldering for several decades. In the late forties, a revival of Al Jolson favorites caught the fancy of the American public; in the early fifties, the big bands were temporarily revived for a new generation, exhibited in a string of motion-picture biographies like "The Glenn Miller Story" and exploited in a treasury of albums; in the late fifties, "golden oldies" entered the lexicon of radio programming; and in the sixties, top-forty radio dedicated entire weekends to the sounds of "solid gold." Richard Nader's evening in New York City unified all these previous efforts.

Combing the metropolitan area, Nader unearthed the retired Five Satins and pasted them back together again. He convinced Chuck Berry to change the date of an appearance at a New Hampshire college; he negotiated with Buck Ram's "new" Platters, prevailing upon them to alter a Saturday night show in South Carolina to a Sunday; and he made arrangements to transport the Coasters back and forth across Long Island for two performances in one breath. In a major coup, where others had failed, Nader brought Bill Haley and the Comets out of retirement, enjoined the Shirelles to return to active performing, and signed Sha Na Na, a chorale that satirized the fifties. With firm belief in his brainchild,

109

Richard Nader pulled off a night of nostalgic insanity and cataloged a pile of rave reviews.

For the next three years, the nostalgia phenomenon continued to build steam; imitators transshipped rock revivals to the smallest villages, and, with a varying degree of interest, brought America back to happier days. Companies like K-Tel and Telehouse rummaged through the archives, invented the "stonewall" method of advertising, and released ceaseless packages of TV limited-time offers; these were resplendent with classics by Jerry Lee Lewis, Chuck Berry, the Platters, and a dusting of questionable gems by the Mello-Tones and the Quotations. Chubby Checker's career, like a spectre, ascended from the cinders when he appeared on national television to pitch, in the best tradition of the huckster, one of these historical volumes. The best of these albums—the Warner Brothers' "Superstar" series and Art Laboe's "Oldies But Goodies" compendium—utilized original masters, and their technical quality was worth the investment; the lesser efforts crammed a baker's dozen on one side of an LP and resulted in a sound comparable to crushed wax paper in the hands of a short-order cook.

Back in 1968, the record hop had given way to live performances, but with the meteoric rise of nostalgia, disc jockeys would revive the interest in dancing. Young and old alike were gyrating to "The Twist" again. In 1972, I grabbed a stack of oldies, repaired to a Chrysler-Plymouth dealer's showroom, and presented a six-hour marathon that resulted in the sale of twenty cars in one night—it was hard to believe that yesterday's rock & rollers could now afford an Imperial. This, and thousands of similar efforts, led to club dates as the radio robber barons jumped on the bandwagon. Within the year, "disco" became the child of the nostalgia romance.

Statistics were the baneful mainstay of nostalgia buffs—as these pages testify—and were often packaged in the form of trivia. If you were worth your salt, you knew that the Clovers were the forerunners of Bobby Vee's "Devil or Angel," Charlie Gracie's follow-up to "Butterfly" was "Fabulous," and Country Joe and the Fish's recording, "Feel Like I'm Fixin' to Die Rag" was one of the first antiwar records. Radio personalities resurrected trivia from cocktail party insignificance to the collective podiums of broadcasting. Adding to this statistical madness, radio stations and newspapers surveyed public opinion and composed catalogs of all-time favorites.

Three members of the media in Baltimore, Maryland, released simultaneous surveys and deduced contrary denouements—three different number-one songs, "In The Still of the Night" by the Five Satins, "Rock Around The Clock" by Bill Haley and the Comets, and "Somewhere, My Love" by Ray Conniff. The discrepancies attested to the formats of each individual broadcaster—one a soul station, one a rocker, the other a "middle of the road" advocate. Nationally, one trade magazine proclaimed "Mack the Knife" by Bobby Darin the all-time champion, as another periodical praised "Don't Be Cruel" by Elvis Presley. In Syracuse, New York, a public survey indicated Del Shannon's "Runaway" undoubtedly was the favorite; and, down in the warmer climes of North Carolina, another poll declared a Tams' recording the unqualified medalist. *Billboard Magazine*'s 1976 Bicentennial special crowned "The Twist" the all-time classic. Demographics, regionalism, and personal taste demonstrated that a definitive survey was impossible.

Amid this subjectivity, trade books of rock & roll trivia (*So You Think You Know Rock & Roll*, by Brown and Freidrich), volumes of early rock history (*Rock On*, by Norn N. Nite), and personal declarations (*The Rock Encyclopedia*, by Lillian Roxon), became best sellers. A renaissance Dick Clark appeared in full costume on late-night television with a nostalgic recreation of the early American Bandstand days, quickly followed by a series of "Goldie" albums under his banner. A plethora of syndicated radio programs were unleashed across the nation; they were lengthy histories of artists like Elvis Presley, Buddy Holly, the Beatles, and the monotonous Burt Bacharach. Rating-conscious stations changed formats completely and were reborn as "golden oldie" outlets—WCBS-FM, New York, an excellent example.

As the seventies hiked past the halfway mark, the nostalgia fad beckoned more and more deaf ears. Radio, in particular, learned that Chuck Berry's "School Days," that was once despised by half the population, still had the same amount of detractors lurking in the older generation and had little appeal to younger

111

audiences, now enthralled by Donnie and Marie Osmond. One trade magazine columnist commented: "1975, with bright hopes for the delayed future, is the year that "nostalgia" died."

Its total absence is unlikely. The year 1976, with its bicentennial ardor, offered nostalgia a temporary reprieve.

1. "American Pie," Don McLean
2. "First Time Ever I Saw Your Face," Roberta Flack
3. "Alone Again (Naturally)," Gilbert O'Sullivan
4. "Without You," Nilsson
5. "Brandy (You're A Fine Girl)," Looking Glass
6. "I Gotcha," Joe Tex
7. "Lean On Me," Bill Withers
8. "Baby, Don't Get Hooked On Me," Mac Davis
9. "Let's Stay Together," Al Green
10. "Candy Man," Sammy Davis, Jr.
11. "Brand New Key," Melanie
12. "Oh Girl," Chi-Lites
13. "My Ding-A-Ling," Chuck Berry
14. "Nice to Be with You," Gallery
15. "Betcha, By Golly, Wow," Stylistics
16. "Daddy Don't You Walk Too Fast," Wayne Newton
17. "I'll Take You There," Staple Singers
18. "Ben," Michael Jackson
19. "Long Cool Woman (In a Black Dress)," Hollies
20. "Heart of Gold," Neil Young
21. "Outta Space," Billy Preston
22. "How Do You Do?" Mouth & MacNeal
23. "Slippin' Into Darkness," War
24. "A Horse with No Name," America
25. "Song Sung Blue," Neil Diamond
26. "Everybody Plays the Fool," Main Ingredient
27. "The Lion Sleeps Tonight," Robert John
28. "Nights in White Satin," Moody Blues
29. "Garden Party," Rick Nelson
30. "Precious & Few," Climax
31. "Go All the Way," Raspberries
32. "I Can See Clearly Now," Johnny Nash
33. "Burning Love," Elvis Presley
34. "(Last Night) I Didn't Get to Sleep At All," Fifth Dimension
35. "Back Stabbers," O'Jays
36. "Starting All Over Again," Mel & Tim

113

37. "Day After Day," Bad Finger
38. "Rocket Man," Elton John
39. "Too Late to Turn Back Now," Cornelius Brothers with Sister Rose
40. "Sunshine," Johnathon Edwards
41. "Scorpio," Dennis Coffey & Detroit Guitar Band
42. "Rockin' Robin," Michael Jackson
43. "Hold Your Head Up," Argent
44. "Beautiful Sunday," Daniel Boone
45. "City of New Orleans," Arlo Guthrie
46. "I Am Woman," Helen Reddy
47. "Happiest Girl in the Whole USA," Donna Fargo
48. "Layla," Derek & Dominos
49. "Papa Was a Rolling Stone," Temptations
50. "Black & White" Three Dog Night

Number-One Songs of '72 *(Billboard)*

"Brand New Key" (2), Melanie
"American Pie" (4), Don McLean
"Let's Stay Together" (1), Al Green
"Without You" (4), Nilsson
"Heart of Gold" (1), Neil Young
"A Horse with No Name," (3), America
"First Time Ever I Saw Your Face" (6), Roberta Flack
"Oh Girl" (1), Chi-Lites
"I'll Take You There" (1), Staple Singers
"Candy Man" (3), Sammy Davis, Jr.
"Song Sung Blue" (1), Neil Diamond
"Lean On Me" (3), Bill Withers
"Alone Again (Naturally)" (6), Gilbert O'Sullivan
"Brandy (You're A Fine Girl)" (1), Looking Glass
"Black & White" (1), Three Dog Night
"Baby, Don't Get Hooked On Me" (3), Mac Davis
"Ben" (1), Michael Jackson

"My Ding-A-Ling" (2), Chuck Berry
"I Can See Clearly Now" (4), Johnny Nash
"Papa Was a Rollin' Stone" (1), Temptations
"I Am Woman" (1), Helen Reddy
"Me & Mrs. Jones" (3), Billy Paul

Most Significant Artists of '72

Roberta Flack
Three Dog Night
Al Green
Don McLean
Gilbert O'Sullivan

Academy Award (Oscar) Winning Song of '72

"The Morning After,"
    from *The Poseidon Adventure*

Major recording: Maureen McGovern

NARAS (Grammy) Major Category Winners of '72

Record of the Year:
    "The First Time Ever I Saw Your Face," Roberta Flack

Album of the Year:
    "The Concert For Bangla Desh," George Harrison & Others

Song of the Year:
    "The First Time Ever I Saw Your Face," Ewan MacColl

Where Have All the Children Gone 1973

The untimely death of Jim Croce inspired a Maryland radio station to endeavor a controversial and intriguing broadcasting first. Assisted by a priest, a parapsychologist, and several mediums, WFBR radio presented a journalistic seance—an attempted communication with the dead and lamented artists—Janis Joplin, Jim Morrison, and Jimmi Hendrix. The results of the program were inconclusive, but the interest generated indicated the public's keen fascination with the score of tragic deaths that had preoccupied the music world for two decades.

Catastrophic aviation disasters were one of the causes of the music industry's flirtation with death. Buddy Holly ("Peggy Sue"), Ritchie Valens ("Donna"), and the Big Bopper ("Chantilly Lace"), perished in a private plane transporting them to a rock concert in 1959. In 1963 similar circumstances took the lives of three country & western stars—Patsy Cline ("I Fall to Pieces"), Cowboy Copas, and Hawkshaw Hawkins. One year later, Jim Reeves, a longtime pop and country artist ("He'll Have to Go"), died in the wreckage of a small plane. In 1968 super-soul star Otis Redding ("Dock of the Bay") and his band the Bar-Kays ("Soul Finger") would all lose their lives in the air. And then, folk-rock prodigy Jim Croce ("Bad, Bad Leroy Brown") would meet a similar fate in 1973. An automobile collision ended the career of rhythm & blues singer Billy Stewart ("Summertime"), at the height of his success.

The deaths of many rock and pop stars were senseless, the bottom-line of a varying degree of insanity. A month before his

117

"Pledging My Love" became a national hit, Johnny Ace committed "accidental suicide" while playing Russian roulette on Christmas Eve, 1954. Another bizarre incident took the life of Sam Cooke ("You Send Me"); he was shot to death in a Los Angeles motel in 1960 under suspicious "unclad" circumstances. Rock singer Johnny Burnette ("Dreamin' ") drowned in a freak fishing incident in 1964. And in 1976 Sal Mineo ("Start Movin' ") was "mugged" and stabbed to death outside his Los Angeles apartment —earlier, a similar attack had almost taken the life of folk-singer Jimmie Rodgers ("Honeycomb") on a southern California freeway, and he has since retired from the public limelight.

Certainly, senseless extinction befell the multitude of artists who trifled with drugs, whose detrimental powers were far from respected. The jazz-pop lark Dinah Washington ("What a Difference a Day Makes") succumbed to an overdose of sleeping pills in 1963. The early seventies headlined drug-oriented death for three of the highly esteemed stars of the "new rock" scene—Jimmi Hendrix ("Purple Haze"), famous for his antics atop a flaming guitar, Janis Joplin ("Me And Bobby McGee"), idolized by thousands of rock concert devotees, and Jim Morrison, neurotic lead singer of the Doors ("Light My Fire"), all perished from suspected drug overdoses. Suicides? No one has clearly ascertained.

Death was sometimes the direct consequence of required surgery. In 1958 Chuck Willis, whose last release was ironically titled "What Am I Living For," did not survive his physician's operating procedures. Bobby Darin ("Mack The Knife") died after serious open-heart surgery. Death, resulting from "neglect," snuffed out the lives of Tommy Edwards ("It's All in the Game"), and Florence Ballard, a member of the once incredibly popular Supremes ("Up the Ladder to the Roof"). Tommy died in 1969, and Florence in 1976; it was rumored that both died penniless and victims of alcoholism.

Other leading singers departed in their prime, dying of natural causes. Roy Hamilton ("You'll Never Walk Alone") passed away from a stroke in 1969. Nat "King" Cole ("Mona Lisa"), after a cameo role in the movie "Cat Ballou", succumbed to cancer in 1965. In the early seventies, after a long illness, Tammi Terrell ("Ain't Nothing Like the Real Thing") died from a brain tumor. Clyde McPhatter (Treasures Of Love") was gone in 1972; the same year, television and recording artist Billy Williams ("I'm Gonna Sit Right Down and Write Myself a Letter") joined the parade of passing songsters.

For some mysterious reason, an inordinate amount of young musical talent has died in the past two decades. Their deaths attract attention because of their vast popularity. In 1974, the Righteous Brothers eulogized many of the aforementioned in their recording "Rock & Roll Heaven."

1. "Tie a Yellow Ribbon 'Round the Old Oak Tree," Tony Orlando & Dawn
2. "Bad, Bad Leroy Brown," Jim Croce
3. "My Love," Paul McCartney & Wings
4. "Killing Me Softly with His Song," Roberta Flack
5. "Let's Get It On," Marvin Gaye
6. "Crocodile Rock," Elton John
7. "Will it Go Round in Circles," Billy Preston
8. "You're So Vain," Carly Simon
9. "Why Me," Kris Kristofferson
10. "The Night the Lights Went Out in Georgia," Vicki Lawrence
11. "Brother Louie," Stories
12. "Delta Dawn," Helen Reddy
13. "Playground in My Mind," Clint Holmes
14. "Touch Me in the Morning," Diana Ross
15. "Me & Mrs. Jones," Billy Paul
16. "Frankenstein," Edgar Winter Group
17. "You Are the Sunshine of My Life," Stevie Wonder
18. "Drift Away," Dobie Gray
19. "Little Willy," Sweet
20. "That Lady," Isley Brothers
21. "Pillow Talk," Sylvia
22. "We're an American Band," Grand Funk
23. "Half Breed," Cher
24. "Right Place, Wrong Time," Dr. John
25. "Superstition," Stevie Wonder
26. "Wildflower," Skylark
27. "Loves Me Like a Rock," Paul Simon
28. "Rocky Mountain High," John Denver
29. "Stuck in the Middle with You," Stealer's Wheel
30. "The Morning After," Maureen McGovern
31. "Shambala," Three Dog Night
32. "Keep On Truckin'," Eddie Kendricks
33. "Love Train," O'Jays
34. "Danny's Song," Anne Murray
35. "I'm Gonna Love You Just a Little More," Barry White

120

36. "Dancing in the Moonlight," King Harvest
37. "Natural High," Bloodstone
38. "Diamond Girl," Seals & Crofts
39. "Give Me Love (Give Me Peace on Earth)," George Harrison
40. "Neither One of Us (Wants to Say Goodbye)," Gladys Knight & Pips
41. "Long Train Running," Doobie Brothers
42. "I'm Doing Fine," New York City
43. "Daddy's Home," Jermaine Jackson
44. "Daniel," Elton John
45. "If You Want Me to Stay," Sly & Family Stone
46. "Smoke on the Water," Deep Purple
47. "Midnight Train to Georgia," Gladys Knight & Pips
48. "Your Mama Don't Dance," Loggins & Messina
49. "Behind Closed Doors," Charlie Rich
50. "Angie," Rolling Stones

Number-One Songs of '73 *(Billboard)*

"You're So Vain" (3), Carly Simon
"Superstition" (1), Stevie Wonder
"Crocodile Rock" (3), Elton John
"Killing Me Softly with His Song" (5), Roberta Flack
"Love Train" (1), O'Jays
"The Night the Lights Went Out in Georgia" (2), Vicki Lawrence
"Tie a Yellow Ribbon 'Round the Old Oak Tree" (4), Tony Orlando & Dawn
"You Are the Sunshine of My Life" (1), Stevie Wonder
"Frankenstein" (1), Edgar Winter Group
"My Love" (4), Paul McCartney & Wings
"Give Me Love (Give Me Peace on Earth)" (1), George Harrison
"Will it Go Round in Circles" (2), Billy Preston
"Bad, Bad Leroy Brown" (2), Jim Croce
"The Morning After" (2), Maureen McGovern
"Touch Me in the Morning" (1), Diana Ross

"Brother Louie" (2), Stories
"Let's Get It On" (2), Marvin Gaye
"Delta Dawn" (1), Helen Reddy
"We're an American Band" (1), Grand Funk
"Half Breed" (2), Cher
"Angie" (1), Rolling Stones
"Midnight Train to Georgia" (2), Gladys Knight & Pips
"Keep on Truckin' " (2), Eddie Kendricks
"Photograph" (1), Ringo
"Top of the World" (2), Carpenters
"The Most Beautiful Girl" (2), Charlie Rich
"Time in a Bottle" (1), Jim Croce

Most Significant Artists of '73

Tony Orlando & Dawn
Stevie Wonder
Jim Croce
Carly Simon
Paul McCartney & Wings

Academy Award (Oscar) Winning Song of '73

"The Way We Were,"
    from *The Way We Were*

Major recording: Barbra Streisand

122

Record of the Year:
    "Killing Me Softly with His Song," Robert Flack

Album of the Year:
    "Innervisions," Stevie Wonder

Song of the Year:
    "Killing Me Softly with His Song," Norman Gimbel, Charles
        Fox

The Discotheque and Re-emergence of the Black Singer

It is here noted that Richard Nixon became President in January of 1969 and left that executive position in August of 1974. During that apocalyptic five-year period, "soul" music took a back seat to its pop and country relatives. Certainly, Mr. Nixon cannot be blamed personally for the white backlash that "censored" most black music on the white radio stations, but the entire philosophy of his administration and the resulting public sentiment were contributing causes. Middle America reacted vehemently to the civil rights disturbances of the sixties, and many radio programmers solemnly believed an avoidance of the black product might keep things quiet in the streets. This ideology, and its repressive spirit, was based on needless fear, to the detriment of top-forty radio.

In 1973, inspired by the nostalgia passion, people danced in every sort of public environment; and a trend that had emerged more than a decade before returned. Across the nation, discotheques replaced "band" bars, and to these niteries came the healthy return of soul—the music with a beat. Artists like Eddie Kendricks ("Boogie Down"), the Jackson Five ("Dancing Machine"), and the O'Jays ("Love Train") were the primary factors in the emergence of a new dance, the "Bump." The Bump possessed the same simplicity as the "twist"; any damn fool could do it! There followed a series of new dances—the "Hustle," exploited by Van McCoy; the "Bus Stop," a tantalizing combination of choreographics that reminded one of the "big boss line" dances of

125

the sixties; and, the most popular, a spontaneity that, for lack of any other name, is called the "boogie."

Discotheques developed the art of wrap-around sound, and most clubs installed sound equipment that not only challenged the vibrations of a live-band but, in many cases, surpassed it. Utilizing mixers, equalizers, amplifiers, and gargantuan speaker units, some clubs budgeted more than $50,000 for stereo rigs. Added to this, incredibly splashy light shows often turned a tavern into a "Shambala," hosted by the resident guru, the "disco jock." The disco deejay was the counterpart of his radio brethren, yet he was not hindered by managerial conservatism and the stringent rules of the Federal Communications Commission—listen to the lyrics of the Isley Brother's "Fight the Power," and you will see what I mean. New record releases were presented to the public ear without reference to the definitive trade magazine chart. Shirley and Company, Kool and the Gang, the O'Jays, K.C. and the Sunshine Band, the Salsoul Orchestra, the Peoples Choice, Gloria Gaynor, and hundreds more profited from hit records that might never have been heard on the radio. Live acts like Disco-Tex and the Sex-O-Lettes became big drawing cards. The Armada Orchestra, Bohannon, and MFSB were suddenly high-priced performers—all this with little exposure on top-forty radio. FM stations—notably WPIX in New York City and WRC-FM in Washington—invaded the scene with disco formats, acquiring their rhythms from local nightclubs.

For years, rock albums had sold millions without much aid from broadcasters; soul singles and albums had been marketed successfully in areas without black-oriented stations; and now, disco captured more of the limelight from top-forty stations. Many announcers, like myself, temporarily left contemporary radio—and its high-pressure politics—to pursue more lucrative careers in the discotheques of America. "Salaries" varied from club to club; many of these, with their own house stereo systems, hired youngsters to "segue" music for three or four dollars an hour, but other nightspots, seeking unique formats, paid up to three hundred dollars a night to a kindred spirit with portable equipment, his own records, and a gift for gab. Several "on-the-air" personalities banked more weekly loot from the local discotheque than from their station paychecks. Women, too, found themselves in demand.

126

As they had with soul music, some top-forty outlets developed an aversion to disco music, but despite their castigation of hitmakers like Johnny Taylor ("Disco Lady") and Kool and the Gang ("Jungle Boogie"), their records would sell millions of copies. Eventually, stations relented and, as they had with many a "hard-rock" song, added disco favorites to their playlists. By 1976, a handful of "pop" stations deluded for years by the supposed benefits of demographic programming, were spinning Aerosmith and Sweet records back-to-back with the Temptations and Donna Summer.

Discotheques—more than fifty thousand were estimated to exist in one form or another in 1976—proved that a hit record is just that, a hit record; the public purchases phonograph records because of the enjoyment they offer, not because someone takes to the air and proclaims their future potential. Like a rose, a hit is a hit is a hit.

The music of discotheques, though not by initial design, splintered in 1975. Soul discos featured the new-and-old of artists like Stevie Wonder and Archie Bell. Rock discos ran the gamut from Silver Convention to the Rolling Stones. Gay discos, bless their hearts, found the Wing and a Prayer Fife and Drum Corps and Crown Heights Affair "attractive." And oldie discos amplified the tried and true classics by Dion, Sam and Dave, and the Everly Brothers. Disco music was widely diversified and not a redundant clamor underneath a crystal ball; the common denominator was danceability, and its motivating spirit was the public's desire to, in the words of Willie Hutch, "Party Down."

1. "The Way We Were," Barbra Streisand
2. "Seasons in the Sun," Terry Jacks
3. "Come & Get Your Love," Redbone
4. "Love's Theme," Love Unlimited Orchestra
5. "Dancing Machine," Jackson Five
6. "T S O P," MFSB
7. "The Streak," Ray Stevens
8. "Bennie & The Jets," Elton John
9. "I Honestly Love You," Olivia Newton-John
10. "Jungle Boogie," Kool & The Gang
11. "One Hell of a Woman," Mac Davis
12. "Midnight at the Oasis," Maria Muldaur
13. "You Make Me Feel Brand New," Stylistics
14. "Spiders & Snakes," Jim Stafford
15. "Show & Tell" Al Wilson
16. "Sunshine on My Shoulder," John Denver
17. "Hooked on a Feeling," Blue Swede
18. "Rock On," David Essex
19. "Sideshow," Blue Magic
20. "Billy Don't Be A Hero," Bo Donaldson & Heywoods
21. "Band on the Run," Paul McCartney & Wings
22. "The Most Beautiful Girl," Charlie Rich
23. "Time in a Bottle," Jim Croce
24. "Annie's Song," John Denver
25. "(You're) Having My Baby," Paul Anka
26. "Rock the Boat," Hues Corporation
27. "Let Me Be There," Olivia Newton-John
28. "Rock Me Gently," Andy Kim
29. "Loco-Motion," Grand Funk
30. "Boogie Down," Eddie Kendricks
31. "You're Sixteen," Ringo Starr
32. "The Best Thing That Ever Happened," Gladys Knight & Pips
33. "If You Love Me (Let Me Know)," Olivia Newton-John
34. "Sundown," Gordon Lightfoot
35. "Rock Your Baby," George McCrae
36. "Just Don't Want To Be Lonely," Main Ingredient

37. "Top of the World," Carpenters
38. "Nothing from Nothing," Billy Preston
39. "The Joker" Steve Miller Band
40. "Livin' for the City," Stevie Wonder
41. "Then Came You," Dionne Warwick & Spinners
42. "Smokin' in the Boys' Room," Brownsville Station
43. "The Entertainer," Marvin Hamlisch
44. "The Night Chicago Died," Paper Lace
45. "Waterloo," Abba
46. "Help Me," Joni Mitchell
47. "I Shot the Sheriff," Eric Clapton
48. "For the Love of Money," O'Jays
49. "Rikki Don't Lose That Number," Steely Dan
50. "Eres Tu (Touch The Wind)," Mocedades

Number-One Songs of '74 *(Billboard)*

"Time in a Bottle" (1), Jim Croce
"The Joker" (1), Steve Miller Band
"Show & Tell" (1), Al Wilson
"You're Sixteen" (1), Ringo Starr
"The Way We Were" (3), Barbra Streisand
"Love's Theme" (1), Love Unlimited Orchestra
"Seasons in the Sun" (3), Terry Jacks
"Dark Lady" (1), Cher
"Sunshine on My Shoulder" (1), John Denver
"Hooked on a Feeling" (1), Blue Swede
"Bennie & the Jets" (1), Elton John
"T S O P" (2), MFSB
"The Loco-Motion" (2), Grand Funk
"The Streak" (3), Ray Stevens
"Band on the Run" (1), Paul McCartney & Wings
"Billy, Don't Be a Hero" (2), Bo Donaldson & Heywoods
"Sundown" (1), Gordon Lightfoot
"Rock the Boat" (1), Hues Corporation

"Rock Your Baby" (2), George McCrae
"Annie's Song" (2), John Denver
"Feel Like Makin' Love" (1), Roberta Flack
"The Night Chicago Died" (1), Paper Lace
"(You're) Having My Baby" (3), Paul Anka
"I Shot the Sheriff" (1), Eric Clapton
"Can't Get Enough of Your Love Baby" (1), Barry White
"Rock Me Gently" (1), Andy Kim
"I Honestly Love You" (2), Olivia Newton-John
"Nothing From Nothing" (1), Billy Preston
"Then Came You" (1), Dionne Warwick & Spinners
"You Haven't Done Nothin' " (1), Stevie Wonder
"You Ain't Seen Nothing Yet" (1), Backman-Turner Overdrive
"Whatever Gets You Through the Night," John Lennon
"I Can Help" (2), Billy Swan
"Kung Fu Fighting" (2), Carl Douglas
"Cat's in the Cradle" (1), Harry Chapin
"Angie Baby" (1), Helen Reddy

Most Significant Artists of '74

Elton John
Olivia Newton-John
John Denver
Stevie Wonder
Kool & The Gang

130

Academy Award (Oscar) Winning Song of '74

"We May Never Love like this Again,"
    from *The Towering Inferno*

Major Recording: Maureen McGovern

NARAS (Grammy) Major Category Winners of '74

Record of the Year:
    "I Honestly Love You," Olivia Newton-John

Album of the Year:
    "Fulfillingness' First Finale," Stevie Wonder

Song of the Year:
    "The Way We Were," Marilyn & Alan Bergman, Marvin
       Hamlisch

The hits have kept on comin' since the inception of top-forty radio, led by the Gordon McClendon's in 1955. Styles and variations have evolved and mutated in the past and will take new forms in the future. We have discussed some of the detours and hurdles that popular music has faced in two decades; it might be interesting to enumerate some of the gigantic, larger-than-life occurrences and "records" of this period, 1955 to 1976. So, from the files of the Flying Dutchman's "Believe It or Don't," here are some subjective observations.

The lengthiest 45 rpm record to sell a million copies is "Hey Jude" (7:06) by the Beatles, with other gems of longevity including "Like a Rolling Stone" (6:06) by Bob Dylan and, just short of a gold record, "MacArthur Park" (7:20) by Richard Harris—an album version of Donna Summer's million-seller and disco classic, "Love To Love You Baby," is sixteen minutes and fifty seconds in duration.

Stepping out of our twenty-two year period of study, we note that a Frenchman, Charles Cros, was the first to conceive the phonograph in 1877, but it took the relentless efforts of Thomas Alva Edison, in the same year, to construct the first working model. The first recorded song, on a cone of tin alloy, was "Mary Had a Little Lamb," featuring Edison himself. The first record to sell a million copies was Enrico Caruso's "Vesta La Giubba" from *Pagliacci*, initially released in 1902. One of the earliest artists to acquire a collection of gold records was Gene Austin with hits like

"My Blue Heaven." Unfortunately, million seller auditing didn't officially begin till 1958.

Bing Crosby holds the record for most discs marketed by an individual, more than four hundred million internationally. The group with the largest sales is the Beatles, with over five hundred million singles sold around the world—this in a period of ten years. Meanwhile, Elton John has earned the most money from his total sales in the record industry. The Beatles have recorded the most industry-audited million sellers, thirty-eight (the 1976 release of "Got to Get You into My Life" will make that thirty-nine); Elvis holds the record for most million sellers by an individual, twenty-eight—auditing is done by the RIAA. Elvis just keeps on truckin', recently converting his affections to the over-thirty crowd. It is likely the "El" will break the abovementioned Bing Crosby statistic before his career terminates. (Note: "Der Bingle" keeps selling, too.)

Hoagy Carmichael's "Stardust" is the most-recorded song with over one thousand various recordings in the catalogs. Recent competitors have included the Lennon-McCartney composition, "Yesterday," John Hartford's "Gentle on My Mind," and Paul Simon's "Bridge Over Troubled Water." Also in the running, the song "Volare" has zoomed to the top of the charts several times, with versions by Domenico Modugno, Dean Martin, Bobby Rydell, and Al Martino. "Mack the Knife" has also reached the top ten several times with recordings by Bobby Darin, Louis Armstrong, Owen Bradley, and others—it is sometimes called "Moritat" or "The Theme from *The Three Penny Opera*." Other perennial favorites include Bill Haley's "Rock Around the Clock," the Five Satins' "In the Still of the Night," Bobby Pickett's "Monster Mash," Brian Wilson's "Help Me Rhonda," and Bobby Helms's "Jingle Bell Rock."

Bing Crosby's recording of Irving Berlin's "White Christmas," in several different updated editions, is the largest-selling single of all time. The largest selling "pop" single is Bill Haley's "Rock Around the Clock."

For the statistician who loves the music charts and their "records" that have become awe-inspiring over the years: The Beatles have had the most number-one records, more than twenty; Elvis has been in the top ten the most times, well over thirty-five

134

journeys; and, once again, Elvis Presley holds the distinction of having some sort of chart appearance every year for twenty-one years, from "Heartbreak Hotel" in 1956 to "Hurt" in 1976.

In the album department, the "established" records are not so easily established. Carole King's "Tapestry" recently passed Capitol's "Sound of Music" LP in total sales—Ode Records reports Carole's sales at over seventeen million. Also in the competition is "The Little Drummer Boy" by the Harry Simeone Chorale— Christmas sales could put this back on top. The distinction of longest residence on *Billboard*'s LP chart, the accepted authority, also belongs to Carole King's album "Tapestry," the origin of several hit singles. Previously, the record has been held by the original cast recording of "My Fair Lady" and the "Johnny Mathis' Greatest Hits" album. "Tapestry" has made a nonstop appearance on the *Billboard* chart since 1971.

In the first week of October, 1976, the young sensation, Peter Frampton, set the all-time "Record World" mark for an LP sustaining itself in the number-one position of that trade magazine's chart. Peter's "Frampton Comes Alive!" album topped the survey for the fifteenth week on October 2. Previously, that record was held by Carole King when her "Tapestry" LP was number-one for fourteen weeks.

Elvis Presley, with several back-to-back smashes, captured the number-one position on *Billboard*'s singles-chart for twenty-eight weeks in 1956, more than half the year, despite the fact his first hit didn't come until spring of that year. The Beatles held down the number-one position for fifteen weeks in 1964. That same year, they captured all top-five positions on the *Billboard* "Hot 100" with "I Want To Hold Your Hand," "Twist and Shout," "She Loves You," "Can't Buy Me Love," and "Please Please Me." At the same time, they had the number-one and number-two bestselling albums in the nation. It all happened in March of that crazy year, 1964.

From our department of off-beat trivia: The longest LP ever produced is "The Complete Works of Shakespeare" with more than 125 discs in the set.

Beatles fans purchased more than two million copies of "Can't Buy Me Love" before the record was released—advance orders were tremendous.

The first gentleman to uncover a cache of superstars was Sam Phillips of Sun Records in Memphis; he discovered Elvis Presley, Johnny Cash, Carl Perkins, Roy Orbison, Charlie Rich, Jerry Lee Lewis, and several others. Berry Gordy, Jr., probably has coordinated more successful acts than any other living person, and he's not done yet! Other artist gold miners have included: "Mitch Miller," (Columbia), "Bernie Lowe" (Cameo), "Randy Wood" (Dot), and Archie Bleyer (Cadence).

Fats Domino has had over twenty million sellers (unofficial) but has yet to achieve a number-one song. Fats has been churning out hits since the mid-40s.

It took the Five Satins more than fifteen years—and a return from retirement—to turn "In the Still of the Night" into a million seller.

The oldest "standard disc" record companies still in existence are Columbia and RCA Victor (Victor Talking Machine Company, incorporated in 1901, took Emile Berliner's gramaphone and revolutionized the infant industry).

The most prolific hitmaker in a short span has been Berry Gordy, Jr., from his Motown—Tamla complex in Detroit. Bernie Lowe's Cameo-Parkway compound in Philadelphia previously possessed the distinction.

Subjectively, the most successful recording, aired and often considered a single, is Led Zeppelin's album selection, "Stairway to Heaven," which Atlantic Records has wisely never released at 45 rpm. Led Zeppelin holds the record for the largest purse at a live performance; they received three hundred and nine thousand dollars for their appearance at Tampa Stadium in 1973. Before that, the Beatles held the record for their performance at Shea Stadium.

Discs that have achieved great sales, but have been vigorously censored by the broadcast industry, include "Annie Had a Baby" by Hank Ballard and the Midnighters, "Honey Love" by Clyde McPhatter and the Drifters, Redd Foxx comedy albums, "Shaving Cream" by Bennie Bell, "Let's Spend the Night Together" by the Rolling Stones, "Lay Lady Lay" by Bob Dylan, "Baby, Let Me Bang Your Box" by Doug Clark and the Hot Nuts, and a variety of recordings by the Mothers of Invention—somehow, I have managed to air all of them, though I must admit that it was usually late at night or when the program director was on vacation.

The biggest "put-on" record of recent times is considered to be the Beatles' "Lucy in the Sky With Diamonds"—John Lennon, with a wink, still denies that it is about the use of LSD.

The two fastest-selling LPs of all time are both about President John Fitzgerald Kennedy. Vaughn Meader's "First Family Album," a smash during the Christmas season of 1962, ironically, was surpassed by "John Fitzgerald Kennedy—A Memorial Album" in the Christmas rush of 1963. The latter sold four million copies in less than one week. Some political experts feel that if the unexpurgated Watergate tapes are ever released in album form, they may smash this existing record.

The "most significant" case of blind luck goes to the writer of "I Left My Heart in San Francisco," who submitted this "provincial" travelog to Tony Bennett by mail; Tony subsequently made it a long-run favorite and a Grammy winner.

And, finally, the credit for triggering the pop scene of today, that has been upon us for the past twenty years or so, is given to Alan Freed, a Cleveland disc jockey who failed to ignore the needs of teenagers. Nightly, he kept beat to the music, tapped vigorously on a phonebook, and screamed "rock & roll, rock & roll, rock & roll!" To him this whole era must be dedicated.

1. "Love Will Keep Us Together," Captain & Tennille
2. "Rhinestone Cowboy," Glen Campbell
3. "Philadelphia Freedom," Elton John
4. "My Eyes Adored You," Frankie Valli
5. "Some Kind Of Wonderful," Grand Funk
6. "Shining Star," Earth Wind & Fire
7. "Fame," David Bowie
8. "Laughter in the Rain," Neil Sedaka
9. "One Of These Nights," Eagles
10. "Thank God I'm a Country Boy," John Denver
11. "Jive Talkin'," Bee Gees
12. "Best Of My Love," Eagles
13. "Lovin' You," Minnie Riperton
14. "Kung Fu Fighting," Carl Douglas
15. "Black Water," Doobie Brothers
16. "Ballroom Blitz," Sweet
17. "He Don't Love You (Like I Love You)," Tony Orlando & Dawn
18. "At Seventeen," Janis Ian
19. "Pick Up the Pieces," Average White Band
20. "The Hustle," Van McCoy
21. "Lady Marmalade," Labelle
22. "Why Can't We Be Friends?" War
23. "Love Won't Let Me Wait," Major Harris
24. "Miracles," Jefferson Starship
25. "Whatever Gets You Through the Night," John Lennon
26. "Boogie On Reggae Woman," Stevie Wonder
27. "Before the Next Teardrop Falls," Freddy Fender
28. "Angie Baby," Helen Reddy
29. "Fight the Power," Isley Brothers
30. "Jackie Blue," Ozark Mountain Daredevils
31. "Fire," Ohio Players
32. "Bad Blood," Neil Sedaka
33. "Sister Golden Hair," America
34. "Please, Mr. Postman," Carpenters
35. "Wasted Days & Wasted Nights," Freddy Fender

36. "Who Loves You," Four Seasons
37. "Mandy," Barry Manilow
38. "Have You Never Been Mellow," Olivia Newton-John
39. "Could It Be Magic," Barry Manilow
40. "Listen to What the Man Said," Paul McCartney & Wings
41. "Another Somebody Done Somebody Wrong Song," B. J. Thomas
42. "Lucy in the Sky with Diamonds," Elton John
43. "I'm Not Lisa," Jessi Colter
44. "Magic," Pilot
45. "I Can Help," Billy Swan
46. "Falling In Love," Hamilton, Joe Frank & Reynolds
47. "When Will I Be Loved," Linda Ronstadt
48. "Get Down Tonight," K.C. & The Sunshine Band
49. "You're the First, the Last, My Everything," Barry White
50. "Cat's in the Cradle," Harry Chapin

Number-One Songs of '75 *(Billboard)*

"Lucy in the Sky with Diamonds" (2), Elton John
"Mandy" (1), Barry Manilow
"Please, Mr. Postman" (1), Carpenters
"Laughter in the Rain" (1), Neil Sedaka
"Fire" (1), Ohio Players
"You're No Good" (1), Linda Ronstadt
"Pick Up the Pieces" (1), Average White Band
"Best Of My Love" (1), Eagles
"Have You Never Been Mellow" (1), Olivia Newton-John
"Black Water" (1), Doobie Brothers
"My Eyes Adored You" (1), Frankie Valli
"Lady Marmalade" (1), Labelle
"Lovin' You" (1), Minnie Riperton
"Philadelphia Freedom" (2), Elton John
"Another Somebody Done Somebody Wrong Song" (1), B. J. Thomas

"He Don't Love You (Like I Love You)" (3), Tony Orlando & Dawn
"Shining Star" (1), Earth Wind & Fire
"Before the Next Teardrop Falls" (1), Freddy Fender
"Thank God, I'm a Country Boy" (1), John Denver
"Sister Golden Hair" (1), America
"Love Will Keep Us Together" (4), Captain & Tennille
"Listen to What the Man Said" (1), Paul McCartney & Wings
"The Hustle" (1), Van McCoy & Soul City Symphony
"One Of These Nights" (1), Eagles
"Jive Talkin' " (2), Bee Gees
"Fallin' In Love" (1), Hamilton, Joe Frank & Reynolds
"Get Down Tonight" (1), K.C. & Sunshine Band
"Rhinestone Cowboy" (2), Glen Campbell
"Fame" (1), David Bowie
"Bad Blood" (3), Neil Sedaka
"Island Girl" (3), Elton John
"That's the Way (I Like It)" (2), K.C. & Sunshine Band
"Fly Robin Fly" (3), Silver Convention
"Let's Do It Again" (1), Staple Singers

Most Significant Artists of '75

John Denver
Eagles
Captain & Tennille
Elton John
Neil Sedaka

140

Academy Award (Oscar) Winning Song of '75

"I'm Easy,"
    from *Nashville*

Major recording: Keith Carradine

NARAS (Grammy) Major Category Winners of '75

Record of the Year:
    "Love Will Keep Us Together," Captain & Tennille

Album of the Year:
    "Still Crazy After All These Years," Paul Simon

Song of the Year:
    "Send In the Clowns," Stephen Sondheim

141

Two Hundred Years Of "Yankee Doodle Dandy" 1976

1976! What a year it was! Lost in all this variety of national cele-
bration are the pace and tempo of popular music. Where the devil
is it all heading? If I turn on my radio—and believe me, it depends
on what facet of my radio—it's hard to tell the established forms
from the emerging trends.

On AM, top-forty formats seem to be losing their historic
foothold. The variety of top-forty spinoffs runs from "M-O-R
Contemporary" to "City-oriented top-forty country & western,"
and if these euphemistic descriptions seem inane, they are for real.
The AM spectrum of the radio dial is caught up in its annual rating
race, and the rating services have ironically put the cart before the
horse. Listeners once bought products, but now advertisers buy
listeners—and not just any listener. It is a listener selected by the
new science, demographics, the art of stuffing Americans into the
right age and social bracket, selected exclusively for the promotion
of the sponsor's product.

Let us say you are between eighteen and thirty-four years of
age—you might appeal to the friendly folks at Coca-Cola. If you
are twenty-five to forty-nine—you are probably a target for the
purveyors of automobiles. If you just happen to be on either side
of these age barriers, you are peripheral and don't appeal to anyone in the advertising community. Add to this rating isolation the
broadcaster's necessity of programming music to fit this mold, and
you have "Who's on first, who's on second?" Theoretically, if you
drench your face with blemish cream, AM radio concludes you are

ready for the chants of new potential artists like Heart, Starbuck, and Henry Gross; but if you drive a Buick and have clear skin, the "broadcast computer" plans a milder diet for you, with servings of John Denver, Karen Carpenter, and Wayne Newton. Unfortunately, if you are under thirteen and adore the "Bay City Rollers" or you are fifty-one and find charm in "Lawrence Welk"—the Hell with you, you are "dead weight"!

Today a majority of AM radio stations zero in on some human calibration of this overall advertisers' delight, the demographic group, eighteen to forty-nine. Because of it, there is money in country & western (male 25 and up), all-white harmony (female 25-34), all-black harmony (minority 18-34), no harmony—all news (male 34-49), hum-drum non-harmony or telephone talk (belligerent 34-49), and the old standby, mix and match harmony, which is all or none of the above (male and female 1-99). Of course, if all this demographic deviation doesn't appeal to you, there is always the FM spectrum.

What about FM radio? The answer is: "The same game, the same ratings, and the same programmers." Oh, yes, there are some differences, but slight and hardly secure for the future. FM broadcasters today offer us "Progressive Rock"—"head shops" and rock show promoters need some advertising outlet, "Beautiful Music"—funeral homes and colonial furniture stores must get their messages home to the older folks who appreciate "elevator" arrangements of stock goodies, and "Contemporary Classical"—a nice niche for the institutional commercial, the stock in trade of corporations with images to uphold. Yet, don't be deluded—the big-money operators set the trend, and slowly, but guaranteed surely, their demands for attractive demographics that tantalize their palates are being felt even in the FM strongholds of unique good taste.

"Watch out! Here they come, coast to coast, the "carousel" (that's "automation" in English) programmers, and they have lots of music and very little talk. Sounds great, doesn't it? But why is all that non-stop music served up in day parts, neat little sections of musical fruit sliced to suit "the proper audience for the 'correct' part of the day"? Translation for the layman: Ladies who listen to Olivia Newton-John are very likely to buy bras from Macys! Fantastic! Let's give the ladies 10-11 A.M. to think about that.

144

Elton John advocates are quite likely into Yamahas! Good! Let's give the guys 3-4 P.M. The Guy Lombardo and Percy Faith fans? They are very heavy users of Poligrip! Good! They get the shaft—about the same size as the one used on the bubble-gummers.

This incredible thought process emanates from the glass palaces of Madison Avenue and echoes in the computerized secret briefing rooms of the giant rating services like ARB and Pulse. The results of this "1984 Theology" are not really too difficult to comprehend—if you like Helen Reddy, Glen Campbell, or John Travolta, run up your victory flag, because in the jargon of advertisers, you "fit nicely," and your electrodes are in place. On the other hand, perchance you love jazz, hard-rock, lush strings, classical, comedy, or some other diversified musical approach, well—"Gosh, you don't have to be a weatherman to see which way the wind is blowing."

Maybe our advertising community—between "red hot" sessions of digital readout—should take pause in this bicentennial era and realize: here we are, two hundred years away from "Yankee Doodle Dandy," and that song, by today's standards was a hit of enormous proportions, an international smash! To trace its origins is nigh impossible. The British had their version, the Spanish claimed they danced to it, the French drank to their version, and our very own American patriots fought to it. In Colonial America, if you were twelve or eighty, you loved this musical delight. It stayed on the "charts" for decades; without the benefit of radio, record, or eight-track tape, "Yankee Doodle Dandy" was as popular as Frankie, Elvis, and the Beatles at their charismatic heights. I'm not too sure that one of our leading advertising agencies could —or would want to—understand this loyalty to simplicity.

Imagine! You, Mr. Retailer, could sell almost anything under the sun to a "Yankee Doodle Dandy" fan, from cribs to caskets. I wonder how the rating services of 1976 would handle that kind of 1776 hit song; "Yankee Doodle Dandy" was big box-office across the demographic scale. Even the legendary fife and drum trio that was most identified with the song defied age classification and social standing. In fact, almost all of the 1776 hits crossed the spectrum from teen to elder. Were our forefathers that naive that they actually believed a good, catchy tune or even a love ballad was universally acceptable? Rot! Our 1976 social leaders would be shocked and their population-trend projections and "calculated perceptions" would tumble from their walnut veneer desks.

I have a feeling that just maybe, two hundred years after the advent of "Mr. Dandy," we, as a nation of wide race-sex-age diversification, aren't quite as musically sophisticated as our product-pushers demand us to be. Occasionally, Mom does sneak a listen to Junior's "Wings" album, little sister enjoys that "odd" Guy Lumbardo on New Year's Eve, and—though this may seem a heresy—the folks over fifty aren't totally committed to "Muzak." If this be the case, let us hope that we can get back to the "Spirit of '76" some day. I speculate that a "pop" song by definition is universally popular, and that its universality is not determined by the quantity of frozen orange juice it sells on the radio.

Number-One Songs of '76 *(Billboard)* (to October 15)

"Saturday Night" (1), Bay City Rollers
"Convoy" (1), C. W. McCall
"I Write the Songs" (1), Barry Manilow
"Theme from *Mahogany* (1), Diana Ross
"Love Rollercoaster" (1), Ohio Players
"Fifty Ways to Leave Your Lover" (3), Paul Simon
"Theme from S.W.A.T." (1), Rhythm Heritage
"Love Machine" (1), Miracles
"December 1963 (Oh, What A Night)" (3), Four Seasons
"Disco Lady" (4), Johnny Taylor
"Let Your Love Flow" (1), Bellamy Brothers
"Welcome Back" (1), John Sebastian
"Boogie Fever" (1), Sylvers
"Love Hangover" (2), Diana Ross
"Silly Love Songs" (5), Paul McCartney & Wings
"Afternoon Delight" (1), Starland Vocal Band
"Kiss and Say Goodbye" (2), Manhattans
"Don't Go Breaking My Heart" (4), Elton John & Kiki Dee
"You Should Be Dancing" (1), Bee Gees
"Shake Your Booty" (1), K.C. & The Sunshine Band
"Play That Funky Music" (3), Wild Cherry
"A Fifth of Beethoven" (1), Walter Murphy & The Big Apple Band
"Disco Duck (Part 1)" (1), Rick Dees & His Cast of Idiots

Most Significant Artists of '76 (to October 15)

Diana Ross
Paul McCartney & Wings
Captain & Tennille
Johnny Taylor
Neil Sedaka/Elton John

147

New Artists of '76 (Projected hitmakers of the future)

Heart
Bellamy Brothers
Sylvers
Starland Vocal Band
Starbuck
Gary Wright
Eric Carmen
Brothers Johnson
Bob Marley & The Wailers
Henry Gross
George Benson
Boz Scaggs

PHOTOS

Photos

BILL HALEY AND THE COMETS. "Peepin' in a Seafood Store." *Courtesy Michael Ochs Archives*

Above left: CHUCK BERRY. ''Just Give Me Some of that Rock and Roll Music.'' *Courtesy Chess Records*

Above: PAT BOONE. 1955-1976 and still going. *Courtesy Michael Ochs Archives*

Left: FATS DOMINO. The fat man. *Courtesy United Artists*

Facing page, top: ELVIS PRESLEY. The ''King.'' *Courtesy RCA*

Facing page, bottom: THE PLATTERS. Harmony in the '50s. *Courtesy Mercury Records*

BUDDY HOLLY. The inspiration.   RAY CHARLES. The "Genius."
Courtesy Michael Ochs Archives   *Courtesy Michael Ochs Archives*

JOHNNY MATHIS. A maestro for
lovers. *Courtesy Michael Ochs Archives*

CONNIE FRANCIS. The "Million-Dollar Paisano." *Courtesy Michael Ochs Archives*

BOBBY DARIN. "Mack the Knife." *Courtesy Michael Ochs Archives*

NEIL SEDAKA. Two generations of excellence. *Courtesy Michael Ochs Archives*

DION. Pop music's most under-
estimated superstar! *Courtesy
Michael Ochs Archives*

GENE PITNEY. The voice
of Connecticut. *Courtesy
Michael Ochs Archives*

CHUBBY CHECKER. "Mr. Twist." *Courtesy Michael Ochs Archives*

THE BEACH BOYS. "Surfin' USA." *Courtesy Michael Ochs Archives*

LEN BARRY. Because Philly wasn't closed. *Courtesy Alan White "Great American Music Machine"*

THE BEATLES. The second colonization of America. *Courtesy Michael Ochs Archives*

Facing page, top: DAVE CLARK
FIVE. The second British Regiment
of Red Coats. *Courtesy Michael Ochs
Archives*

Facing page, bottom: THE ROLL-
ING STONES. The world's most
consistent hit-makers. *Courtesy
Michael Ochs Archives*

Right: PETULA CLARK. A sign of
her times. *Courtesy Michael Ochs Archives*

Below: HERMAN'S HERMITS.
Where "Bubble Gum" began. *Courtesy Michael Ochs Archives*

Top left: ARETHA FRANKLIN. Lady soul. *Courtesy Michael Ochs Archives*

Top right: OTIS REDDING. The big "O." *Courtesy Michael Ochs Archives*

Left: TOMMY JAMES AND THE SHONDELLS. The New York sound of the '60s. *Courtesy Michael Ochs Archives*

Facing page, top: THE MONKEES. Rock comes to television. *Courtesy Michael Ochs Archives*

Facing page, bottom: THREE DOG NIGHT. "Jeremiah was a Bullfrog." *Courtesy Michael Ochs Archives*

Facing page, top: "LATE" BEATLES. Down "The Long and Winding Road." *Courtesy Capitol Records*

Facing page, middle: CREEDENCE CLEARWATER REVIVAL. They brought rock into the '70s. *Courtesy Michael Ochs Archives*

Facing page, bottom: BLOOD, SWEAT, AND TEARS. Big band rock. *Courtesy Michael Ochs Archives*

Right: JIM CROCE. "Bad, Bad, Leroy Brown." *Courtesy Michael Ochs Archives*

Below: JEFFERSON STARSHIP. Gracie Slick spaketh twice. *Courtesy RCA*

ELTON JOHN. The all-time breadwin-
ner. *Courtesy Michael Ochs Archives*

JOHN DENVER. "Take Me Home,
Country Roads." *Courtesy RCA*

A DISCOGRAPHY OF POPULAR HITS, 1955–1976

A Discography of Popular Hits, 1955–1976

This discography is an alphabetical treasure of the major recording artists and their greatest musical achievements from 1955 to 1976. Individual artists are entered under their proper names (Cash, Johnny) and vocal groups and bands are posted by the first letter of their entire title (Fifth Dimension). In the cases where individual singers recorded with well-known groups (Dion and the Belmonts) or the group had a distinctive lead (Alpert, Herb, and the Tijuana Brass) the listing is based on the proper name of the lead. Accordingly, many artists have several different listings.

Those songs selected for each artist are determined by the aggregate popularity they reached at their peak (usually, national top-forty status was the standard). These indexed compositions are their greatest hits (songs of regional popularity are excluded). Many of the well-known stars that are cataloged here attained hits prior to 1955, but the time span of this book does not allow for their mention in this discography.

In most instances, we list the title and the year of a record's greatest popularity: these years are not release dates or the date they achieved million-seller status. If a cataloged tune sold one million copies, as audited by the Recording Industry Assocation of America (RIAA), this achievement is noted directly after its year of popular acceptance (Johnny Horton's "Battle of New Orleans," 1959, RIAA '66). There are many examples of songs that took ten years to sell that legendary million copies.

The hit recordings of the Motown–Tamla labels (Supremes,

169

Temptations, etc.) are not, and never have been, audited by RIAA, and Motown-Tamla would not make their sales figures available, though many of their hits have surely surpassed minimum requirements for gold status.

It might be wise to keep in mind that RIAA did not start their audit processes until 1958, and even then, not all hits were immediately submitted to them for evaluation. Throughout the following pages, if any song has no date of popularity indicated, it is because the tune's public acceptance varied greatly in different parts of the country: if it has two dates, it was a hit more than once ("The Twist").

Since this book is based solely on single recordings, we have made little reference to long-playing albums, an important facet in the over-all success of an artist. In this discography we have listed under each artist's separate heading the albums that have achieved gold awards or sales of 500,000 copies or more.

In 1976, the RIAA added a new twist to their certification of LPs and singles, by adding the "Platinum Record Award." Singles that have sold two million copies, and albums that have sold one million copies, qualify. In this discography that distinction has been noted in specific listings under the artist's name. Formerly, gold certification indicated a single-marketed one million copies and an LP that achieved one million dollars in manufacturer's sales.

Abba, "Waterloo," 1974; "S O S," 1975; "I Do, I Do, I Do," 1976; "Mama Mia," 1976; "Fernando," 1976
Ace, "How Long (Has This Been Going On)," 1975
Ace, Johnny, "Pledging My Love," 1955
Acklin, Barbara, "Love Makes a Woman," 1968
Adams, Johnny, "Reconsider Me," 1969
Adderly, Cannonball, "Mercy, Mercy, Mercy," 1967
Addrisi Brothers, "Cherrystone," 1959; "We've Got to Get It on Again," 1972
Ad-Libs, "The Boy from New York City," 1965
Aerosmith, "Dream On," 1976; "Lady Child," 1976
Aerosmith, RIAA Gold Albums, "Get Your Wings," 1975; "Toys in the Attic," 1975; "Aerosmith," 1975; "Rocks," 1976

170

Aerosmith, RIAA Platinum Album, "Rocks," 1976

Akens, Jewel, "The Birds and the Bees," 1965

Alaimo, Steve, "Everyday I Have to Cry," 1963

Albert, Morris, "Feelings (Dime)," 1975; RIAA 75

Alexander, Arthur, "You Better Move On," 1962; "Anna," 1962

Alive 'n' Kicking, "Tighter and Tighter," 1970

Allan, Davie, and the Arrows, "Blues Theme," 1967

Allen, Lee, "Walkin' with Mr. Lee," 1958

Allen, Rex, "Don't Go Near the Indians," 1962

Allen, Steve, "Autumn Leaves," 1955

Allman Brothers, "Ramblin' Man," 1973

Allman Brothers Band, RIAA Gold Albums, "The Allman Brothers Band at Fillmore East," 1971; "Eat a Peach," 1972; "Brothers & Sisters," 1973; "Beginnings," 1973; "Win, Lose or Draw," 1975

Allman, Duane, RIAA Gold Album, "An Anthology," 1972

Allman, Gregg, RIAA Gold Album, "Laid Back," 1974

Alpert, Herb, & The Tijuana Brass, "The Lonely Bull," 1962; "Taste of Honey," 1965; "3rd Man Theme," 1965; "Zorba The Greek/Tijuana Taxi," 1966; "The Work Song," 1966; "What Now My Love/Spanish Flea," 1966; "Flamingo," 1966; "Mame," 1966; "Casino Royale," 1967; "Wade in the Water," 1967; "A Banda," 1967; "This Guy's in Love with You," 1968, RIAA 68

Alpert, Herb, & The Tijuana Brass, RIAA Gold Albums, "Going Places," 1965; "Whipped Cream & Other Delights," 1965; "South of the Border," 1966; "The Lonely Bull," 1966; "What Now My Love," 1966; "Herb Alpert's Tijuana Brass, Vol. 2," 1966; "S. R. O.," 1967; "Sounds Like," 1967; "Herb Alpert's Ninth," 1967; "The Beat of the Brass," 1968; "The Christmas Album," 1968; "Warm," 1970; "Greatest Hits," 1971

Amazing Rhythm Aces, "Third Rate Romance," 1975

Amboy Dukes, "Journey to the Center of the Mind," 1968

America, "A Horse with No Name," 1972, RIAA 72; "Ventura Highway," 1972; "I Need You," 1972; "Lonely People," 1974; "Tin Man," 1974; "Sister Golden Hair," 1975; "Woman Tonight," 1975; "Daisy Jane," 1975; "Today Is the Day," 1976

America, RIAA Gold Albums, "America," 1972; "Homecoming," 1972; "Holiday," 1974; "Hearts," 1975; "History—America's Greatest Hits," 1975

American Breed, "Step Out of Your Mind," 1967; "Bend Me, Shape Me," 1968, RIAA 68

Ames Brothers, "My Bonnie Lassie," 1955; "It Only Hurts for a Little While,"

1956; "Tammy," 1957; "Melodie D'Amour," 1957; "Pussy Cat," 1958

Ames, Ed (see Ames Brothers), "Try to Remember," 1965; "My Cup Runneth Over," 1967; "Who Will Answer," 1967

Ames, Ed, RIAA Gold Albums, "My Cup Runneth Over," 1967; "Who Will Answer?" 1969

Anderson, Bill, "Still," 1963

Anderson, Lynn, "Rose Garden," 1970, RIAA 71; "How Can I Unlove You," 1971

Anderson, Lynn, RIAA Gold Album, "Rose Garden," 1971

Andrea True Connection, "More, More, More," 1976, RIAA 76

Andrews, Julie, & Dick Van Dyke, "Super-Cali-Fragil-Istic-Expi-Ali-Docious," 1965

Andrews, Lee, & The Hearts, "Long Lonely Nights," 1957; "Teardrops," 1957; "Try the Impossible," 1958

Angels, "Til," 1961; "Cry Baby Cry," 1962; "My Boyfriend's Back," 1963; "I Adore Him," 1963

Animals, "House of the Rising Sun," 1964; "I'm Crying," 1964; "Boom Boom," 1964; "We Gotta Get Out of This Place," 1965; "Don't Let Me Be Misunderstood," 1965; "It's My Life," 1965; "Bring It On Home To Me," 1965; "Inside-Looking Out," 1966; "Don't Bring Me Down," 1966; "See See Rider," 1966; "San Franciscan Nights," 1967; "When I Was Young," 1967; "Monterrey," 1967; "Sky Pilot," 1968

Animals, RIAA Gold Album, "The Best of the Animals," 1966

Anka, Paul, "Diana," 1957; "You Are My Destiny," 1958; "Crazy Love," 1958; "(All of a Sudden) My Heart Sings," 1958; "I Miss You So," 1959; "It's Time to Cry," 1959; "Lonely Boy," 1959; "Put Your Head On My Shoulder," 1959; "My Hometown," 1960; "Summer's Gone," 1960; "Puppy Love," 1960; "The Story of My Love," 1961; "Tonight, My Love, Tonight," 1961; "Dance On Little Girl," 1961; "Love Me Warm & Tender," 1962; "Eso Beso," 1962; "A Steel Guitar & a Glass of Wine," 1962; "Goodnight My Love," 1962; "You're Having My Baby," 1974, RIAA 74; "I Don't Like to Sleep Alone," 1975; "One Man Woman (One Woman Man)," 1975; "Times of Your Life," 1976; "Anytime," 1976

Anka, Paul, RIAA Gold Album, "Anka," 1974

Anka, Paul, George Hamilton IV, Johnny Nash, "The Teen Commandments," 1958

Annette, "Tall Paul," 1959; "First Name Initial," 1959; "O Dio Mio," 1960; "Pineapple Princess," 1960

Ann Margret, "I Just Don't Understand," 1961

Anthology Albums, RIAA Gold Albums, "Dick Clark: 20 Years of Rock & Roll," 1973; "American Graffiti," 1973

Anthony, Ray, "Theme From 'Peter Gunn'," 1959

Apollo 100, "Joy," 1972

Applejacks, "Mexican Hat Rock," 1958; "Rocka-Conga," 1958

April Wine, "You Could Have Been a Lady," 1972

Aquatones, "You," 1958

Arbors, "Symphony For Susan," 1966; "Graduation Day," 1967; "The Letter," 1969

Archies, "Bang Shang A Lang," 1968; "Sugar, Sugar," 1969, RIAA 69; "Jingle Jangle," 1970, RIAA 70

Arden, Toni, "Padre," 1958

Argent, "Hold Your Head Up," 1972

Arms, Russell, "Cinco Robles," 1957

Armstrong, Louis, "Mack the Knife," 1956; "Blueberry Hill," 1956; "Hello, Dolly," 1964; "Mame," 1966

Armstrong, Louis, RIAA Gold Album, "Hello, Dolly," 1964

Arnold, Eddy, "The Cattle Call," 1955; "I've Been Thinking," 1955; "Tennessee Stud," 1959; "What's He Doing In My World," 1965; "Make the World Go Away," 1965; "I Want To Go With You," 1966; "The Last Word In Lonesome Is Me," 1966; "The Tip of My Fingers," 1966

Arnold, Eddy, RIAA Gold Albums, "My World," 1966; "The Best of Eddy Arnold," 1968

Assembled Multitude, "Overture From *Tommy*," 1970

Association, "Along Comes Mary," 1966; "Cherish," 1966, RIAA 66; "Pandora's Golden Heebie Jeebies," 1966; "Windy," 1967, RIAA 67; "Never My Love," 1967, RIAA 67; "Everything That Touches You," 1968; "Time For Livin'," 1968; "Six Man Band," 1968

Association, RIAA Gold Albums, "Along Comes The Association," 1967; "Insight Out," 1967; "The Association's Greatest Hits," 1969

Austin, Sil, "Slow Walk," 1956

Autry, Gene, "Rudolph The Red Nosed Reindeer," RIAA 69

Avalon, Frankie, "De De Dinah," 1958; "Gingerbread," 1958; "I'll Wait For You," 1958; "Venus," 1959; "A Boy Without a Girl," 1959; "Bobby Sox to Stockings," 1959; "Just Ask Your Heart," 1959; "Why," 1959; "Don't Throw Away All Those Teardrops," 1960; "Togetherness," 1960; "You Are Mine," 1962; "Venus (Disco Version)," 1976

Avant-Garde, "Naturally Stoned," 1968

Average White Band (AWB), "Pick Up the Pieces," 1975, RIAA 75; "Cut the Cake," 1975; "School Boy Crush," 1976

Average White Band (AWB), RIAA Gold Albums, "Average White Band," 1975; "Cut the Cake," 1975; "Soul Searchin'," 1976

B. Bumble & The Stingers, "Bumble Boogie," 1961; "Nut Rocker," 1962

B. T. Express, "Do It ('Til You're Satisfied)," 1974, RIAA 74; "Express," 1975, RIAA 75; "Peace Pipe," 1975; "Can't Stop Groovin. . .," 1976

B. T. Express, RIAA Gold Album, "Do It ('Til You're Satisfied)," 1975

Bacharach, Burt, RIAA Gold Albums, "Butch Cassidy & The Sundance Kid," 1970; "Make It Easy On Yourself," 1970; "Reach Out," 1970; "Burt Bacharach," 1971

Bachelors, "Diane," 1964; "No Arms Can Ever Hold You," 1964; "Marie," 1965; "Chapel in the Moonlight," 1965; "Love Me With All of Your Heart," 1966

Bachman-Turner Overdrive, "Taking Care of Business," 1974; "Let It Ride," 1974; "You Ain't Seen Nothin' Yet," 1974, RIAA 74; "Lookin' Out For #1," 1976

Bachman-Turner Overdrive, RIAA Gold Albums, "Bachman-Turner Overdrive," 1974; "Bachman-Turner Overdrive II," 1974; "Not Fragile," 1974; "Four Wheel Drive," 1975; "Head On," 1975; "Best of BTO (So Far)," 1976

Backus, Jim, & Friend, "Delicious!" 1958

Bad Company, "Can't Get Enough Of Your Love," 1974; "Feel Like Makin' Love," 1975; "Young Blood," 1976

Bad Company, RIAA Gold Albums, "Bad Company," 1974; "Straight Shooter," 1975; "Run With the Pack," 1976

Badfinger, "Come & Get It," 1970; "No Matter What," 1970; "Day After Day," 1971, RIAA 72; "Baby Blue," 1972

Baez, Joan, "The Night They Drove Old Dixie Down," 1971, RIAA 71; "Diamonds & Rust," 1975

Baez, Joan, RIAA Gold Albums, "Joan Baez," 1966; "Joan Baez, Vol. 2," 1966; "Joan Baez in Concert," 1966; "Blessed Are," 1972; "Any Day Now," 1972; "Diamonds & Rust," 1975

Baja Marimba Band, "Comin' in the Back Door," 1963

Baker, George, Selection, "Little Green Bag," 1970; "La Paloma Blanca," 1976

Baker, Laverne, "Tweedle Dee," 1955; "I Can't Love You Enough," 1956; "Jim Dandy," 1956; "I Cried a Tear," 1958; "I Waited Too Long," 1959; "Saved," 1961; "See See Rider," 1962

174

Ball, Kenny, "Midnight in Moscow," 1962

Ballard, Hank, & The Midnighters, "The Twist," 1959-1960; "Finger Poppin' Time," 1960; "Let's Go, Let's Go, Let's Go," 1960; "The Hoochi Coochi Coo," 1960; "The Continental Walk," 1961; "The Switch-a-Roo," 1961

Band, "Up on Cripple Creek," 1969; "Don't Do It," 1972

Band, RIAA Gold Albums, "The Band," 1969; "Stage Fright," 1970; "Rock of Ages," 1972

Banks, Darrell, "Open the Door to Your Heart," 1966

Barber, Chris, Jazz Band, "Petite Fleur," 1959

Bare, Bobby, "The All-American Boy (as Bill Parsons)," 1958; "Shame on Me," 1962; "500 Miles (Away From Home)," 1963; "Detroit City," 1963; "Miller's Cave," 1964

Bar-Kays, "Soul Finger," 1967

Barnum, H. B., "Lost Love," 1961

Barretto, Ray, "El Watusi," 1963

Barry & The Tamerlanes, "I Wonder What She's Doing Tonight," 1963

Barry, Joe, "I'm a Fool to Care," 1961

Barry, Len (see The Dovells), "1-2-3," 1965; "Like a Baby," 1966; "Somewhere," 1966

Basie, Count, "April in Paris," 1956

Baskerville Hounds, "Hold Me," 1969

Bass, Fontella, "Rescue Me," 1965; "Recovery," 1965

Bass, Fontella, & Bobby McClure, "Don't Mess Up a Good Thing," 1965

Bassey, Shirley, "Goldfinger," 1965; "Something," 1970; "Diamonds Are Forever," 1972

Baxter, Les, Orchestra, "Unchained Melody," 1955; "Wake the Town & Tell the People," 1955; "Poor People of Paris," 1956

Bay City Rollers, "Saturday Night," 1975 RIAA 76; "Money Honey," 1976; "Rock and Roll Love Letter," 1976; "I Only Want to be with You," 1976

Bay City Rollers, RIAA Gold Album, "Bay City Rollers," 1975

Bazuka, "Dynomite," 1975

Beach Boys, "Surfin' Safari"/"409," 1962; "Surfin' U.S.A."/"Shut Down," 1963; "Surfer Girl"/"Little Deuce Coupe," 1963; "In My Room"/"Be True to Your School," 1963; "Fun, Fun, Fun," 1964; "I Get Around"/"Don't Worry Baby," 1964; "When I Grow Up," 1964; "Wendy"/"Little Honda," 1964; "Dance, Dance, Dance," 1964; "Do You Wanna Dance," 1965; "Help Me Rhonda," 1965; "California Girls," 1965; "The Little Girl I Once Knew," 1965; "Barbara Ann," 1966; "Sloop John B," 1966; "God Only Knows"/"Wouldn't It Be Nice," 1966; "Good Vibrations," 1966, RIAA 66; "Heroes &

Villains," 1967; "Wild Honey," 1967; "Darlin'," 1967; "Do It Again," 1968; "I Can Hear Music," 1969; "Rock & Roll Music," 1976

Beach Boys, RIAA Gold Albums, "Beach Boys in Concert," 1965; "All Summer Long," 1965; "The Beach Boys Today," 1965; "Surfer Girl," 1965; "Surfin' USA," 1965; "Summer Days," 1966; "Little Deuce Coupe," 1966; "Shut Down, Vol. 2," 1966; "Best of the Beach Boys," 1967; "Beach Boys in Concert," 1974; "Spirit of America," 1976; "Endless Summer," 1976; "15 Big Ones," 1976

Bear, Edward, "Last Song," 1973, RIAA 73; "Close Your Eyes," 1973

Beatles, "I Want to Hold Your Hand"/"I Saw Her Standing There," 1964, RIAA 64; "Can't Buy Me Love," 1964, RIAA 64; "She Loves You," 1964; "Please Please Me"/"From Me to You," 1964; "Do You Want to Know A Secret"/"Thank You Girl," 1964; "Twist & Shout," 1964; "Love Me Do," 1964; "P.S. I Love You," 1964; "My Bonnie" (with Tony Sheridan), 1964; "Ain't She Sweet," 1964; "Roll Over Beethoven," 1964; "All My Loving," 1964; "A Hard Day's Night," 1964, RIAA 64; "And I Love Her," 1964; "I'll Cry Instead," 1964; "Matchbox"/"Slowdown," 1964; "I Feel Fine"/"She's A Woman," 1964, RIAA 64; "Eight Days A Week," 1965, RIAA 65; "Ticket to Ride," 1965; "Help!" 1965, RIAA 65; "Yesterday"/"Act Naturally," 1965, RIAA 65; "We Can Work It Out"/"Day Tripper," 1965, RIAA 65; "Nowhere Man," 1966, RIAA 66; "Paperback Writer"/"Rain," 1966, RIAA 66; "Yellow Submarine"/"Eleanor Rigby," 1966, RIAA 66; "Penny Lane"/"Strawberry Fields Forever," 1967, RIAA 67; "All You Need Is Love"/"Baby You're a Rich Man," 1967, RIAA 67; "Hello Goodbye," 1967, RIAA 67; "Lady Madonna," 1968, RIAA 68; "Hey Jude"/"Revolution," 1968, RIAA 68; "Get Back"/"Don't Let Me Down" (with Billy Preston), 1969, RIAA 69; "Ballad of John & Yoko," 1969, RIAA 69; "Come Together"/"Something," 1969, RIAA 69; "Let It Be," 1970, RIAA 70; "Long and Winding Road"/"For You Blue," 1970, RIAA 70; "Got to Get You Into My Life"/"Helter Skelter," 1976

Beatles, RIAA Gold Albums, "Meet The Beatles," 1964; "Beatles' 2nd Album," 1964; "Something New," 1964; "Beatles '65," 1964; "The Beatles' Story," 1964; "Beatles VI," 1965; "Help!" 1965; "Rubber Soul," 1965; "Yesterday & Today," 1966; "Revolver," 1966; "Sergeant Pepper's Lonely Hearts Club Band," 1967; "Magical Mystery Tour," 1967; "The Beatles," 1968; "Yellow Submarine," 1969; "Abbey Road," 1969; "Hey Jude," 1970; "Let It Be," 1970; "The Beatles 1962-1966," 1973; "The Beatles 1966-1970," 1973; "The Early Beatles," 1974; "Rock 'N' Roll Music," 1976

Beatles, RIAA Platinum Album, "Rock 'N' Roll Music," 1976

Beau Brummels, "Laugh Laugh," 1965; "Just A Little," 1965; "You Tell Me Why," 1965

176

Beck, Jeff, RIAA Gold Albums, "Blow by Blow," 1975; "Wired," 1976

Beckham, Bob, "Just As Much As Ever," 1959; "Crazy Arms," 1960

Bee Gees, "1941 New York Mining Disaster," 1967; "To Love Somebody,"
1967; "Holiday," 1967; "(The Lights Went Out In) Massachusetts,"
1967; "Words," 1968; "I've Gotta Get a Message to You," 1968; "I
Started a Joke," 1968; "First of May," 1969; "Lonely Days," 1970,
RIAA 71; "How Can You Mend a Broken Heart," 1971, RIAA 71;
"My World," 1972; "Run to Me," 1972; "Alive," 1972; "Jive Talk-
in'," 1975, RIAA 75; "Nights On Broadway," 1975; "Fanny," 1976;
"You Should Be Dancing," 1976; "Love so Right," 1976

Bee Gees, RIAA Gold Albums, "Best of the Bee Gees," 1969; "Main Course,"
1975; "You Should Be Dancing," 1976; "Children of the World,"
1976

Beginning Of The End, "Funky Nassau, Part 1," 1971

Belafonte, Harry, "Jamaica Farewell," 1956; "Mary's Little Boy Child,"
1956; "Banana Boat (Day-O)," 1957; "Mama Look At Bubu,"
1957; "Island in the Sun," 1957

Belafonte, Harry, RIAA Gold Albums, "Belafonte at Carnegie Hall," 1961;
"Calypso," 1963; "Belafonte Returns to Carnegie Hall," 1963;
"Belafonte," 1963; "Jump Up Calypso," 1963; "An Evening With
Belafonte," 1967

Bell, Archie, & The Drells, "Tighten Up, Part 1," 1968, RIAA 68; "I Can't
Stop Dancing," 1968; "There's Gonna Be a Showdown," 1968;
"Soul City Walk," 1976; "Let's Groove," 1976

Bell Notes, "I've Had It," 1959

Bell, Vincent, "Airport Love Theme," 1970

Bellamy Brothers, "Let Your Love Flow," 1976, RIAA 76

Bells, "Stay Awhile," 1971, RIAA 71

Bellus, Tony, "Robbin' the Cradle," 1959

Belmonts, "Tell Me Why," 1961; "Come on Little Angel," 1962

Belvin, Jesse, "Goodnite My Love," 1956; "Guess Who," 1959

Bennett, Joe, & The Sparkletones, "Black Slacks," 1957; "Penny Loafers &
Bobby Socks," 1957

Bennett, Robert Russell, RIAA Gold Album, "Victory at Sea, Vol. 1," 1964

Bennett, Tony, "Can You Find It in Your Heart," 1956; "Just in Time,"
1956; "One for My Baby (One for the Road)," 1957; "In the Middle
of an Island," 1957; "Firefly," 1958; "I Left My Heart in San Francisco," 1962; "I Wanna Be Around," 1963; "The Good Life," 1963;
"Who Can I Turn To," 1964

Bennett, Tony, RIAA Gold Albums, "I Left My Heart in San Francisco,"
1963; "Tony Bennett's Greatest Hits, Vol. 3," 1967

Benson, George, "This Masquerade," 1976

Benson, George, RIAA Platinum Album, "Breezin'," 1976

Benson, George, RIAA Gold Album, "Breezin'," 1976

Benton, Brook, "A Million Miles from Nowhere," 1958; "Thank You, Pretty Baby," 1959; "It's Just a Matter of Time," 1959; "So Many Ways," 1959; "Endlessly"/"So Close," 1959; "Kiddio," 1960; "Fools Rush In," 1960; "Think Twice," 1961; "For My Baby," 1961; "The Boll Weevil Song," 1961; "Frankie & Johnny," 1961; "Revenge," 1961; "Shadrack," 1962; "Lie to Me," 1962; "Hotel Happiness," 1962; "I Got What I Wanted," 1963; "My True Confession," 1963; "Two Tickets to Paradise," 1963; "Rainy Night in Georgia," 1970, RIAA 70; "Don't It Make You Want to Go Home," 1970

Benton, Brook, & Dinah Washington, "Baby, (You've Got What It Takes)," 1960; "A Rockin' Good Way," 1960

Bernard, Rod, "This Should Go on Forever," 1959

Berry, Chuck, "Maybellene," 1955; "Thirty Days," 1955; "Too Much Monkey Business," 1956; "Roll Over Beethoven," 1956; "School Day," 1957; "Rock & Roll Music," 1957; "Sweet Little Sixteen," 1958; "Johnny B. Goode," 1958; "Carol," 1958; "Sweet Little Rock & Roll," 1958; "Run Rudolph Run," 1958; "Almost Grown," 1959; "Back in the U.S.A.," 1959; "Too Pooped to Pop," 1960; "Nadine," 1960; "No Particular Place to Go," 1964; "You Never Can Tell," 1964; "Promised Land," 1964; "My Ding-a-Ling," 1972, RIAA 72; "Reelin' & Rockin'," 1972

Berry, Chuck, RIAA Gold Album, "The London Chuck Berry Session," 1972

Biddu Orchestra, "Summer of '42," 1975; "Jump for Joy," 1976

Big Bopper, "Chantilly Lace," 1958; "Big Bopper's Wedding," 1958

Big Brother & The Holding Company, (See Janis Joplin), "Piece of My Heart," 1968; "Down on Me," 1968

Bilk, Mr. Acker, "Stranger on the Shore," 1962, RIAA 67

Bilk, Mr. Acker, RIAA Gold Album, "Stranger on the Shore," 1967

Billy & Lillie, "La Dee Dah," 1957; "Lucky Ladybug," 1958

Billy Joe & The Checkmates, "Percolater," 1962

Bishop, Elvin, "Fooled Around and Fell in Love," 1976, RIAA 76

Black, Bill, Combo, "Smokie," 1959; "White Silver Sands," 1960; "Josephine," 1960; "Don't Be Cruel," 1960; "Blue Tango," 1960; "Hearts of Stone," 1961; "Ole Buttermilk Sky," 1961; "Twist-Her," 1961

Black, Cilla, "You're My World," 1964

Black, Jeanne, "He'll Have to Stay," 1960

Black Oak Arkansas, RIAA Gold Albums, "Black Oak Arkansas," 1974; "Raunch 'N Roll," 1975; "High on the Hog," 1976

Black Sabbath, "Paranoid," 1970; "Iron Man," 1970

Black Sabbath, RIAA Gold Albums, "Paranoid," 1971; "Black Sabbath,"

1971; "Master of Reality," 1971; "Black Sabbath-Vol. IV," 1972; "Sabbath, Bloody Sabbath," 1974

Blackbyrds, "Walking in Rhythm," 1975; "Happy Music," 1976

Blackbyrds, RIAA Gold Album, "City Life," 1976

Blanchard, Jack, & Misty Morgan, "Tennessee Bird Walk," 1970

Bland, Billy, "Let the Little Girl Dance," 1960

Bland, Bobby "Blue," "Turn on Your Lovelight," 1961; "I Pity the Fool," 1961; "Don't Cry No More," 1961; "Call on Me," 1963; "Sometimes You Gotta Cry," 1963; "Ain't Nothing You Can Do," 1964

Bland, Bobby, & B. B. King, RIAA Gold Album, "Together for the First Time," 1975

Blane, Marcie, "Bobby's Girl," 1962

Blind Faith, RIAA Gold Album, "Blind Faith," 1969

Blood, Sweat, & Tears, "You've Made Me So Very Happy," 1969, RIAA 69; "Spinning Wheel," 1969, RIAA 69; "And When I Die," 1969, RIAA 70; "Hi-De-Ho," 1970; "Lucretia McEvil," 1970; "Go Down Gamblin'," 1971; "Got To Get You Into My Life," 1975

Blood, Sweat & Tears, RIAA Gold Albums, "Blood, Sweat & Tears," 1969; "The Child Is the Father of Man," 1969; "Blood, Sweat & Tears 3," 1970; "B S & T 4," 1971; "Blood, Sweat & Tears Greatest Hits," 1972

Bloodrock, "D.O.A.," 1971

Bloodstone, "Natural High," 1973, RIAA 73

Bloom, Bobby, "Montego Bay," 1970

Bloomfield/Kooper/Stills, RIAA Gold Album, "Super Session," 1970

Blue Cheer, "Summertime Blues," 1968

Blue Haze, "Smoke Gets in Your Eyes," 1972

Blue Jays, "Lover's Island," 1961

Blue Magic, "Sideshow," 1974, RIAA 74

Blue Oyster Cult, "(Don't Fear) the Reaper," 1976

Blue Ridge Rangers, "Jambalaya (On the Bayou), 1972; "Hearts of Stone," 1973

Blue Stars, "Lullaby of Birdland," 1955

Blue Swede, "Hooked on a Feeling," 1974, RIAA 74; "Never My Love," 1974

Blues Image, "Ride Captain Ride," 1970, RIAA 70

Blues Magoos, "(We Ain't Got) Nothin' Yet," 1966

Bob B. Soxx & The Blue Jeans, "Zip-A-Dee-Do-Dah," 1962; "Why Do Lovers Break Each Other's Heart," 1963

Bobbettes, "Mr. Lee," 1957; "I Shot Mr. Lee," 1960

Bond, Johnny, "Hot Rod Lincoln," 1960; "Ten Little Bottles," 1965

Bonds, Gary U.S., "New Orleans," 1960; "Quarter to Three," 1961; "School

Is Out," 1961; "School Is In," 1961; "Dear Lady Twist," 1961; "Twist Twist Senora," 1962; "Seven Day Weekend," 1962

Booker T. & The MG's, "Green Onions," 1962; "Hip Hug-Her," 1967; "Groovin'," 1967; "Soul Limbo," 1968; "Hang 'Em High," 1968; "Time Is Tight," 1969; "Mrs. Robinson," 1969

Boone, Daniel, "Beautiful Sunday," 1972

Boone, Pat, "Ain't That a Shame," 1955; "At My Front Door," 1955; "No Other Arms," 1955; "Gee Whittakers'," 1955; "I'll Be Home"/"Tutti Fruiti," 1956; "Long Tall Sally," 1956; "I Almost Lost My Mind," 1956; "Friendly Persuasion"/"Chains Of Love," 1956; "Don't Forbid Me"/"Anastasia," 1956; "Why Baby Why"/"I'm Waiting Just For You," 1957; "Love Letters in the Sand"/"Bernadine," 1957; "Remember You're Mine"/"Gold Mine in the Sky," 1957; "April Love"/ "When the Swallows Come Back To Capistrano," 1957; "A Wonderful Time Up There"/"It's Too Soon to Know," 1958; "Sugar Moon," 1958; "If Dreams Come True," 1958; "For My Good Fortune," 1958; "With the Wind & the Rain in Your Hair"/"Good Rockin' Tonight," 1959; "For a Penny," 1959; "Twixt Twelve & Twenty," 1959; "Fools Hall of Fame," 1959; "(Welcome) New Lovers," 1960; "Moody River," 1961; "Big Cold Wind," 1961; "Johnny Will," 1961; "Speedy Gonzales," 1962

Boone, Pat, RIAA Gold Album, "Pat's Great Hits," 1960

Boston, "More than a Feeling," 1976

Boston Pops Orchestra (with Arthur Fiedler), "I Want to Hold Your Hand," 1964

Bowen, Jimmy, "I'm Sticking with You," 1957

Bowie, David, "Space Oddity," 1973; "Young Americans," 1975; "Fame," 1975, RIAA 75; "Golden Years," 1976

Bowie, David, RIAA Gold Albums, "Ziggy Stardust," 1974; "Diamond Dogs," 1974; "David 'Live'," 1974; "The Young Americans," 1975; "Station to Station," 1976; "Changesonbowie," 1976

Box Tops, "The Letter," 1967, RIAA 67; "Neon Rainbow," 1967; "Cry Like a Baby," 1968, RIAA 68; "Sweet Cream Ladies," 1968; "Soul Deep," 1969

Boyce, Tommy, & Bobby Hart, "Out & About," 1968; "I Wonder What She's Doing Tonight," 1968

Bradley, Jan, "Mama Didn't Lie," 1963

Brass Construction, RIAA Gold Album, "Brass Construction," 1976

Brass Ring, "The Phoenix Love Theme," 1966; "The Dis-advantages of You," 1967

Braun, Bob, "Till Death Do Us Part," 1962

Bread, "Make It with You," 1970, RIAA 70; "It Don't Matter to Me," 1970; "If," 1971; "Baby, I'm a Want You," 1972, RIAA 72; "Everything

180

I Own," 1972; "Diary," 1972; "The Guitar Man," 1972; "Sweet
Surrender," 1972; "Aubrey," 1973

Bread, RIAA Gold Albums, "Baby, I'm a Want You," 1972; "Guitar Man,"
1972; "Manna," 1972; "On the Waters," 1972; "The Best of Bread,"
1973; "The Best of Bread, Vol. 2," 1974

Bremers, Beverly, "Don't Say You Don't Remember," 1972

Brennan, Walter, "Dutchman's Gold," 1960; "Old Rivers," 1962

Brenda & The Tabulations, "Dry Your Eyes," 1967; "Right on the Tip of My
Tongue," 1971

Brewer, Teresa, "A Tear Fell," 1956; "Bo Weevil," 1956; "A Sweet Old
Fashioned Girl," 1956; "Empty Arms," 1957

Brewer and Shipley, "One Toke Over the Line," 1971

Brighter Side of Darkness, "Love Jones," 1973, RIAA 73

Bristol, Johnny, "Hang on in There Baby," 1974

Broadway Original Casts, RIAA Gold Albums, "The Music Man," 1959;
"Sound of Music," 1960; "West Side Story," 1962; "Camelot,"
1962; "Flower Drum Song," 1962; "My Fair Lady," 1964; "Hello,
Dolly!" 1964; "Funny Girl," 1964; "Fiddler on the Roof," 1965;
"Oliver," 1966; "South Pacific," 1966; "Mame," 1967; "Man of
la Mancha," 1967; "Hair," 1969; "Jesus Christ Superstar," 1970;
"Godspell," 1972

Brooklyn Bridge, "The Worst That Can Happen," 1969, RIAA 69

Brooks, Donnie, "Mission Bell," 1960; "Doll House," 1960

Brotherhood Of Man, "United We Stand (Divided We Fall)," 1970; "Save
Your Kisses For Me," 1976

Brothers Four, "Greenfields," 1960; "The Green Leaves of Summer," 1960

Brothers Johnson, "I'll Be Good to You," 1976; "Get the Funk Out Ma
Face," 1976

Brothers Johnson, RIAA Gold Album, "Lookin' Out for #1," 1976

Brothers Johnson, RIAA Platinum Album, "Lookin' Out for #1," 1976

Brown's, Al, Tunetoppers, "The Madison," 1960

Brown, Arthur, Crazy World Of, "Fire," 1968, RIAA 68

Brown, Buster, "Fannie Mae," 1960

Brown, James (& The Famous Flames), "Please Please Me," 1956; "Try Me,"
1958; "Night Train," 1962; "Prisoner of Love," 1963; "Papa's Got a
Brand New Bag," 1965; "I Got You (I Feel Good)," 1965; "Ain't
That a Groove," 1966; "It's a Man's Man's World," 1966; "Cold
Sweat," 1967; "I Got the Feelin'," 1968; "Licking Stick," 1968;
"Say It Loud, I'm Black & I'm Proud," 1968; "Give It Up or Turn It
Loose," 1969; "The Popcorn," 1969; "Mother Popcorn," 1969;
"Get Up (Like a Sex Machine)," 1970; "Super Bad," 1970; "Make It
Funky," 1971; "Hot Pants," 1971; "The Good Foot," 1972, RIAA

72; "I Got Ants in My Pants," 1973; "The Payback," 1974, RIAA
   74; "Sex-Machine," 1975; "Get Up Offa That Thing," 1976

Brown, James, RIAA Gold Album, "The Payback," 1974

Brown, Jim Ed (see The Browns), "Morning," 1970

Brown, Maxine, "All in My Mind," 1961; "Funny," 1961; "Oh No Not My
   Baby," 1964; "If You Gotta Make a Fool of Somebody," 1965

Brown, Nappy, "Don't Be Angry," 1955; "Little By Little," 1957

Brown, Roy, "Let the Four Winds Blow," 1957

Brown, Ruth, "Lucky Lips," 1957; "This Little Girl's Gone Rockin'," 1958

Browne, Jackson, "Doctor My Eyes," 1972

Browne, Jackson, RIAA Gold Albums, "Late for the Sky," 1974; "For Every
   man," 1975

Browns, The, "The Three Bells," 1959; "Scarlet Ribbons," 1959; "The Old
   Lamplighter," 1960

Brownsville Station, "Smokin' in the Boys Room," 1974, RIAA 74

Brubeck, Dave, Quartet, "Take Five," 1961

Brubeck, Dave, Quartet, RIAA Gold Album, "Time Out," 1963

Bryant, Anita, "Til There Was You," 1959; "Paper Roses," 1960; "In My
   Little Corner of the World," 1960; "Wonderland by Night," 1960

Bubble Puppy, "Hot Smoke and Sassafrass," 1969

Buchanan Brothers, "Medicine Man," 1969

Buchanan & Goodman (see Dickie Goodman), "The Flying Saucer," 1956;
   "Flying Saucer, the 2nd," 1957

Buckinghams, "Kind of a Drag," 1966; "Don't You Care," 1967; "Mercy,
   Mercy, Mercy," 1967; "Hey Baby," 1967; "Susan," 1967

Buffalo Springfield, "For What It's Worth," 1967

Bulldog, "No," 1972

Bullet, "White Lies, Blue Eyes," 1971

Buoys, "Timothy," 1971

Burden, Eric, & War, "Spill the Wine," 1970, RIAA 70

Burke, Solomon, "Just Out of Reach," 1961; "Cry to Me," 1962; "Everybody Needs Somebody to Love," 1964; "Got to Get You Off My
   Mind," 1965; "Tonight's the Night," 1965

Burnette, Dorsey, "Tall Oak Tree," 1960; "Hey Little One," 1960

Burnette, Johnny, "Dreamin'," 1960; "You're Sixteen," 1960; "Little Boy
   Sad," 1961; "Big Big World," 1961

Busters, "Bust Out," 1963

Butler, Jerry, "For Your Precious Love (with the Impressions)," 1958; "He
   Will Break Your Heart," 1960; "Moon River," 1961; "Make It Easy
   On Yourself," 1962; "Hey, Western Union Man," 1968; "Never Give

You Up," 1968; "Only the Strong Survive," 1969, RIAA 69;
  "Moody Woman," 1969; "What's the Use of Breaking Up," 1969
Butler, Jerry, & Brenda Lee Eager, "Ain't Understanding Mellow," 1972,
  RIAA 72
Byrds, "Mr. Tambourine Man," 1965; "Turn, Turn, Turn," 1965; "Eight
  Miles High," 1966; "So You Want to Be a Rock & Roll Star," 1967;
  "My Back Pages," 1967
Byrds, RIAA Gold Album, "The Byrds' Greatest Hits," 1968
Byrnes, Ed "Kookie," "Kookie, Kookie, Lend Me Your Comb," 1959

Cadets, "Stranded in the Jungle," 1956
Cadillacs, "Speedo (But His Real Name Is Mr. Earl)," 1955; "Peek-A-Boo,"
  1958
Caesar & Cleo (Sonny & Cher), "Love Is Strange," 1965
Caiola, Al, "Magnificent Seven," 1960; "Bonanza," 1961
Cale, J. J., "Crazy Mama," 1972
Campbell, Glen, "Turn Around, Look at Me," 1961; "Gentle on My Mind,"
  1967 & 1968; "By the Time I Get to Phoenix," 1967; "Hey Little
  One," 1968; "I Wanna Live," 1968; "Dreams of the Everyday House-
  wife," 1968; "Wichita Lineman," 1968, RIAA 69; "Galveston,"
  1969, RIAA 69; "Where's the Playground Susie," 1969; "True Grit,"
  1969; "Try a Little Kindness," 1969; "Honey Come Back," 1970;
  "Oh Happy Day," 1970; "It's Only Make Believe," 1970; "Dream
  Baby," 1971; "Rhinestone Cowboy," 1975, RIAA 75; "Country
  Boy," 1976; "Don't Pull Your Love"/"Then You Can Tell Me Good-
  bye," 1976; "See You On Sunday," 1976
Campbell, Glen, RIAA Gold Albums, "By the Time I Get to Phoenix," 1968;
  "Gentle on My Mind," 1968; "Wichita Lineman," 1968; "Hey Little
  One," 1969; "Galveston," 1969; "Glen Campbell—Live," 1969;
  "Try a Little Kindness," 1970; "Glen Campbell's Greatest Hits,"
  1972; "Rhinestone Cowboy," 1975
Campbell, Glen, & Bobbie Gentry, "Let It Be Me," 1969; "All I Have To Do
  Is Dream," 1970
Campbell, Glen, & Bobbie Gentry, RIAA Gold Album, "Gentry/Campbell,"
  1969
Campbell, Jo Ann, "(I'm the Girl) On Wolverton Mountain," 1962; "Mother,
  Please!" 1963
Canned Heat, "On the Road Again," 1968; "Going Up the Country," 1968;
  "Let's Work Together," 1970

Cannibal & The Headhunters, "Land Of 1000 Dances," 1965

Cannon, Ace, "Tuff," 1961

Cannon, Freddy, "Tallahassee Lassie," 1959; "Way Down Yonder in New Orleans," 1959; "Chattanooga Shoe Shine Boy," 1960; "Jump Over," 1960; "Muskrat Ramble," 1961; "Buzz Buzz A-Diddle-It," 1961; "Transistor Sister," 1961; "Palisades Park," 1962; "Abigail Beecher," 1964; "Action," 1965

Capitols, "Cool Jerk," 1966

Capris, "There's a Moon Out Tonight," 1961

Captain & Tennille, "Love Will Keep Us Together," 1975, RIAA 75; "The Way I Want to Touch You," 1975, RIAA 75; "Lonely Night (Angel Face," 1976, RIAA 76; "Shop Around," 1976, RIAA 76

Captain & Tennille, RIAA Gold Albums, "Love Will Keep Us Together," 1975; "Song Of Joy," 1976

Captain & Tennille, RIAA Platinum Album, "Song of Joy," 1976

Caravelles, "You Don't Have To Be A Baby To Cry," 1963

Carefrees, "We Love You Beatles (Yes, We Do)," 1964

Cargill, Henson, "Skip A Rope," 1967

Carlin, George, RIAA Gold Records, "FM & AM," 1972; "Class Clown," 1973

Carlos, Walter, RIAA Gold Album, "Switched On Bach," 1969

Carmen, Eric (see Raspberries), "All By Myself," 1976, RIAA 76; "Never Gonna Fall In Love Again," 1976; "Sunrise," 1976

Carosone, Renato, "Torero," 1958

Carpenters, "Ticket to Ride," 1970; "(They Long to Be) Close to You," 1970, RIAA 70; "We've Only Just Begun," 1970, RIAA 70; "For All We Know," 1971, RIAA 71; "Rainy Days & Mondays," 1971, RIAA 71; "Superstar," 1971, RIAA 71; "Hurting Each Other," 1972, RIAA 72; "It's Going to Take Some Time," 1972; "Goodbye to Love," 1972; "Sing," 1973; "Yesterday Once More," 1973, RIAA 73; "Top of the World," 1973, RIAA 73; "I Won't Last a Day Without You," 1974; "Please Mr. Postman," 1975, RIAA 75; "Kind of a Hush," 1976; "I Need to Be in Love," 1976; "Goofus," 1976

Carpenters, RIAA Gold Albums, "Close to You," 1970; "Carpenters," 1971; "A Song for You," 1972; "Now & Then," 1973; "The Singles (1969-1973)," 1973; "Horizon," 1975; "A Kind of Hush," 1976

Carr, Cathy, "Ivory Tower," 1956

Carr, Joe "Fingers," "Portuguese Washerwomen," 1956

Carr, Vikki, "It Must Be Him," 1967; "With Pen In Hand," 1969

Carradine, Keith, "I'm Easy," 1976

Carroll, David, "Melody Of Love," 1955; "It's Almost Tomorrow," 1955

Carson, Kit, "Band Of Gold," 1955

Carter, Clarence, "Slip Away," 1968, RIAA 68; "Too Weak To Fight," 1968, RIAA 69; "Patches," 1970, RIAA 70

Carter, Mel, "Hold Me, Thrill Me, Kiss Me," 1965; "Band Of Gold," 1966

Cascades, "Rhythm of the Rain," 1963

Cash, Alvin, & The Crawlers, "Twine Time," 1965

Cash, Johnny, "I Walk the Line," 1956; "Ballad of a Teenage Queen," 1958; "Guess Things Happen That Way," 1958; "The Ways of a Woman in Love," 1958; "All Over Again," 1958; "Don't Take Your Guns to Town," 1959; "Ring of Fire," 1963; "Understand Your Man," 1964; "The One on the Right is on the Left," 1966; "Folsom Prison Blues," 1968; "Daddy Sang Bass," 1968; "A Boy Named Sue," 1969, RIAA 69; "What is Truth," 1970; "Sunday Morning Coming Down," 1970; "One Piece at a Time," 1976

Cash, Johnny, RIAA Gold Albums, "Ring of Fire," 1965; "I Walk the Line," 1967; "Johnny Cash at Folsom Prison," 1968; "Johnny Cash's Greatest Hits," 1969; "Johnny Cash at San Quentin," 1969; "Hello, I'm Johnny Cash," 1970; "The World of Johnny Cash," 1971

Cash, Johnny, & June Carter, "If I Were a Carpenter," 1970

Cashman & West, "American City Suite," 1972

Casinos, "Then You Can Tell Me Goodbye," 1967

Cassidy, David, "Cherish," 1971; "Could It Be Forever," 1972; "How Can I Be Sure," 1972; "Rock Me Baby," 1972

Cassidy, David, RIAA Gold Album, "Cherish," 1972

Castaways, "Liar, Liar," 1965

Castells, "Sacred," 1961; "So This Is Love," 1962

Castor, Jimmy, "Hey, Leroy, Your Mama's Callin' You," 1966; "Troglodyte (Cave Man)," 1972, RIAA 72; "Bertha Butt Boogie," 1975

Cate Brothers, "Union Man," 1976

Cates, George, "Moonglow," "Theme from *Picnic*," 1956

Cathy Jean & The Roommates, "Please Love Me Forever," 1961

Cat Mother & The All Night News Boys, "Good Old Rock & Roll," 1969

C Company (see Terry Nelson)

Chad & Jeremy, "Yesterday's Gone," 1964; "Summer Song," 1964; "Willow Weep for Me," 1964; "If You Loved Me," 1965; "Before & After," 1965; "Distant Shores," 1966

Chairmen of the Board, (See The Showmen), "Give Me Just a Little More Time," 1970, RIAA 70; "Pay to the Piper," 1970

Chakachas, "Jungle Fever," 1972, RIAA 72

Chamberlain, Richard, "Theme from 'Dr. Kildare'," 1962; "Love Me Tender," 1962; "All I Have to Do Is Dream," 1963

Chambers Brothers, "Time Has Come Today," 1968

Chambers Brothers, RIAA Gold Album, "The Time Has Come," 1968

Champs, "Tequila," 1958; "El Rancho Rock," 1958; "Too Much Tequila," 1960; "Limbo Rock," 1962

Chandler, Gene, "Duke of Earl," 1962; "Rainbow," 1963; "Just Be True," 1964; "Nothing Can Stop Me," 1965; "Groovy Situation," 1970, RIAA 70

Channel, Bruce, "Hey Baby," 1962

Chantays, "Pipeline," 1963

Chantels, "Maybe," 1958; "Look in My Eyes," 1961; "Well, I Told You," 1961

Chapin, Harry, "Taxi," 1972; "Cat's in the Cradle," 1974, RIAA 74; "W-O-L-D," 1974

Chapin, Harry, RIAA Gold Album, "Verities & Balderdash," 1974

Charles, Jimmy, "A Million to One," 1960

Charles, Ray, "I've Got a Woman," 1955; "Hallelujah! I Love Her So," 1956; "Swanee River Rock," 1957; "What'd I Say," 1959; "I'm Movin' On," 1959; "Sticks & Stones," 1960; "Georgia on My Mind," 1960; "Ruby," 1960; "One Mint Julep," 1961; "Hit the Road Jack," 1961; "Unchain My Heart," 1961; "Hide Nor Hair," 1962; "I Can't Stop Loving You," 1962, RIAA 62; "Born to Lose," 1962; "You Don't Know Me," 1962; "You Are My Sunshine," 1962; "Your Cheating Heart," 1962; "Don't Set Me Free," 1963; "Take These Chains from My Heart," 1963; "No One"/"Without Love," 1963; "Busted," 1963; "That Lucky Old Sun," 1963; "My Heart Cries for You," 1964; "Crying Time," 1965; "Together Again," 1966; "Let's Go Get Stoned," 1966; "I Chose to Sing the Blues," 1966; "Here We Go Again," 1967; "In the Heat of the Night," 1967; "Yesterday," 1967; "Eleanor Rigby," 1968; "Don't Change On Me," 1971

Charles, Ray, RIAA Gold Albums, "Modern Sounds in Country & Western Music," 1962; "Modern Sounds In Country & Western Music, Vol. 2," 1968; "Greatest Hits," 1968; "A Man & His Soul," 1968

Charles, Ray, Orchestra, "Booty Butt," 1971

Charles, Ray, Singers, "Love Me With All Your Heart," 1964; "Al Di La," 1964

Charles, Sonny, & The Checkmates, "Black Pearl," 1969

Chartbusters, "She's the One," 1964

Charts, "Deserie"/"Zoop," 1957

Checker, Chubby, "The Class," 1959; "The Twist," 1960; "The Hucklebuck," 1960; "Pony Time," 1961; "Dance the Mess Around," 1961; "Let's Twist Again," 1961; "The Fly," 1961; "The Twist," 1961-1962; "Let's Twist Again," 1961-1962; "Slow Twistin'," 1962; "Dancin' Party," 1962; "Limbo Rock," 1962; "Popeye the Hitchhiker," 1962; "Twenty Miles," 1963; "Let's Limbo Some More," 1963; "Birdland," 1963; "Twist It Up," 1963; "Loddy Lo," 1963; "Hooka Tooka," 1963; "Hey, Bobba Needle," 1964

Cheech & Chong, "Basketball Jones," 1973; "Earache My Eye," 1975

Cheech & Chong, RIAA Gold Albums, "Cheech & Chong," 1972; "Big Bambu," 1972; "Los Cochinos," 1973

Cheers, "Black Denim Trousers," 1955

Cher (see Sonny & Cher), "All I Really Want to Do," 1965; "Where Do You Go," 1965; "Bang, Bang," 1966; "Alfie," 1966; "You Better Sit Down Kids," 1967; "Gypsys, Tramps, & Thieves," 1971, RIAA 71; "The Way of Love," 1972; "Living in a House Divided," 1972; "Half Breed," 1973, RIAA 73; "Dark Lady," 1974, RIAA 74

Cher, RIAA Gold Albums, "Cher," 1972; "Half Breed," 1974

Cherry, Don, "Band of Gold," 1955; "Wild Cherry," 1956; "Ghost Town," 1956

Cherry People, "And Suddenly," 1968

Chicago, "Questions 67 & 68," 1969; "Make Me Smile," 1970; "25 or 6 to 4," 1970; "Does Anybody Really Know What Time It Is?" 1970; "Free," 1971; "Lowdown," 1971; "Beginnings"/"Colour My World," 1971; "I'm a Man"/"Questions 67 & 68," 1971; "Saturday in the Park," 1972, RIAA 72; "Dialogue," 1972; "Feeling Stronger Everyday," 1973; "Call on Me," 1974; "Just You & Me," 1974, RIAA 74; "I've Been Searchin' So Long," 1974; "Old Days," 1975; "Brand New Love Affair," 1975; "Rainy Day in New York City," 1976; "If You Leave Me Now," 1976

Chicago, RIAA Gold Albums, "Chicago Transit Authority," 1969; "Chicago," 1970; "Chicago III," 1971; "Live at Carnegie Hall," 1971; "Chicago V," 1972; "Chicago VI," 1973; "Chicago VII," 1974; "Chicago VIII," 1975; "Chicago IX–Chicago's Greatest Hits," 1975; "Chicago X," 1976

Chicago, RIAA Platinum Album, "Chicago X," 1976

Chiffons, "He's So Fine," 1963; "One Fine Day," 1963; "Sweet Talkin' Guy," 1966

Chi-Lites, "(For God's Sake) Give More Power to the People," 1971; "Have You Seen Her," 1971; "Oh Girl," 1972

Chimes, "Once in a While," 1960

Chipmunks (with David Seville), "The Chipmunk Song," 1958; "Alvin's Harmonica," 1959; "Ragtime Cowboy Joe," 1959; "Alvin's Orchestra," 1960; "Rudolph The Red Nosed Reindeer," 1960; "The Alvin Twist," 1962

Choir, "It's Cold Outside," 1967

Chordettes, "Mr. Sandman," 1955; "Eddie My Love," 1956; "Born to Be with You," 1956; "Lay Down Your Arms," 1956; "Just Between

You & Me," 1957; "Lollipop," 1958; "Zorro," 1958; "No Other Arms," 1959; "Never on Sunday," 1961

Christie, "Yellow River," 1970

Christie, Lou, "The Gypsy Cried," 1963; "Two Faces Have I," 1963; "Lightning Strikes," 1965, RIAA 66; "Rhapsody in the Rain," 1966; "I'm Gonna Make You Mine," 1969

Christie, Susan, "I Love Onions," 1966

Church, Eugene, "Pretty Girls Everywhere," 1958

Clanton, Jimmy, "Just a Dream," 1958; "A Letter to an Angel," 1958; "My Own True Love," 1959; "Go Jimmy Go," 1959; "Another Sleepless Night," 1960; "Venus in Blue Jeans," 1962

Clapton, Eric, "After Midnight," 1970; "Let It Rain," 1972; "I Shot the Sheriff," 1974, RIAA 74

Clapton, Eric, RIAA Gold Albums, "History of Eric Clapton," 1972; "461 Ocean Boulevard," 1974

Clark, Claudine, "Party Lights," 1962

Clark, Dave, Five, "Glad All Over," 1964; "Bits & Pieces," 1964; "Can't You See That She's Mine," 1964; "Because," 1964; "Everybody Knows," 1964; "Any Way You Want It," 1964; "Come Home," 1965; "Reelin' & Rockin'," 1965; "I Like It Like That," 1965; "Catch Us If You Can," 1965; "Over & Over," 1965; "At the Scene," 1966; "Try Too Hard," 1966; "Please Tell Me Why," 1966; "You Got What It Takes," 1967; "Everybody Knows," 1967

Clark, Dave Five, RIAA Gold Albums, "Glad All Over," 1965; "Dave Clark's Greatest Hits," 1966

Clark, Dee, "Nobody But You," 1958; "Just Keep It Up," 1959; "Hey Little Girl," 1959; "Raindrops," 1961

Clark, Petula, "Downtown," 1964, RIAA 65; "I Know A Place," 1965; "You'd Better Come Home," 1965; "Round Every Corner," 1965; "My Love," 1965; "A Sign of the Times," 1966; "I Couldn't Live Without Your Love," 1966; "Who Am I," 1966; "Color My World," 1967; "This Is My Song," 1967; "Don't Sleep in the Subway," 1967; "The Other Man's Grass Is Always Greener," 1967; "Kiss Me Goodbye," 1968; "Don't Give Up," 1968

Clark, Roy, "Tips of My Fingers," 1963; "Yesterday, When I Was Young," 1969; "Think Summer," 1976

Clark, Sanford, "The Fool," 1956

Clarke, Tony, "The Entertainer," 1965

Classics, "Til Then," 1963

Classics IV (featuring Dennis Yost), "Spooky," 1968; "Stormy," 1968, RIAA 69; "Traces," 1969; "Everyday With You Girl," 1969

Clay, Tom, "What the World Needs Now Is Love," 1971

Clayton, Merry, "Keep Your Eye on the Sparrow," 1975

Clean Living, "In Heaven There Is No Beer," 1972

Cleftones, "Heart & Soul," 1961

Cliff, Jimmy, "Wonderful World, Beautiful People," 1969

Clifford, Buzz, "Baby Sittin' Boogie," 1961

Clifford, Mike, "Close to Cathy," 1962

Climax, "Precious & Few," 1972, RIAA 72

Cline, Patsy, "Walkin' After Midnight," 1957; "I Fall to Pieces," 1961; "Crazy," 1961; "She's Got You," 1962

Clique, "Sugar on Sunday," 1969

Clovers, "Blue Velvet," 1955; "Devil or Angel," 1955; "Love Potion #9," 1959

Coasters, "Searchin' "/"Young Blood," 1957; "Yakety Yak," 1958; "Charlie Brown," 1959; "Along Came Jones," 1959; "Poison Ivy," 1959; "I'm a Hog for You," 1959; "Little Egypt," 1961

Cochran, Eddie, "Sittin' in the Balcony," 1957; "Summertime Blues," 1958; "C'mon Everybody," 1958; "Somethin' Else," 1959

Cocker, Joe, "With a Little Help from My Friends," 1968; "She Came in Through the Bathroom Window," 1969; "The Letter," 1970; "Cry Me a River," 1970; "High Time We Went," 1971; "Midnight Rider," 1972; "You Are So Beautiful," 1975

Cocker, Joe, RIAA Gold Albums, "Joe Cocker," 1970; "Mad Dogs & Englishmen," 1970; "With a Little Help from My Friends," 1970

Coffey, Dennis, The Detroit Guitar Band, "Scorpio," 1971, RIAA 71; "Taurus," 1972

Colder, Ben, "Almost Persuaded Number 2," 1966

Cole, Cozy, "Topsy I," 1958; "Topsy II," 1958; "Turvy II," 1958

Cole, Nat King, "Darling Je Vous Aime Beaucoup," 1955; "A Blossom Fell," 1955; "Forgive My Heart," 1955; "Ask Me," 1956; "Too Young to Go Steady," 1956; "That's All There Is to That," 1956; "Night Lights," 1956; "To the Ends of the Earth," 1956; "Ballerina," 1957; "Send for Me," 1957; "Looking Back," 1958; "Non Dimenticar," 1958; "Midnight Flyer," 1959; "Time & the River," 1960; "Ramblin' Rose," 1962; "Dear Lonely Hearts," 1962; "Those Lazy-Hazy-Crazy Days of Summer," 1963; "That Sunday, That Summer," 1963; "I Don't Want to Be Hurt Anymore," 1964; "L-O-V-E," 1964

Cole, Nat King, RIAA Gold Albums, "Love Is the Thing," 1960; "Ramblin' Rose," 1964; "Unforgettable," 1964; "The Christmas Song," 1969

Cole, Natalie, "This Will Be," 1975; "Sophisticated Lady," 1976

Cole, Natalie, RIAA Gold Albums, "Inseparable," 1976; "Natalie," 1976

Collins, Dave & Ansil, "Double Barrel," 1971

Collins, Dorothy, "My Boy Flat Top," 1955; "Seven Days," 1956

Collins, Judy, "Both Sides Now," 1968; "Amazing Grace," 1970; "Send in the Clowns," 1975

Collins, Judy, RIAA Gold Albums, "Wildflowers," 1969; "Who Knows Where the Time Goes," 1969; "In My Life," 1970; "Whales & Nightingales," 1971; "Colors of the Day," 1974; "Judith," 1975

Colter, Jesse, "I'm Not Lisa," 1975

Coltrane, Chi, "Thunder & Lightning," 1972

Commander Cody & His Lost Planet Airmen, "Hot Rod Lincoln," 1972; "Don't Let Go," 1975

Commodores, "I Feel Sanctified," 1975; "Slippery When Wet," 1975; "Sweet Love," 1976; "Just to be Close to You," 1976

Como, Perry, "Ko Ko Mo," 1955; "Tina Marie," 1955; "All At Once You Love Her," 1955; "Hot Diggity," 1956; "Juke Box Baby," 1956; "Glendora," 1956; "More," 1956; "Somebody Up There Likes Me," 1956; "Dream Along With Me," 1956; "Round & Round," 1957; "The Girl with the Golden Braids," 1957; "Just Born," 1957; "Catch a Falling Star," 1958; "Magic Moments," 1958; "Kewpie Doll," 1958; "Moon Talk," 1958; "Love Makes the World Go 'Round," 1958; "Tomboy," 1959; "Delaware," 1960; "Caterina," 1962; "Dream on Little Dreamer," 1965; "Seattle," 1969; "It's Impossible," 1970; "I Think Of You," 1971; "And I Love You So," 1973; "Christmas Dream," 1974

Como, Perry, RIAA Gold Albums, "Seasons Greetings from Perry Como," 1963; "Perry Como Sings Merry Christmas Music," 1966

Comstock, Bobby, & The Counts, "Tennessee Waltz," 1959; "Let's Stomp," 1963

Conley, Arthur, "Sweet Soul Music," 1967, RIAA 67; "Funky Street," 1968

Conniff, Ray, " 'S Wonderful," 1957

Conniff, Ray, RIAA Gold Albums, "Memories Are Made of This," 1962; "Concert in Rhythm," 1962; " 'S Marvelous," 1962; "So Much in Love," 1962; "Christmas with Conniff," 1963; "Somewhere My Love," 1966; "Merry Christmas to All," 1967; "It Must Be Him," 1969; "Honey," 1969

Conniff, Ray, & The Singers, "Invisible Tears," 1964; "Somewhere My Love," 1966

Conner, Chris, "I Miss You So," 1956

Consumer Rapport, "Ease on Down the Road," 1975

Contino, Dick, "Pledge of Love," 1957

Contours, "Do You Love Me," 1962

Cooke, Sam, "You Send Me"/"Summertime," 1957; "I'll Come Running Back to You," 1957; "For Sentimental Reasons," 1957; "Lonely

190

Island," 1958; "Win Your Love for Me," 1958; "Love You Most of All," 1958; "Everybody Likes to Cha Cha Cha," 1959; "Only Sixteen," 1959; "Wonderful World," 1960; "Chain Gang," 1960; "Sad Mood," 1960; "Cupid," 1961; "Twistin' the Night Away," 1962; "Bring It on Home to Me"/"Havin' a Party," 1962; "Nothing Can Change This Love," 1962; "Send Me Some Lovin'," 1963; "Another Saturday Night," 1963; "Frankie & Johnnie," 1963; "Little Red Rooster," 1963; "Good News," 1964; "Good Times," 1964; "Tennessee Waltz," 1964; "Shake," 1965; "Sugar Dumpling," 1965

Cookies, "Chains," 1962; "Don't Say Nothing Bad About My Baby," 1963; "Girls Grow Up Faster Than Boys," 1963

Cooley, Eddie, & The Dimples, "Priscilla," 1956

Cooper, Alice, "I'm Eighteen," 1971; "School's Out," 1972; "Only Women (Bleed)," 1975

Cooper, Alice, RIAA Gold Albums, "Killer," 1972; "School's Out," 1972; "Love It to Death," 1972; "Billion Dollar Babies," 1973; "Muscle of Love," 1973; "Alice Cooper's Greatest Hits," 1974; "Welcome to My Nightmare," 1975

Cooper, Les, "Wiggle Wobble," 1962

Copeland, Ken, "Pledge of Love," 1957

Corey, Jill, "I Love My Baby," 1956; "Love Me to Pieces," 1957

Cornelius Brothers (with Sister Rose), "Treat Her Like a Lady," 1971, RIAA 71; "Too Late to Turn Back Now," 1972, RIAA 72; "Don't Ever Be Lonely (A Poor Little Fool Like Me)," 1972

Cornell, Don, "Love Is a Many Splendored Thing," 1955; "The Bible Tells Me So," 1955; "Young Abe Lincoln," 1955

Cornerstone, "Holly Go Softly," 1970

Corsairs, "Smoky Places," 1961

Cortez, Dave "Baby," "The Happy Organ," 1959; "Rinky Dink," 1962

Cosby, Bill, "Little Ole Man (Uptight, Everything's Alright)," 1967; "Yes, Yes, Yes," 1976

Cosby, Bill, RIAA Gold Albums, "I Started Out as a Child," 1966; "Wonderfulness," 1966; "Why Is There Air?" 1966; "Bill Cosby Is A Very Funny Fellow, Right?" 1966; "Revenge," 1967; "To Russell, My Brother, Whom I Slept With," 1968; "200 MPH," 1969

Costa, Don, "I Walk the Line," 1959; "Theme from *The Unforgiven*," 1960; "Never on Sunday," 1960

Count Five, "Psychotic Reaction," 1966

Covay, Don, & The Good Timers, "Mercy, Mercy," 1964; "See Saw," 1965; "No Tell Motel," 1976

Coven, "One Tin Soldier," 1971

Cowsills, "The Rain, the Park & Other Things," 1967, RIAA 67; "We Can

Fly," 1968; "Indian Lake," 1968; "Hair," 1969, RIAA 69

Crabby Appleton, "Go Back," 1970

Cramer, Floyd, "Last Date," 1960; "On the Rebound," 1961; "San Antonio Rose," 1961; "Chattanooga Choo Choo," 1962

Crane, Les, "Desiderata," 1971

Crawford, Johnny, "Cindy's Birthday," 1962; "Your Nose Is Gonna Grow," 1962; "Rumors," 1962; "Proud," 1963

Crazy Elephant, "Gimme, Gimme, Good Lovin'," 1969

Cream, "Sunshine of Your Love," 1968, RIAA 68; "White Room," 1968; "Crossroads," 1969

Cream, RIAA Gold Albums, "Disraeli Gears," 1968; "Wheels of Fire," 1968; "Fresh Cream," 1968; "Goodbye," 1969; "Best of Cream," 1969

Creedence Clearwater Revival, "Suzie Q," 1968; "Proud Mary," 1969, RIAA 76; "Bad Moon Rising," 1969, RIAA 70; "Green River," 1969; "Down on the Corner"/"Fortunate Son," 1969, RIAA 70; "Travelin' Band"/"Who'll Stop the Rain," 1970, RIAA 70; "Up Around the Bend"/"Run Through the Jungle," 1970, RIAA 70; "Lookin' Out My Back Door," 1970; "Have You Ever Seen the Rain"/"Hey Tonight," 1971, RIAA 71; "Sweet Hitch-Hiker," 1971; "Someday Never Comes," 1972; "I Heard It Through The Grapevine," 1976

Creedence Clearwater Revival, RIAA Gold Albums, "Cosmo's Factory," 1970; "Willie & the Poor Boys," 1970; "Green River," 1970; "Bayou Country," 1970; "Pendulum," 1970; "Mardi Gras," 1972; "Creedence Gold," 1973

Crescendos, "Oh Julie," 1957

Crests, "Sixteen Candles," 1958; "Six Nights a Week," 1959; "The Angels Listened In," 1959; "Step by Step," 1960; "Trouble in Paradise," 1960

Crewcuts, "Earth Angel," 1955; "A Story Untold," 1955; "Angels in the Sky," 1955; "Mostly Martha," 1955; "Seven Days," 1956; "Young Love," 1957

Crewe, Bob, Generation, "Music to Watch Girls By," 1966; "Street Talk," 1976

Crickets (featuring Buddy Holly), "That'll Be the Day," 1957, RIAA 69; "Oh Boy," 1957; "Maybe Baby," 1958; "It's So Easy," 1958; "Think It Over," 1958

Critters, "Younger Girl," 1966; "Mr. Dieingly Sad," 1966

Croce, Jim, "You Don't Mess Around with Jim," 1972; "Operator (That's Not the Way It Feels)," 1972; "Bad, Bad Leroy Brown," 1973, RIAA 73; "One Less Set of Footsteps," 1973; "Time in a Bottle," 1974, RIAA 74; "I'll Have to Say I Love You in a Song," 1974; "Chain Gang Medley," 1976

Croce, Jim, RIAA Gold Albums, "Life & Times," 1973; "You Don't Mess

192

Around with Jim," 1973; "I Got a Name," 1973; "Photographs &
Memories, His Greatest Hits," 1974

Crosby, Bing, "In a Little Spanish Town," 1956; "True Love" (with Grace
Kelly), 1956; "Around the World," 1957; "White Christmas,"
(standard)

Crosby, Bing, RIAA Gold Album, "Merry Christmas," 1970

Crosby, David, RIAA Gold Album, "If I Could Only Remember My Name,"
1971

Crosby, David, & Graham Nash, RIAA Gold Album, "Wind on the Water,"
1976

Crosby, Stills, & Nash, "Marrakesh Express," 1969; "Suite: Judy Blue Eyes,"
1969

Crosby, Stills & Nash, RIAA Gold Album, "Crosby, Stills, & Nash," 1969

Crosby, Stills, Nash & Young, "Woodstock," 1970; "Teach Your Children,"
1970; "Ohio," 1970; "Our House," 1970

Crosby, Stills, Nash & Young, RIAA Gold Albums, "Deja Vu," 1970; "Four
Way Street," 1971; "So Far," 1974

Cross Country, "In the Midnight Hour," 1973

Crow, "Evil Woman Don't Play Your Games With Me," 1969

Crown Heights Affair, "Dreamin' a Dream," 1975; "Every Beat of My Heart,"
1975

Crows, "Gee," 1954-55

Crusaders, "Put It Where You Want It," 1972

Crystals, "There's No Other," 1961; "Uptown," 1962; "He's a Rebel," 1962;
"He's Sure the Boy I Love," 1962; "Da Doo Ron Ron," 1963;
"Then He Kissed Me," 1963

Cuff Links, "Tracy," 1969

Curb, Mike, Congregation, "Burning Bridges," 1970

Curry, Clifford, "She Shot a Hole in My Soul," 1967

Curtola, Bobby, "Fortuneteller," 1962

Cymarron, "Rings," 1971

Cymbal, Johnny (see Derek), "Mr. Bass Man," 1963

Cyrkle, "Red Rubber Ball," 1966; "Turn Down Day," 1966

Daddy Dewdrop, "Chick-a-Boom," 1971

Daddy-O's, "Got a Match?" 1958

Dale & Grace, "I'm Leaving It Up to You," 1963; "Stop and Think It Over,"
1964

Damon, Liz, Orient Express, "1900 Yesterday," 1970

Damone, Vic, "On the Street Where You Live," 1956; "An Affair to Remember," 1957; "You Were Only Fooling," 1965

Dana, Vic, "Little Altar Boy," 1961; "I Will," 1962; "Shangri-La," 1964; "Red Roses for a Blue Lady," 1965; "I Love You Drops," 1966

Dancer, Prancer & Nervous, "The Happy Reindeer," 1959

Daniels, Charlie, Band, "Uneasy Rider," 1973; "The South's Gonna Do It," 1975

Daniels, Charlie, Band, RIAA Gold Album, "Fire on the Mountain," 1975

Danleers, "One Summer Night," 1958

Danny & The Jrs., "At the Hop," 1957; "Rock & Roll Is Here to Stay," 1958; "Twistin' USA," 1960

Dante & The Evergreens, "Alley Oop," 1960

Darensburg, Joe, & The Dixie Flyers, "Yellow Dog Blues," 1958

Darin, Bobby, "Splish Splash," 1958; "Queen of the Hop," 1958; "Plain Jane," 1959; "Dream Lover," 1959; "Mack the Knife," 1959; "Beyond the Sea," 1960; "Clementine," 1960; "Won't You Come Home, Bill Bailey"/"I'll Be There," 1960; "Artificial Flowers," 1960; "Christmas Auld Lang Syne," 1960; "Lazy River," 1961; "You Must Have Been a Beautiful Baby," 1961; "Irresistible You"/ "Multiplication," 1961; "What'd I Say," 1962; "Things," 1962; "Baby Face," 1962; "If a Man Answers," 1962; "You're the Reason I'm Living," 1963; "18 Yellow Roses," 1963; "If I Were a Carpenter," 1966; "Lovin' You," 1967

Darren, James, "Gidget," 1959; "Goodbye Cruel World," 1961; "Her Royal Majesty," 1962; "Conscience," 1962; "Mary's Little Lamb," 1962; "All," 1967

Dartells, "Hot Pastrami," 1963

David & Jonathan, "Michelle," 1966

Davidson, John, "Everytime I Sing A Love Song," 1976

Davis, Mac, "Whoever Finds This, I Love You," 1970; "Baby Don't Get Hooked on Me," 1972, RIAA 72; "One Hell of a Woman," 1974; "Stop and Smell the Roses," 1974; "Rock and Roll (I Gave You the Best Years of My Life)," 1975

Davis, Mac, RIAA Gold Albums, "Baby Don't Get Hooked on Me," 1973; "Stop and Smell the Roses," 1974; "All the Love in the World," 1976

Davis, Miles, RIAA Gold Album, "Bitches Brew," 1976

Davis, Paul, "Ride 'Em, Cowboy," 1974; "Superstar," 1976

Davis, Sammy, Jr., "Something's Gotta Give," 1955; "That Old Black Magic," 1955; "What Kind of Fool Am I," 1962; "The Shelter of Your Arms," 1963; "Don't Blame the Children," 1967; "I've Gotta Be

Me," 1968; "Candy Man," 1972, RIAA 72; "Keep Your Eye on the Sparrow," 1975

Davis, Skeeter, "My Last Date (With You)," 1960; "The End Of The World," 1963; "I Can't Stay Mad at You," 1963

Davis, Spencer, Group, (See Spencer Davis Group)

Davis, Tyrone, "Can I Change My Mind," 1969, RIAA 69; "Turn Back the Hands of Time," 1970, RIAA 70; "Give it Up (Turn it Loose)," 1976

Dawn (see Tony Orlando & Dawn)

Day, Bobby (see The Hollywood Flames), "Rockin Robin"/"Over & Over," 1958

Day Doris, "Whatever Will Be, Will Be (Que Sera, Sera)," 1956; "Everybody Loves a Lover," 1958

Day, Doris, RIAA Gold Album, "Doris Day's Greatest Hits," 1968

Deal, Bill, & The Rhondells, "May I," 1969; "I've Been Hurt," 1969; "What Kind of Fool Do You Think I Am," 1969

Dean & Jean, "Tra La La La Suzy," 1963; "Hey Jean, Hey Dean," 1964

Dean, Jimmy, "Big Bad John," 1961, RIAA 61; "Dear Ivan," 1962; "The Cajun Queen," 1962; "To a Sleeping Beauty," 1962; "P.T. 109," 1962; "Little Black Book," 1962; "I. O. U.," 1976, RIAA 76

Dee, Joey, & The Starlighters, "Peppermint Twist," 1961; "Hey, Let's Twist," 1962; "Shout," 1962; "What Kind of Love Is This," 1962; "Hot Pastrami (With Mashed Potatoes)," 1963

Dee, Johnny, "Sittin' in the Balcony," 1957

Dee, Tommy (with Carol Kay & The Teen-Aires), "Three Stars," 1959

Deep Purple, "Hush," 1968; "Kentucky Woman," 1968; "Smoke on the Water," 1973, RIAA 73; "Woman from Tokyo," 1973

Deep Purple, RIAA Gold Albums, "Machine Head," 1972; "Who Do You Think We Are," 1973; "Made in Japan," 1973; "Burn," 1974; "Stormbringer," 1975

Dees, Rick, & His Cast of Idiots, "Disco Duck," RIAA 76

De Franco Family, "Heartbeat—It's a Lovebeat," 1973, RIAA 73

Dekker, Desmond, & The Aces, "Israelites," 1969

Delaney & Bonnie & Friends, "Never Ending Song of Love," 1971; "Only You Know and I Know," 1971

Delegates, "Convention '72," 1972

Del-Fonics, "La La Means I Love You," 1968; "Didn't I (Blow Your Mind This Time)," 1970, RIAA 70

Dells, "Oh What a Night," 1956; "There Is," 1968; "Stay in My Corner," 1968; "Always Together," 1968; "I Can Sing a Rainbow"/"Love Is Blue," 1969; "Oh What a Night" (re-release), 1969; "The Love We Had (Stays on My Mind)," 1971; "Give Your Baby a Standing Ovation," 1973, RIAA 73

Dell-Vikings, "Come Go with Me," 1957; "Whispering Bells," 1957; "Cool Shake," 1957

Demensions, "Over the Rainbow," 1960

Denny, Martin, "Quiet Village," 1959; "The Enchanted Sea," 1959

Denver, John, "Take Me Home, Country Roads," 1971, RIAA 71; "Friends with You," 1971; "Rocky Mountain High," 1972; "Sunshine on My Shoulder," 1974, RIAA 74; "Annie's Song," 1974, RIAA 74; "Back Home Again," 1974, RIAA 75; "Thank God, I'm a Country Boy," 1975, RIAA 75; "I'm Sorry"/"Calypso," 1975, RIAA 75; "Fly Away," 1976; "Looking for Space," 1976; "It Makes Me Giggle," 1976; "Like a Sad Song," 1976

Denver, John, RIAA Gold Albums, "Poems, Prayers & Promises," 1971; "Aerie," 1972; "Rocky Mountain High," 1972; "Farewell Andromeda," 1973; "John Denver's Greatest Hits," 1973; "Back Home Again," 1974; "An Evening with John Denver," 1975; "Windsong," 1975; "Rocky Mountain Christmas," 1975

Denver, John, RIAA Platinum Album, "Spirit," 1976

Deodato, "2001," (also, "Sprach Zarathustra"), 1973; "Caravan"/"El Watusi," 1976

Derek (see Cymbal, Johnny), "Cinnamon," 1968; "Back Door Man," 1969

Derek & The Dominos, "Layla," 1972

Derek & The Dominos, RIAA Gold Albums, "Layla," 1971; "In Concert," 1973

DeShannon, Jackie, "Needles & Pins," 1963; "What the World Needs Now Is Love," 1965; "Put a Little Love in Your Heart," 1969, RIAA 69; "Love Will Find a Way," 1969

Detergents, "Leader of the Laundromat," 1964

Detroit Emaralds, "Baby Let Me Take You (In My Arms)," 1972

DeVaughn, William, "Be Thankful for What You Got," 1974, RIAA 74

DeVorzon, Barry, and Perry Botkin, Jr., "Nadia's Theme," 1976

Devotions, "Rip Van Winkle," 1964

Diamond, Neil, "Cherry, Cherry," 1966; "I Got the Feelin'," 1966; "You Got to Me," 1967; "Girl, You'll Be a Woman Soon," 1967; "Thank the Lord for the Night Time," 1967; "Kentucky Woman," 1967; Brother Love's Traveling Salvation Show," 1969; "Sweet Caroline," 1969, RIAA 69; "Holy, Holy," 1969, RIAA 69; "Shilo," 1970; "Soolaimon," 1970; "Solitary Man," 1970; "Cracklin' Rosie," 1970, RIAA 70; "He Ain't Heavy, He's My Brother," 1970; "Do It," 1970; "I Am . . . I Said," 1971; "Stones"/"Crunchy Granola Suite," 1971; "Song Sung Blue," 1972, RIAA 72; "Play Me," 1972; "Walk on Water," 1972; "Cherry, Cherry" (from "Hot August Night"), 1973; "Longfellow Serenade," 1974; "If You Know What I Mean," 1976

Diamond, Neil, RIAA Gold Albums, "Gold," 1970; "Touching You, Touching You," 1970; "Taproot Manuscript," 1971; "Stones," 1972; "Moods," 1972; "Hot August Night," 1972; "Jonathan Livingston Seagull," 1973; "His 12 Greatest Hits," 1974; "Serenade," 1974; "Beautiful Noise," 1976

Diamond, Neil, RIAA Platinum Album, "Beautiful Noise," 1976

Diamonds, "Why Do Fools Fall in Love," 1956; "Church Bells May Ring," 1956; "Love, Love, Love," 1956; "Soft Summer Breeze," 1956; "Ka Ding Dong," 1956; "Little Darlin'," 1957; "The Stroll," 1957; "Walking Along," 1958; "She Say (Oom Dooby Doom)," 1959; "One Summer Night," 1961

Dick & DeeDee, "The Mountain's High," 1961; "Tell Me," 1962; "Young & in Love," 1963; "Turn Around," 1963; "Thou Shall Not Steal," 1964

Dickens, Little Jimmy, "May the Bird of Paradise Fly Up Your Nose," 1965

Diddley, Bo, "Bo Diddley"/"I'm a Man," 1955; "Say Man," 1959

Dinning, Mark, "Teen Angel," 1959

Dino, Desi & Billy, "I'm a Fool," 1965; "Not the Lovin' Kind," 1965; "If You're Thinking What I'm Thinking," 1966

Dino, Kenny, "Your Ma Said You Cried in Your Sleep Last Night," 1961

Dion (see Dion & The Belmonts), "Lonely Teenager," 1960; "Runaround Sue," 1961; "The Wanderer"/"The Majestic," 1961; "Lovers Who Wander," 1962; "Little Diane," 1962; "Love Came to Me," 1962; "Sandy," 1963; "Ruby Baby," 1963; "This Little Girl," 1963; "Be Careful of the Stones That You Throw," 1963; "Donna, the Prima Donna," 1963; "Drip, Drop," 1963; "Abraham, Martin, & John," 1968, RIAA 69

Dion & The Belmonts, (See Dion), (See The Belmonts), "I Wonder Why," 1958; "No One Knows," 1958; "A Teenager in Love," 1959; "Where or When," 1960; "When You Wish Upon a Star," 1960

Dirksen, Senator Everett McKinley, "Gallant Men," 1966

Disco-Tex & The Sex-o-Lettes, "Get Dancin'," 1974; "Dancin' Kid," 1976

Dixiebells, "Down at Papa Joe's," 1963; "Southtown, USA," 1964

Dixie Cups, "Chapel of Love," 1964; "People Say," 1964; "Iko Iko," 1965

Dobkins, Jr., Carl, "My Heart is an Open Book," 1959; "Lucky Devil," 1959

Doggett, Bill, "Honky Tonk," 1956; "Slow Walk," 1956

Domino, Fats, "Ain't That a Shame," 1955; "All by Myself," 1955; "Bo Weevil," 1956; "I'm in Love Again"/"My Blue Heaven," 1956; "When My Dreamboat Comes Home"/"So Long," 1956; "Blueberry Hill," 1956; "Blue Monday," 1956; "I'm Walkin'," 1957; "Valley of Tears"/"It's You I Love," 1957; "Wait & See"/"I Still Love You," 1957; "The Big Beat," 1957; "Sick & Tired," 1958; "Whole Lotta Loving"/"Coquette," 1958; "I'm Ready," 1959; "I Want to Walk

You Home"/"I'm Gonna Be a Wheel Someday," 1959; "Be My Guest"/"I've Been Around," 1959; "Country Boy," 1960; "Walking to New Orleans"/"Don't Come Knockin'," 1960; "Three Nights a Week," 1960; "My Girl Josephine"/"Natural Born Lover," 1960; "What a Price," 1961; "Shu Rah"/"Fell in Love on Monday," 1961; "Let the Four Winds Blow"/"It Keeps Rainin'," 1961; "What a Party," 1961; "Jambalaya"/"I Hear You Knocking," 1961; "You Win Again," 1962; "Red Sails in the Sunset," 1963; "Lady Madonna," 1968

Don & Juan, "What's Your Name," 1962

Donaldson, Bo. & The Heywoods, "Billy, Don't Be a Hero," 1974, RIAA 74; "Who Do You Think You Are," 1974

Donegan, Lonnie, "Rock Island Line," 1956; "Does Your Chewing Gum Lose Its Flavor," 1961

Donner, Ral, "Girl of My Best Friend," 1961; "You Don't Know What You Got (Until You Lose It)," 1961; "She's Everything," 1961

Donovan, "Catch the Wind," 1965; "Colours," 1965; "Sunshine Superman," 1966; "Mellow Yellow," 1966, RIAA 67; "Epistle to Dippy," 1967; "There Is a Mountain," 1967; "Wear Your Love Like Heaven," 1967; "Jennifer Juniper," 1968; "Hurdy Gurdy Man," 1968; "Lalena," 1968; "To Susan on the West Coast Waiting," 1969; "Atlantis," 1969; "Goo Goo Barabajagal," 1969

Donovan, RIAA Gold Albums, "Donovan's Greatest Hits," 1969; "A Gift from a Flower to a Garden," 1970

Doo, Dickey, & The Don'ts, "Click Clack," 1958; "Nee Nee Na Na Na Na Nu Nu," 1958; "Flip Top Box," 1958; "Leave Me Alone (Let Me Cry)," 1958

Doobie Brothers, "Listen to the Music," 1972; "Long Train 'Running," 1973; "China Grove," 1973; "Another Park, Another Sunday," 1974; "Black Water," 1975, RIAA 75; "Take Me in Your Arms," 1975; "Taking It to the Streets," 1976

Doobie Brothers, RIAA Gold Albums, "The Captain & Me," 1973; "Toulouse Street," 1973; "What Were Once Vices Are Now Habits," 1974; "Stampede," 1975; "Takin' It to the Streets," 1976

Doors, "Light My Fire," 1967, RIAA 67; "People Are Strange," 1967; "Love Me Two Times," 1967; "The Unknown Soldier," 1968; "Hello, I Love You," 1968, RIAA 68; "Touch Me," 1969, RIAA 69; "Love Her Madly," 1971; "Riders on the Storm," 1971

Doors, RIAA Gold Albums, "The Doors," 1967; "Strange Days," 1968; "Waiting for the Sun," 1968; "The Soft Parade," 1969; "Morrison Hotel," 1970; "Absolutely Live," 1970; "L.A. Woman," 1971; "Thirteen," 1972

Dorman, Harold, "Mountain of Love," 1960

Dorsey, Jimmy, "So Rare," 1957; "June Night," 1957; "Jay Dee's Boogie Woogie," 1957

Dorsey, Lee, "Ya, Ya," 1961; "Do-Re-Mi," 1961; "Ride Your Pony," 1965; "Working in the Coal Mine," 1966; "Holy Cow," 1966

Dorsey, Tommy, Orchestra (with Warren Covington), "Tea for Two Cha Cha," 1958

Douglas, Carl, "Kung Fu Fighting," 1974, RIAA 74

Douglas, Carol, "Doctor's Orders," 1975

Douglas, Mike, "The Men in My Little Girl's Life," 1965

Dove, Ronnie, "Say You," 1964; "Right or Wrong," 1964; "One Kiss for Old Times' Sake," 1965; "A Little Bit of Heaven," 1965; "I'll Make All Your Dreams Come True," 1965; "Kiss Away," 1965; "When Liking Turns to Loving," 1966; "Let's Start All Over Again," 1966; "Happy Summer Days," 1966; "I Really Don't Want to Know," 1966; "Cry," 1966; "One More Mountain to Climb," 1967

Dovells (see Len Barry), "Bristol Stomp," 1961; "Do the New Continental," 1962; "Bristol Twistin' Annie," 1962; "Hully Gully Baby," 1962; "You Can't Sit Down," 1963

Dowell, Joe, "Wooden Heart," 1961; "Little Red Rented Rowboat," 1962

Dozier, Lamont, "Trying to Hold on to My Woman," 1974

Dr. Feelgood & The Interns, "Doctor Feelgood," 1962

Dr. Hook, "Sylvia's Mother" (with The Medicine Show), 1972, RIAA 72; "Cover of the Rolling Stone" (with The Medicine Show), 1972, RIAA 73; "Only Sixteen," 1976, RIAA 76; "A Little Bit More," 1976

Dr. West's Medicine Show & Junk Band, "The Eggplant That Ate Chicago," 1966

Drake, Charlie, "My Boomerang Won't Come Back," 1962

Drake, Pete, "Forever," 1964

Dramatics, "Whatcha See Is Whatcha Get," 1971; "In the Rain," 1972

Draper, Rusty, "The Shifting Whispering Sands," 1955; "Are You Satisfied," 1955; "In the Middle of the House," 1956; "Freight Train," 1957; "Night Life," 1963

Dreamlovers, "When We Get Married," 1961

Dreamweavers, "It's Almost Tomorrow," 1955; "A Little Love Can Go a Long, Long Way," 1956

Drew, Patti, "Tell Him," 1967

Drifters, "White Christmas," 1955; "Fools Fall in Love," 1957; "Moonlight Bay"/"Drip Drop," 1958; "There Goes My Baby," 1959; "Dance with Me"/"True Love, True Love," 1959; "This Magic Moment," 1960; "Save the Last Dance for Me," 1960; "I Count The Tears," 1960; "Some Kind of Wonderful," 1961; "Please Stay," 1961;

"Sweets for My Sweet," 1961; "When My Little Girl Is Smiling," 1962; "Up on the Roof," 1962; "On Broadway," 1963; "I'll Take You Home," 1963; "Vaya Con Dios," 1964; "Under the Boardwalk," 1964; "I've Got Sand in My Shoes," 1964; "Saturday Night at the Movies," 1964

Driscoll, Julie, & Brian Auger's Trinity, "This Wheel's on Fire," 1968

Drusky, Roy, "Three Hearts in a Tangle," 1961

Duals, "Stick Shift," 1961

Dudley, Dave, "Six Days on the Road," 1963

Dukays, "Nite Owl," 1962

Duke, Patty, "Don't Just Stand There," 1965; "Say Something Funny," 1965

Duprees, "You Belong to Me," 1962; "My Own True Love," 1962; "Why Don't You Believe Me," 1963; "Have You Heard," 1963

Durante, Jimmy, "September Song," 1963

Dyke & The Blazers, "We Got More Soul," 1969; "Let a Woman Be a Woman, Let a Man Be a Man," 1969

Dylan, Bob, "Subterranean Homesick Blues," 1965; "Like a Rolling Stone," 1965; "Positively 4th Street," 1965; "Rainy Day Women #12 & 35," 1966; "I Want You," 1966; "Just Like a Woman," 1966; "Lay Lady Lay," 1969; "Wigwam," 1970; "George Jackson," 1971; "Hurricane," 1975; "Mozambique," 1976

Dylan, Bob, RIAA Gold Albums, "Blonde on Blonde," 1967; "Highway '61," 1967; "Bringing It All Back Home," 1967; "John Wesley Harding," 1968; "Bob Dylan's Greatest Hits," 1968; "Nashville Skyline," 1969; "Self Portrait," 1970; "New Morning," 1970; "The Freewheelin' Bob Dylan," 1970; "Bob Dylan's Greatest Hits, Vol. 2," 1972; "Dylan," 1973; "Planet Waves," 1974; "Blood on the Tracks," 1975; "Desire," 1976; "Hard Rain," 1976

Dylan, Bob, RIAA Platinum Album, "Desire," 1976

Dylan, Bob, & The Band, RIAA Gold Album, "Before the Flood," 1974

Dyson, Ronnie, "(If You Let Me Make Love to You Then) Why Can't I Touch You?" 1970; "I Don't Wanna Cry," 1970

Eagles, "Take It Easy," 1972; "Witchy Woman," 1972; "Peaceful Easy Feeling," 1973; "Best of My Love," 1975; "One of These Nights," 1975; "Lyin' Eyes," 1975; "Take It to the Limit," 1976

Eagles, RIAA Gold Albums, "Eagles," 1974; "On the Border," 1974; "Desperado," 1974; "One of These Nights," 1975; "Eagles"/"Their Greatest Hits 1971-1975," 1976

200

Eagles, RIAA Platinum Album, "Eagles—Their Greatest Hits," 1976

Earls, "Remember Then," 1962

Earth, Wind, & Fire, "Shining Star," 1975, RIAA 75; "The Way of the World," 1975; "Sing a Song," 1976, RIAA 76; "Can't Hide Your Love," 1976; "Get Away," 1976

Earth, Wind & Fire, RIAA Gold Albums, "Head to the Sky," 1973; "Open Our Eyes," 1974; "The Way of the World," 1975; "Gratitude," 1975; "Spirit," 1976

Easybeats, "Friday on My Mind," 1967

Echoes, "Baby Blue," 1961

Ecstasy, Passion & Pain, "One Beautiful Day," 1975

Eddy, Duane, "Rebel Rouser," 1958; "Ramrod," 1958; "Cannonball," 1958; "The Lonely One," 1959; "Yep!" 1959; "Forty Miles of Bad Road," 1959; "Bonnie Come Back," 1960; "Because They're Young," 1960; "Peter Gunn," 1960; "Pepe," 1960; "(Dance with the) Guitar Man," 1962; "Boss Guitar," 1962

Edison Lighthouse, "Love Grows (Where My Rosemary Goes)," 1970, RIAA 70

Edmunds, Dave, "I Hear You Knocking," 1971

Edsels, "Rama Lama Ding Dong," 1961

Edwards, Bobby, "You're the Reason," 1961

Edwards, Jonathan, "Sunshine," 1971, RIAA 72

Edwards, Tommy, "It's All in the Game," 1958; "Please Love Me Forever," 1958; "Love Is All We Need," 1958; "Please Mr. Sun," 1959; "The Morning Side of the Mountain," 1959; "My Melancholy Baby," 1959; "I Really Don't Want to Know," 1960

Eighth Day, "She's Not Just Another Woman," 1971

Elbert, Donnie, "Where Did Our Love Go," 1971; "I Can't Help Myself (Sugar Pie, Honey Bunch)," 1972

El Chicano, "Viva Tirado, Part 1," 1970

El Dorados, "At My Front Door," 1955

Electric Indian, "Keem-O-Sabe," 1969

Electric Light Orchestra, "Roll Over Beethoven," 1973; "Can't Get It Out of My Head," 1975; "Evil Woman," 1976; "Strange Magic," 1976

Electric Light Orchestra, RIAA Gold Albums, "Eldorado," 1975; "Face the Music," 1976; "Ole' ELO," 1976

Electric Prunes, "I Had Too Much to Dream (Last Night)," 1966; "Get Me to the World on Time," 1967

Elegants, "Little Star," 1958

Elgart, Les, "Main Title—Golden Arm," 1956

Elledge, Jimmy, "Funny How Time Slips Away," 1961

Elliman, Yvonne, "I Don't Know How to Love Him," 1971

Ellis, Shirley, "The Nitty Gritty," 1963; "The Name Game," 1964; "The Clapping Song," 1965

Emerson, Lake & Palmer, "Lucky Man," 1971; "From the Beginning," 1972

Emerson, Lake & Palmer, RIAA Gold Albums, "Emerson, Lake & Palmer," 1971; "Tarkus," 1971; "Pictures at an Exhibition," 1972; "Trilogy," 1972; "Brain Salad Surgery," 1973; "Welcome Back, My Friends, to the Show," 1974

Emotions, "So I Can Love You," 1969

England Dan, & John Ford Coley, "I'd Really Love to See You Tonight," 1976; "Nights are Forever Without You," 1976

English Congregation, "Softly Whispering I Love You," 1972

Epps, Preston, "Bongo Rock," 1959; "Bongo, Bongo, Bongo," 1960

Equals, "Baby Come Back," 1970

Ernie (Jim Henson), "Rubber Duckie," 1970

Esquires, "Get On Up," 1967; "And Get Away," 1967

Essex, "Easier Said Than Done," 1963; "A Walkin' Miracle," 1963

Essex, David, "Rock On," 1974, RIAA 74

Evans, Paul, "Seven Little Girls (Sittin' in the Back Seat)," 1959; "Midnite Special," 1960; "Happy-Go-Lucky-Me," 1960

Everett, Betty, "You're No Good," 1963; "The Shoop Shoop Song," 1964; "There'll Come a Time," 1969

Everett, Betty, & Jerry Butler, "Let It Be Me," 1964

Everly Brothers, "Bye Bye Love," 1957; "Wake Up Little Susie," 1957; "This Little Girl of Mine," 1958; "All I Have to Do Is Dream," 1958; "Claudette," 1958; "Bird Dog," 1958; "Devoted to You," 1958; "Problems," 1958; "Take a Message to Mary," 1959; "Poor Jenny," 1959; "(Til') I Kissed You," 1959; "Let It Be Me," 1960; "When Will I Be Loved," 1960; "Be Bop A-Lula," 1960; "Like Strangers," 1960; "Cathy's Clown," 1960; "So Sad," 1960; "Lucille," 1960; "Walk Right Back," 1961; "Ebony Eyes," 1961; "Temptation," 1961; "Don't Blame Me," 1961; "Crying in the Rain," 1962; "That's Old Fashioned," 1962; "Bowling Green," 1967

Every Mother's Son, "Come on Down to My Boat," 1967

Exciters, "Tell Him," 1962

Fabares, Shelly, "Johnny Angel," 1962; "Johnny Loves Me," 1962

Fabian, "I'm a Man," 1959; "Turn Me Loose," 1959; "Tiger," 1959; "Come on and Get Me," 1959; "Hound Dog Man," 1959; "This Friendly World," 1959

Fabric, Bent, "Alley Cat," 1962

Facenda, Tommy, "High School USA," 1959

Faces, "Stay with Me," 1972; "Cindy Incidentally," 1973

Faces, RIAA Gold Album, "A Nod Is as Good as a Wink," 1972

Fairchild, Barbara, "Teddy Bear," 1973

Faith, Hope & Charity, "To Each His Own," 1975

Faith, Percy, "Theme From *A Summer Place*," 1960; "Theme From *A Summer Place*," 1976 (remake)

Faith, Percy, RIAA Gold Albums, "VIVA!" 1963; "Themes for Young Lovers," 1967

Faithfull, Marianne, "As Tears Go By," 1964; "Come and Stay with Me," 1965; "This Little Bird," 1965; "Summer Nights," 1965

Falcons, "You're So Fine," 1959

Fame, George, "Yeh, Yeh," 1965; "The Ballad of Bonnie & Clyde," 1968

Fancy, "Wild Thing," 1974

Fantastic Johnny C., "Boogaloo Down Broadway," 1967

Fardon, Don, "Indian Reservation," 1968

Fargo, Donna, "The Happiest Girl in the Whole USA," 1972, RIAA 72; "Funny Face," 1972, RIAA 72

Fargo, Donna, RIAA Gold Album, "The Happiest Girl in the Whole USA," 1973

Feliciano, Jose, "Light My Fire," 1968; "Hi-Heel Sneakers," 1968; "Rain," 1969; "Feliz Navidad," 1969

Feliciano, Jose, RIAA Gold Albums, "Feliciano," 1968; "Alive Alive-o!" 1970; "Feliciano"/"10 To 23," 1970

Felts, Narvel, "Reconsider Me," 1975

Fender, Freddy, "Before the Next Teardrop Falls," 1975, RIAA 75; "Wasted Days & Wasted Nights," 1975, RIAA 75; "Secret Love," 1976; "You'll Lose a Good Thing," 1976; "Vaya Con Dios," 1976

Fender, Freddy, RIAA Gold Album, "Before the Next Teardrop Falls," 1975

Fendermen, "Mule Skinner Blues," 1960

Ferguson, Johnny, "Angela Jones," 1960

Ferrante & Teicher, "Theme From *The Apartment*," 1960; "Exodus," 1960; "Tonight," 1961; "Midnight Cowboy," 1969

Fields, Ernie, "In the Mood," 1959

Fiestas, "So Fine," 1959

Fifth Dimension, "Go Where You Wanna Go," 1967; "Up, Up and Away," 1967; "Paper Cup," 1967; "Carpet Man," 1968; "Stoned Soul

Picnic," 1968, RIAA 68; "Sweet Blindness," 1968; "California
Soul," 1968; "Aquarius"/"Let the Sunshine In," 1969, RIAA 69;
"Workin' on a Groovy Thing," 1969; "Wedding Bell Blues," 1969,
RIAA 69; "Blowing Away," 1970; "Puppet Man," 1970; "Save
the Country," 1970; "One Less Bell to Answer," 1970, RIAA 70;
"Love's Lines, Angles and Rhymes," 1971; "Never My Love," 1971;
"(Last Night) I Didn't Get to Sleep at All," 1972, RIAA 72; "If I
Could Reach You," 1972; "Love Hangover," 1976

Fifth Dimension, RIAA Gold Albums, "The Age of Aquarius," 1969; "Up,
Up and Away," 1970; "The Fifth Dimension's Greatest Hits," 1970;
"Portrait," 1970; "Love's Lines, Angles and Rhymes," 1971; "Live,"
1971; "Greatest Hits on Earth," 1972

Fifth Estate, "Ding Dong! The Witch Is Dead," 1967

Finnegan, Larry, "Dear One," 1962

Fireballs, "Torquay," 1959; "Bulldog," 1960; "Bottle of Wine," 1968

Firefall, "You are the Woman," 1976

Fireflies, "You Were Mine," 1959

First Class, "Beach Baby," 1974

Fisher, Eddie, "Dungaree Doll," 1955; "On the Street Where You Live,"
1956; "Cindy, Oh Cindy," 1956; "Tonight," 1961; "Games That
Lovers Play," 1966

Fisher, Miss Toni, "The Big Hurt," 1959

Fitzgerald, Ella, "Mack the Knife," 1960

Five Americans, "I See the Light," 1966; "Western Union," 1967

Five Blobs, "The Blob," 1958

Five Du-Tones, "Shake a Tail Feather," 1963

Five Keys, "Close Your Eyes," 1955; "Out of Sight, Out of Mind," 1956;
"Wisdom of a Fool," 1956

Five Man Electrical Band, "Signs," 1971, RIAA 71; "Absolutely Right,"
1971

Five Satins, "In the Still of the Nite," 1956; "To the Aisle," 1957

Five Stairsteps, "O-o-h Child"/"Dear Prudence," 1970, RIAA 70

5000 Volts, "I'm on Fire," 1975

Flack, Roberta, "First Time Ever I Saw Your Face," 1972, RIAA 72; "Killing
Me Softly with His Song," 1973, RIAA 73; "Feel Like Makin' Love,"
1974, RIAA 74; "Jesse," 1974

Flack, Roberta, RIAA Gold Albums, "Chapter Two," 1971; "First Take,"
1972; "Quiet Fire," 1972; "Killing Me Softly," 1973

Flack, Roberta, & Donny Hathaway, "You've Got a Friend," 1971; "Where
Is the Love," 1972, RIAA 72

Flack, Roberta, & Donny Hathaway, RIAA Gold Album, "Roberta Flack &
Donny Hathaway," 1972

Flaming Ember, "Mind, Body & Soul," 1969; "Westbound #9," 1970; "I'm Not My Brothers Keeper," 1970

Flamingos, "Lovers Never Say Goodbye," 1959; "I Only Have Eyes for You," 1959; "Nobody Loves Me Like You," 1960

Flares, "Foot Stomping, Part 1," 1961

Flash Cadillac & The Continental Kids, "Did You Boogie (with Your Baby)," 1976

Flatt, Lester, & Earl Scruggs, "The Ballad of Jed Clampett," 1962; "Foggy Mountain Breakdown (Theme from *Bonnie & Clyde*)," 1968

Fleetwood Mac, "Over My Head," 1975; "Rhiannon," 1976; "Say You Love Me," 1976

Fleetwood Mac, RIAA Gold Albums, "Fleetwood Mac," 1975; "Bare Trees," 1976

Fleetwoods, "Come Softly to Me," 1959; "Mr. Blue," 1959; "Runaround," 1960; "Tragedy," 1961; "(He's) The Great Impostor," 1961

Flint, Shelby, "Angel on My Shoulder," 1961

Flood, Dick, "The Three Bells," 1959

Floyd, Eddie, "Knock on Wood," 1966; "Bring It on Home to Me," 1968

Floyd, King, "Groove Me," 1970, RIAA 71; "Baby Let Me Kiss You," 1971

Flying Machine, "Smile a Little Smile for Me," 1969, RIAA 69

Focus, "Hocus Pocus," 1973

Focus, RIAA Gold Albums, "Moving Waves," 1973; "Focus 3," 1973

Fogelberg, Dan, RIAA Gold Album, "Souvenirs," 1976

Fogerty, John, "Rockin' All Over the World," 1975

Foghat, "Slowride," 1976; "Fool for the City," 1976

Foghat, RIAA Gold Albums, "Energized," 1975; "Foghat," 1975; "Fool for the City," 1976

Fontaine, Frank, RIAA Gold Album, "Songs I Sang on the Jackie Gleason Show," 1968

Fontane Sisters, "Hearts of Stone," 1955; "Rock Love," 1955; "Seventeen," 1955; "Daddy-O," 1955; "Eddie My Love," 1956; "The Banana Boat Song," 1956

Ford, Frankie, "Sea Cruise," 1959

Ford, "Tennessee" Ernie, "Sixteen Tons," 1955

Ford, "Tennessee" Ernie, RIAA Gold Albums, "Hymns," 1959; "Spirituals," 1961; "Star Carol," 1962; "Nearer the Cross," 1962

Fortunes, "You've Got Your Troubles," 1965; "Here It Comes Again," 1965; "Here Come That Rainy Day Feeling Again," 1971

Forum, "The River Is Wide," 1967

Foundations, "Baby, Now That I've Found You," 1967; "Build Me Up Buttercup," 1969, RIAA 69

Four Aces, "Love Is a Many-Splendored Thing," 1955; "A Woman in Love," 1955

Four Coins, "I Love You Madly," 1955; "Memories of You," 1955; "Shangri-La," 1957; "My One Sin," 1957

Four Esquires, "Look Homeward Angel," 1956; "Hideaway," 1958

Four Freshmen, "Graduation Day," 1956

Four Jacks & Jill, "Master Jack," 1968

Four Lads, "Moments to Remember," 1955; "No Not Much," 1956; "Standing on the Corner," 1956; "The Bus Stop Song (A Paper of Pins)," 1956; "A House with Love in It," 1956; "Who Needs You," 1957; "I Just Don't Know," 1957; "Enchanted Island," 1958; "The Mocking Bird," 1958

Four Preps, "26 Miles," 1958; "Big Man," 1958; "Down by the Station," 1960; "More Money for You and Me," 1961

Four Seasons, "Sherry," 1962; "Big Girls Don't Cry," 1962; "Walk Like a Man," 1963; "Ain't That a Shame," 1963; "Candy Girl," 1963; "Stay," 1964; "Dawn," 1964; "Ronnie," 1964; "Rag Doll," 1964, RIAA 64; "Save It For Me," 1964; "Big Man in Town," 1964; "Bye Bye Baby," 1965; "Let's Hang On," 1965; "Working My Way Back to You," 1966; "Opus 17 (Don't You Worry 'Bout Me)," 1966; "I've Got You Under My Skin," 1966; "Tell It to the Rain," 1966; "Beggin'," 1967; "C'mon Marianne," 1967; "Will You Love Me Tomorrow," 1968; "Who Loves You," 1975; "Oh What a Night," 1976, RIAA 76 ("December," 1963); "Silver Star," 1976

Four Seasons, RIAA Gold Albums, "Gold Vault of Hits," 1966; "2nd Vault of Golden Hits," 1967; "Edizione D'Oro," 1970

Four Tops, "Baby I Need Your Loving," 1964; "Ask the Lonely," 1965; "I Can't Help Myself," 1965; "It's the Same Old Song," 1965; "Something About You," 1965; "Shake Me, Wake Me (When It's Over)," 1966; "Reach Out I'll Be There," 1966; "Standing in the Shadows of Love," 1966; "Bernadette," 1967; "7 Rooms of Gloom," 1967; "You Keep Running Away," 1967; "Walk Away Renee," 1968; "If I Were a Carpenter," 1968; "It's All in the Game," 1970; "Still Water (Love)," 1970; "Keeper of the Castle," 1972; "Ain't No Woman (Like the One I Got)," 1973, RIAA 73; "Are You Man Enough," 1974

Four Tunes, "I Understand (Just How You Feel)," 1955

Foxx, Inez, "Mockingbird," 1963

Frampton, Peter, "Show Me the Way," 1976; "Baby, I Love Your Way," 1976; "Do You Feel Like We Do," 1976

Frampton, Peter, RIAA Gold Albums, "Frampton Comes Alive!" 1976; "Frampton," 1976

Frampton, Peter, RIAA Platinum Album, "Frampton Comes Alive!" 1976

Francis, Connie, "Who's Sorry Now," 1958; "Stupid Cupid," 1958; "Fallin'," 1958; "My Happiness," 1958; "If I Didn't Care," 1959; "Lipstick on Your Collar," 1959; "Frankie," 1959; "Among My Souvenirs," 1959; "Mama," 1960; "Teddy," 1960; "Everybody's Somebody's Fool," 1960; "Jealous of You," 1960; "My Heart Has a Mind of Its Own," 1960; "Many Tears Ago," 1960; "Where the Boys Are," 1961; "Breakin' in a Brand New Broken Heart," 1961; "Together," 1961; "(He's My) Dreamboat," 1961; "When The Boy in Your Arms," 1961; "Don't Break the Heart That Loves You," 1962; "Second Hand Love," 1962; "Vacation," 1962; "I'm Gonna Be Warm This Winter," 1962; "Follow the Boys," 1963; "If My Pillow Could Talk," 1963; "Your Other Love," 1963; "Blue Winter," 1964; "Be Anything (But Be Mine)," 1964

Francis, Connie, RIAA Gold Album, "The Very Best of Connie Francis," 1969

Franklin, Aretha, "I Never Loved a Man (The Way I Love You)," 1967, RIAA 67; "Respect," 1967, RIAA 67; "Baby I Love You," 1967, RIAA 67; "A Natural Woman," 1967; "Chain of Fools," 1967, RIAA 68; "(Sweet, Sweet Baby) Since You've Been Gone," 1968, RIAA 68; "Ain't No Way," 1968; "Think," 1968, RIAA 68; "The House That Jack Built," 1968; "I Say a Little Prayer," 1968, RIAA 68; "See Saw," 1968, RIAA 68; "The Weight," 1969; "Share Your Love with Me," 1969; "Eleanor Rigby," 1969; "Call Me"/"Son of a Preacher Man," 1970; "Don't Play That Song," 1970; "You're All I Need to Get By," 1971; "Bridge Over Troubled Water"/"Brand New Me," 1971, RIAA 71; "Spanish Harlem," 1971, RIAA 71; "Rock Steady," 1971, RIAA 71; "Day Dreaming," 1972, RIAA 72; "Until You Come Back to Me," 1974, RIAA 74; "Something He Can Feel," 1976

Franklin, Aretha, RIAA Gold Albums, "I Never Loved a Man The Way I Love You," 1967; "Lady Soul," 1968; "Aretha Now," 1968; "Aretha Franklin at the Fillmore West," 1971; "Young, Gifted & Black," 1972; "Amazing Grace," 1972; "Sparkle," 1976

Freberg, Stan, "The Yellow Rose of Texas," 1955; "Heartbreak Hotel," 1956; "Banana Boat Song (Day-O)," 1957; "Wun'erful Wun'erful," 1957; "Green Christmas," 1959

Fred, John, & His Playboy Band, "Judy in Disguise," 1967, RIAA 68

Freddie & The Dreamers, "I'm Telling You Now," 1965; "You Were Made for Me," 1965; "Do the Freddie," 1965

Free, "All Right Now," 1970

Freeman, Bobby, "Do You Want to Dance," 1958; "Betty Lou Got a New Pair of Shoes," 1958; "C'mon and Swim," 1964

Freeman, Ernie, "Raunchy," 1957

Free Movement, "I've Found Someone of My Own," 1971

Friend & Lover, "Reach Out of the Darkness," 1968

Friends of Distinction, "Grazing in the Grass," 1969, RIAA 69; "Going in Circles," 1969, RIAA 69; "Love or Let Me Be Lonely," 1970

Frijid Pink, "House of the Rising Sun," 1970, RIAA 70

Frizzell, Lefty, "Saginaw, Michigan," 1964

Frogmen, "Underwater," 1961

Frost, Max, & The Troopers, "Shape of Things to Come," 1968

Fuller, Bobby, Four, "I Fought the Law," 1966; "Love's Made a Fool of You," 1966

Fuzz, "I Love You for All Seasons," 1971

Gallery, "Nice to Be with You," 1972, RIAA 72; "I Believe in Music," 1972; "Big City Miss Ruth Ann," 1972

Gallop, Frank, "Got a Match?" 1958; "The Ballad of Irving," 1966

Gardner, Dave, "White Silver Sands," 1957

Gardner, Don, & Dee Dee Ford, "I Need Your Loving," 1962

Garfunkel, Art (see Simon & Garfunkel), "All I Know," 1973; "Second Avenue," 1974; "I Only Have Eyes for You," 1975; "Breakaway," 1976

Garfunkel, Art, RIAA Gold Albums, "Angel Clare," 1973; "Breakaway," 1975

Gari, Frank, "Utopia," 1960; "Lullaby of Love," 1961; "Princess," 1961

Garland, Judy, RIAA Gold Album, "Judy at Carnegie Hall," 1962

Garnett, Gale, "We'll Sing in the Sunshine," 1964

Gaye, Marvin, "Stubborn Kind of Fellow," 1962; "Hitch Hike," 1963; "Pride and Joy," 1963; "Can I Get a Witness," 1963; "I'm Crazy About My Baby," 1963; "You're a Wonderful One," 1964; "Try It Baby," 1964; "How Sweet It Is (To Be Loved By You)," 1964; "I'll Be Doggone," 1965; "Ain't That Peculiar," 1965; "One More Heartache," 1966; "Take This Heart of Mine," 1966; "I Heard It Through the Grapevine," 1968; "Too Busy Thinking About My Baby," 1969; "That's the Way Love Is," 1969; "What's Going On," 1971; "Mercy, Mercy Me (The Ecology)," 1971; "Inner City Blues (Make Me Wanna Holler)," 1971; "Trouble Man," 1972; "Let's Get It On," 1973; "I Want You," 1976

Gaye, Marvin, & Diana Ross, "My Mistake," 1974

Gaye, Marvin, & Kim Weston, "It Takes Two," 1967

Gaye, Marvin, & Mary Wells, "What's the Matter with You Baby," 1964; "Once Upon a Time," 1964

Gaye, Marvin, & Tammi Terrell, "Ain't No Mountain High Enough," 1967;

208

"Your Precious Love," 1967; "If I Could Build My Whole World Around You," 1967; "Ain't Nothing Like the Real Thing," 1968; "You're All I Need to Get By," 1968; "Keep On Lovin' Me Honey," 1968; "Good Lovin' Ain't Easy to Come By," 1969;

Gaynor, Gloria, "Never Can Say Goodbye," 1975; "Reach Out, I'll Be There," (LP cut); "Honey Bee," (LP cut); "How High the Moon," 1976

G Clefs, "Ka-Ding Dong," 1953; "I Understand (Just How You Feel)," 1961

Geddes, David, "Run, Joey, Run," 1975; "Last Game of the Season," 1976

Geils, J., Band, "Looking for Love," 1971; "Give It to Me," 1973; "Must of Got Lost," 1974; "Where Did Our Love Go," 1976

Geils, J., Band, RIAA Gold Albums, "Bloodshot," 1973; "Live Full House," 1974

Gene & Debbie, "Playboy," 1968; "Lovin' Season," 1968

Gentry, Bobbie, "Ode to Billie Joe," 1967, RIAA 67; "Fancy," 1969

Gentry, Bobbie, RIAA Gold Album, "Ode to Billy Joe," 1967

Gentrys, "Keep on Dancing," 1965

George, Barbara, "I Know," 1961

Gerry & The Pacemakers, "Don't Let the Sun Catch You Crying," 1964; "How Do You Do It," 1964; "I Like It," 1964; "I'll Be There," 1964; "Ferry Across the Mersey," 1965; "It's Gonna Be Alright," 1965; "Girl on a Swing," 1966

Getz, Stan & Astrud Gilberto, "The Girl from Ipanema," 1964

Getz, Stan, & Astrud Gilberto, RIAA Gold Album, "Getz/Gilberto," 1965

Getz, Stan & Charlie Byrd, "Desafinado," 1962

Gibbs, Georgia, "Tweedle Dee," 1955; "Dance with Me Henry," 1955; "Kiss Me Another," 1956; "Hula Hoop Song," 1958

Gibson, Don, "Oh Lonesome Me"/"I Can't Stop Lovin' You," 1958; "Blue Blue Day," 1958; "Sea of Heartbreak," 1961

Gilkyson, Terry, & The Easy Riders, "Marianne," 1957

Gilmer, Jimmy, & The Fireballs, "Sugar Shack," 1963, RIAA 63; "Daisy Petal Pickin'," 1963

Gilreath, James, "Little Band of Gold," 1963

Giorgio, "Son of My Father," 1972

Gladiolas, "Little Darlin'," 1957

Glahe, Will, "Liechtensteiner Polka," 1957

Glass Bottle, "I Ain't Got Time Anymore," 1971

Glazer, Tom, & The Children's Chorus, "On Top of Spaghetti," 1963

Gleason, Jackie, RIAA Gold Albums, "Music, Martinis & Memories," 1962; "Music for Lovers Only," 1962

Glencoves, "Hootenanny," 1963

Glitter, Gary, "Rock & Roll, Part 2," 1972

Godspell, "Day By Day," 1972

Golden Earring, "Radar Love," 1974

Golden Earring, RIAA Gold Album, "Moontan," 1974

Goldsboro, Bobby, "See the Funny Little Clown," 1964; "Whenever He Holds You," 1964; "Little Things," 1965; "Voodoo Woman," 1965; "Broomstick Cowboy," 1965; "It's Too Late," 1966; "Honey," 1968, RIAA 68; "Autumn of My Life," 1968; "The Straight Life," 1969; "I'm a Drifter," 1969; "Muddy Mississippi Line," 1969; "Watching Scotty Grow," 1970

Goldsboro, Bobby, RIAA Gold Album, "Honey," 1968

Gone All Stars, "7-11," 1961

Goodman, Dickie, "The Touchables," 1961; "Mr. Jaws," 1975, RIAA 75

Gordon, Rosco, "Nuttin' for Christmas," 1955

Gore, Lesley, "It's My Party," 1963; "Judy's Turn to Cry," 1963; "She's a Fool," 1963; "You Don't Own Me," 1963; "That's the Way Boys Are," 1964; "Maybe I Know," 1964; "Sunshine, Lollipops & Rainbows," 1965; "California Nights," 1967

Gorme, Eydie, "Too Close for Comfort," 1956; "Blame It on the Bossa Nova," 1963; "Tonight I'll Say a Prayer," 1969

Goulet, Robert, "What Kind of Fool Am I," 1962; "My Love Forgive Me," 1964

Goulet, Robert, RIAA Gold Album, "My Love Forgive Me," 1968

Gracie, Charlie, "Butterfly," 1957; "Fabulous," 1957

Graham Central Station, RIAA Gold Album, "Ain't No 'Bout-A-Doubt It," 1975

Grammer, Billy, "Gotta Travel On," 1958

Granahan, Gerry, "No Chemise Please," 1958

Grand Funk (Railroad), "Time Machine," 1969; "Closer to Home," 1970; "Footstompin' Music," 1972; "Rock 'n' Roll Soul," 1972; "We're an American Band," 1973, RIAA 73; "The Loco-Motion," 1974, RIAA 74; "Some Kind of Wonderful," 1975; "Bad Time," 1975

Grand Funk (Railroad), RIAA Gold Albums, "Grand Funk," 1970; "Closer to Home," 1970; "On Time," 1970; "Live Album," 1970; "Survival," 1971; "E Pluribus Funk," 1971; "Mark, Don, & Mel," 1972; "Phoenix," 1972; "We're an American Band," 1973; "Shinin' On," 1974; "All the Girls in the World Beware!" 1974

Grant, Earl, "The End," 1958

Grant, Earl, RIAA Gold Album, "Ebb Tide," 1967

Grant, Gogi, "Suddenly There's A Valley," 1955; "The Wayward Wind," 1956

Grant, Janie, "Triangle," 1961

Grass Roots, "Where Were You When I Needed You," 1966; "Let's Live for

Today," 1967; "Things I Should Have Said," 1967; "Midnight Confessions," 1968, RIAA 68; "Bella Linda," 1968; "The River Is Wide," 1969; "I'd Wait a Million Years," 1969; "Heaven Knows," 1969; "Temptation Eyes," 1970; "Sooner or Later," 1971; "Two Divided By Love," 1971

Grass Roots, RIAA Gold Albums, "Golden Grass," 1970; "Their Sixteen Greatest Hits," 1972

Grateful Dead, "Truckin'," 1971

Grateful Dead, RIAA Gold Albums, "Grateful Dead," 1971; "Europe '72," 1972; "Workingman's Dead," 1974; "American Beauty," 1974

Gray, Dobie, "The 'In' Crowd," 1965; "Drift Away," 1973, RIAA 73

Grean, Charles Randolph, Sounde, "Quentin's Theme," 1969; "Theme from 'Star Trek'," 1976

Greaves, R. B., "Take a Letter Maria," 1969, RIAA 69; "Always Something There to Remind Me," 1970

Greco, Cyndi, "Making Our Dreams Come True," 1976

Green, Al, "Tired of Being Alone," 1971, RIAA 71; "Let's Stay Together," 1971, RIAA 72; "Look What You Done for Me," 1972, RIAA 72; "I'm Still in Love with You," 1972, RIAA 72; "You Ought to Be with Me," 1972, RIAA 72; "Call Me (Come Back Home)," 1973, RIAA 73; "Here I Am (Come Take Me)," 1973, RIAA 73; "Sha-La-La," 1974, RIAA 75; "Full of Fire," 1975

Green, Al, RIAA Gold Albums, "Let's Stay Together," 1972, "I'm Still in Love with You," 1972; "Call Me," 1973; "Livin' for You," 1974; "Al Green Explores Your Mind," 1975

Green, Garland, "Jealous Kind of Fella," 1969

Greenbaum, Norman, "Spirit in the Sky," 1970, RIAA 70

Greene, Jack, "There Goes My Everything," 1967

Greene, Lorne, "Ringo," 1964

Gregg, Bobby, & His Friends, "The Jam," 1962

Grin (see Todd Rundgren)

Groce, Larry, "Junk Food Junkie," 1976

Gross, Henry, "Shannon," 1976, RIAA 76; "Springtime Mama," 1976

Guaraldi, Vince, Trio, "Cast Your Fate to the Wind," 1962

Guess Who, "Shakin' All Over," 1965; "These Eyes," 1969, RIAA 69; "Laughing," 1969, RIAA 69; "Undun," 1969; "No Time," 1969; "American Woman"/"No Sugar Tonight," 1970, RIAA 70; "Hand Me Down World," 1970; "Share the Land," 1970; "Albert Flasher"/ "Broken," 1971; "Rain Dance," 1971; "Clap for the Wolfman," 1974

Guess Who, RIAA Gold Albums, "American Woman," 1970; "Share the Land," 1970; "The Best of the Guess Who," 1971

Guitar, Bonnie, "Dark Moon," 1957

Gunhill Road, "Back When My Hair Was Short," 1973

Gunne, Jo Jo, "Run, Run, Run," 1973

Guthrie, Arlo, "Alice's Restaurant," 1969; "The City of New Orleans," 1972

Guthrie, Arlo, RIAA Gold Albums, "Alice's Restaurant," 1969

Haggard, Merle, & The Strangers, "Okie from Muskogee," 1969

Haggard, Merle, & The Strangers, RIAA Gold Albums, "Okie from Muskogee," 1970; "The Fightin' Side of Me," 1971; "The Best of Merle
Haggard," 1972; "The Best of the Best of Merle Haggard," 1974

Haley, Bill & The Comets, "Shake, Rattle, & Roll," 1954-55; "Dim Dim the
Lights," 1955; "Rock Around the Clock," 1955; "Razzle Dazzle,"
1955; "Burn That Candle," 1955; "Rock-A-Beatin' Boogie," 1955;
"See You Later, Alligator," 1956; "R-O-C-K," 1956; "The Saints'
Rock 'n' Roll," 1956; "Rip It Up," 1956; "Rudy's Rock," 1956;
"Skinny Minnie," 1958

Hall, Daryl, & John Oates, "Sara Smile," 1976, RIAA 76; "She's Gone," 1976

Hall, Daryl, & John Oates, RIAA Gold Album, "Abandoned Luncheonette,"
1976

Hall, Larry, "Sandy," 1959

Hall, Tom T., "I Love," 1974

Halos, "Nag," 1961

Hamilton, George, IV, "A Rose & a Baby Ruth," 1956; "Why Don't They
Understand," 1957; "Abilene," 1963

Hamilton, Joe Frank & Dennison, "Light Up the World with Sunshine," 1976

Hamilton, Joe Frank & Reynolds, "Don't Pull Your Love," 1971, RIAA 71;
"Falling in Love," 1975, RIAA 75; "Winners & Losers," 1976

Hamilton, Roy, "Unchained Melody," 1955; "Without a Song," 1955; "Don't
Let Go," 1958; "Pledging My Love," 1958; "You Can Have Her,"
1961

Hamilton, Russ, "Rainbow," 1957

Hamlisch, Marvin, "The Entertainer (from *The Sting*)," 1974, RIAA 74

Hammond, Albert, "It Never Rains in Southern California," 1972, RIAA 73

Hancock, Herbie, RIAA Gold Albums, "Head Hunters," 1974

Happenings, "See You in September," 1966; "Go Away Little Girl," 1966;
"I Got Rhythm," 1967; "My Mammy," 1967

Hardin, Tim, "Misty Roses," 1967

Hardy, Hagood, "The Homecoming," 1976

Harnell, Joe, "Fly Me to the Moon Bossa Nova," 1962

212

Harpers Bizarre, "59th Street Bridge Song (Feelin' Groovy)," 1967; "Come to the Sunshine," 1967; "Anything Goes," 1967; "Chattanooga Choo Choo," 1967

Harpo, Slim, "Rainin' in My Heart," 1961; "Baby, Scratch My Back," 1966

Harris, Betty, "Cry to Me," 1963

Harris, Eddie, "Exodus," 1961

Harris, Major, "Love Won't Let Me Wait," 1975, RIAA 75

Harris, Richard, "MacArthur Park," 1968; "My Boy," 1971

Harris, Rolf, "Sun Arise," 1963; "Tie Me Kangaroo Down, Sport," 1963

Harris, Thurston, "Little Bitty Pretty One," 1957

Harrison, George, "My Sweet Lord"/"Isn't It a Pity," 1971, RIAA 71; "What Is Life," 1971; "Bangla-Desh"/"Deep Blue," 1971; "Give Me Love (Give Me Peace on Earth)," 1973; "You," 1975

Harrison, George, RIAA Gold Albums, "All Things Must Pass," 1970; "Living in the Material World," 1973; "Dark Horse," 1974; "Extra Texture," 1975

Harrison, George, & Friends, RIAA Gold Album, "The Concert for Bangla-Desh," 1972

Harrison, Noel, "A Young Girl," 1965; "Suzanne," 1967; "Windmills of Your Mind," 1968

Harrison, Wilbert, "Kansas City," 1959

Hart, Freddie, "Easy Loving," 1971, RIAA 71

Hart, Freddie, RIAA Gold Album, "Easy Loving," 1972

Hartford, John, "Gentle on My Mind," 1967

Hathaway, Donny, RIAA Gold Album, "Donny Hathaway Live," 1972

Havens, Ritchie, "Here Comes the Sun," 1971

Hawkin, Dale, "Susie-Q," 1957; "La-Do-Dada," 1958

Hawkins, Ronnie, "Forty Days," 1959; "Mary Lou," 1959

Hawkins, Screamin' Jay, "I Put a Spell on You," 1957

Hawkins', Edwin, Singers, "Oh Happy Day," 1969, RIAA 69

Hawley, Deane, "Look for a Star," 1960

Hayes, Bill, "Ballad of Davy Crockett," 1957

Hayes, Isaac, "Never Can Say Goodbye," 1971; "Theme from *Shaft*," 1971

Hayes, Isaac, RIAA Gold Albums, "Hot Buttered Soul," 1969; "Live at the Sahara Tahoe," 1973; "Joy," 1973; "Chocolate Chip," 1975

Hayman, Richard, & Jan August, "A Theme from *The Three Penny Opera*," 1956

Head, Murray, with the Trinidad Singers, "Superstar," 1971

Head, Roy, "Treat Her Right," 1965

Heart, "Crazy on You," 1976; "Magic Man," 1976

Heart, RIAA Gold Album, "Dreamboat Annie," 1976

Heartbeats, "A Thousand Miles Away," 1956

Heatherton, Joey, "Gone," 1972

Hebb, Bobby, "Sunny," 1966, RIAA 66; "Sunny '76," 1976

Hedgehoppers Anonymous, "It's Good News Week," 1965

Helms, Bobby, "Fraulein," 1957; "Jingle Bell Rock," 1957

Henderson, Joe, "Snap Your Fingers," 1962

Hendricks, Bobby, "Itchy Twitchy Feeling," 1958

Hendrix, Jimi, "Purple Haze," 1967; "Foxey Lady," 1967; "All Along the Watchtower," 1968

Hendrix, Jimi, RIAA Gold Albums, "Are You Experienced," 1968; "Axis: Bold As Love," 1968; "Electric Ladyland," 1968; "Jimi Hendrix Smash Hits," 1969; "Band of Gypsys," 1970; "The Cry of Love," 1971; "Rainbow Bridge," 1971; "Hendrix in the West," 1972

Henry, Clarence ("Frog Man"), "Ain't Got No Home," 1956; "I Don't Know Why (But I Do)," 1961; "You Always Hurt the One You Love," 1961

Herman's Hermits, "I'm Into Something Good," 1964; "Can't You Hear My Heartbeat," 1965; "Silhouettes," 1965; "Mrs. Brown You've Got a Lovely Daughter," 1965, RIAA 65; "Wonderful World," 1965; "I'm Henry VIII, I Am," 1965, RIAA 65; "Just a Little Bit Better," 1965; "A Must to Avoid," 1965; "Listen People," 1966; "Leaning on the Lamp Post," 1966; "This Door Swings Both Ways," 1966; "Dandy," 1966; "There's a Kind of Hush," 1967; "Don't Go Out Into the Rain (You're Going to Melt)," 1967

Herman's Hermits, RIAA Gold Albums, "Introducing Herman's Hermits," 1965; "Herman's Hermits on Tour," 1965; "The Best of Herman's Hermits," 1966; "The Best of Herman's Hermits, Vol. 2," 1969; "There's Kind of a Hush All Over the World," 1969

Heywood, Eddie, "Soft Summer Breeze," 1956

Heywood, Leon, "I Wanna Do Something Freaky to You," 1975

Hibbler, Al, "Unchained Melody," 1955; "He," 1955; "After the Lights Go Down Low," 1956

Hickey, Ersel, "Bluebirds Over the Mountain," 1958

Highlights, "City of Angels," 1956

Highwaymen, "Michael," 1961; "Cotton Fields," 1961

Hill, Jessie, "Ooh Poo Pah Doo, Part II," 1960

Hillside Singers, "I'd Like to Teach the World to Sing (In Perfect Harmony)," 1971

Hilltoppers, "Only You," 1955; "Marianne," 1957

Hinton, Joe, "Funny," 1964

Hirt, Al, "Java," 1964; "Cotton Candy," 1964; "Sugar Lips," 1964

214

Hirt, Al, RIAA Gold Albums, "Honey in the Horn," 1964; "Cotton Candy," 1964; "Sugar Lips," 1965; "The Best of Al Hirt," 1966

Ho, Don, "Tiny Bubbles," 1966

Hodges, Eddie, "I'm Gonna Knock on Your Door," 1961; "(Girls, Girls, Girls) Made to Love," 1962

Holden, Ron, "Love You So," 1960

Holland, Eddie, "Jamie," 1962

Hollies, "Just One Look," 1964; "Look Through Any Window," 1965; "Bus Stop," 1966; "Stop Stop Stop," 1966; "On a Carousel," 1967; "Pay You Back with Interest," 1967; "Carrie-Anne," 1967; "He Ain't Heavy, He's My Brother," 1969; "Long Cool Woman (In a Black Dress)," 1972, RIAA 72; "Long Dark Road," 1972; "The Air That I Breathe," 1974, RIAA 74

Holloway, Brenda, "Every Little Bit Hurts," 1964; "When I'm Gone," 1965

Holly, Buddy (see The Crickets), "Peggy Sue," 1957; "Rave On," 1958; "Early in the Morning," 1958; "Heartbeat," 1959; "It Doesn't Matter Anymore"/"Raining in My Heart," 1959

Holly, Buddy, & The Crickets, RIAA Gold Album, "The Buddy Holly Story," 1969

Hollywood Argyles, "Alley-Oop," 1960

Hollywood Flames (see Bobby Day), "Buzz-Buzz-Buzz," 1957

Holman, Eddie, "Hey There, Lonely Girl," 1969, RIAA 70

Holmes, Clint, "Playground of My Mind," 1973, RIAA 73

Holmes, Jake, "So Close," 1970

Hombres, "Let It Out (Let It All Hang Out)," 1967

Homer & Jethro, "The Battle of Kookamonga," 1959

Hondells, "Little Honda," 1964

Honeycombs, "Have I the Right," 1964

Honey Cone, "Want Ads," 1971, RIAA 71; "Stick-Up," 1971, RIAA 71; "One Monkey Don't Stop No Show," 1971

Hooker, John Lee, "Boom Boom," 1962

Hopkin, Mary, "Those Were the Days," 1968, RIAA 68; "Goodbye," 1969

Horton, Johnny, "The Battle of New Orleans"/"All for the Love of a Girl," 1966, RIAA 66; "Sink the Bismarck," 1960; "North to Alaska," 1960

Horton, Johnny, RIAA Gold Album, "Johnny Horton's Greatest Hits," 1964

Hot Butter, "Popcorn," 1972

Hot Chocolate, "Emma," 1975; "Disco Queen," 1975; "You Sexy Thing," 1976, RIAA 76; "Don't Stop It Now," 1976

Hotlegs, "Neanderthal Man," 1970

Houston, David, "Almost Persuaded," 1966

Hudson Brothers, "So You Are a Star," 1974

Hues Corporation, "Rock the Boat," 1974, RIAA 74; "Rockin' Soul," 1975

Hudson and Landry, "Ajax Liquor Store," 1971

Hughes, Fred, "Oo Wee Baby, I Love You," 1965

Hughes, Jimmy, "Steal Away," 1964; "Neighbor, Neighbor," 1966

Human Beinz, "Nobody But Me," 1967

Humble Pie, RIAA Gold Albums, "Rockin' the Fillmore," 1972; "Smokin'," 1972

Humperdinck, Engelbert, "Release Me," 1967; "There Goes My Everything," 1967; "The Last Waltz," 1967; "Am I That Easy to Forget," 1967; "A Man Without Love," 1968; "Les Bicyclettes De Belsize," 1968; "Winter World of Love," 1969

Humperdinck, Engelbert, RIAA Gold Albums, "Release Me," 1967; "A Man Without Love," 1969; "The Last Waltz," 1969; "Engelbert," 1970; "Engelbert Humperdinck," 1970; "We Made It Happen," 1970; "Sweetheart," 1971

Humphrey, Paul, & His Cool Aid Chemists, "Cool Aid," 1971

Hunt, Tommy, "Human," 1961

Hunter, Ivory Joe, "I Almost Lost My Mind," 1955; "Since I Met You Baby," 1956; "Empty Arms," 1957

Hunter, Tab, "Young Love," 1957; "Red Sails in the Sunset," 1957; "Ninety-Nine Ways," 1957

Husky, Ferlin, "Gone," 1957; "Wings of a Dove," 1960

Hyland, Brian, "Itsy Bitsy Teenie Weenie Yellow Polka Dot Bikini," 1960; "Ginny Come Lately," 1962; "Sealed with a Kiss," 1962; "The Joker Went Wild," 1966; "Gypsy Woman," 1971, RIAA 71

Hyman, Dick, Trio, "Moritat (Theme from *The Three Penny Opera*)," 1956

Ian, Janis, "Society's Child," 1967; "At Seventeen," 1975

Ian, Janis, RIAA Gold Album, "Between the Lines," 1975

Ides of March, "Vehicle," 1970

Ifield, Frank, "I Remember You," 1962

Ikettes, "I'm Blue," 1962

Impalas, "Sorry (I Ran All the Way Home)," 1959

Impressions, "For Your Precious Love" (with Jerry Butler), 1958; "Gypsy Woman," 1961; "It's All Right," 1963; "Talking About My Baby," 1964; "I'm So Proud," 1964; "Keep on Pushing," 1964; "You Must Believe Me," 1964; "Amen," 1964; "People Get Ready," 1965;

"Woman's Got Soul," 1965; "We're a Winner," 1967; "Fool for You," 1968; "This Is My Country," 1968; "Choice of Colors," 1969

Independents, "Leaving Me," 1973, RIAA 73

Ingmann, Jorgen, "Apache," 1961

Ingram, Luther, "(If Loving You Is Wrong) I Don't Want to Be Right," 1972

Innocents, "Honest I Do," 1960; "Gee Whiz," 1960

Intruders, "Cowboys to Girls," 1968, RIAA 68; "(Love Is like a) Baseball Game," 1968

Irish Rovers, "The Unicorn," 1968; "Whiskey on a Sunday," 1968

Iron Butterfly, "In-A-Gadda-Da-Vida," 1968; "Soul Experience," 1969

Iron Butterfly, RIAA Gold Albums, "In-A-Gadda-Da-Vida," 1968; "Ball," 1969

Irwin, Big Dee, "Swinging on a Star," 1963

Islanders, "The Enchanted Sea," 1959

Isley Brothers, "Shout," 1959; "Shout," 1962; "Twist & Shout," 1962; "This Old Heart of Mine (Is Weak for You)," 1966; "It's Your Thing," 1969, RIAA 69; "I Turned You On," 1969; "Love the One You're With," 1971; "Pop That Thing," 1972; "That Lady," 1973, RIAA 73; "Fight the Power," 1975, RIAA 75; "Who Loves You Better," 1976; "Harvest for the World," 1976

Isley Brothers, RIAA Gold Albums, "3 + 3," 1973; "Live It Up," 1974; "The Heat Is On," 1975; "Harvest for the World," 1976

It's a Beautiful Day, RIAA Gold Album, "It's a Beautiful Day," 1972

Ives, Burl, "A Little Bitty Tear," 1961; "Funny Way of Laughin'," 1962; "Call Me Mr. In-Between," 1962

Ivy Three, "Yogi," 1960

Jacks, Terry, "Seasons in the Sun," 1974, RIAA 74

Jackson, Chuck, "I Don't Want To Cry," 1961; "Any Day Now," 1962

Jackson, Deon, "Love Makes the World Go 'Round," 1966

Jackson, Jermaine, "Daddy's Home," 1972

Jackson, J. J. "But It's Alright," 1966

Jackson, Michael, "Got to Be There," 1971; "Rockin' Robin," 1972; "I Wanna Be Where You Are," 1972; "Ben," 1972; "Just a Little Bit of You," 1975

Jackson, Millie, "Ask Me What You Want," 1972

Jackson, Millie, RIAA Gold Album, "Caught Up," 1975

Jackson, Stonewall, "Waterloo," 1959

Jackson, Wanda, "Let's Have a Party," 1960; "Right or Wrong," 1961; "In the Middle of a Heartache," 1961

Jackson 5, "I Want You Back," 1969; "ABC," 1970; "The Love You Save"/ "I Found That Girl," 1970; "I'll Be There," 1970; "Mama's Pearl," 1971; "Never Can Say Goodbye," 1971; "Maybe Tomorrow," 1971; "Sugar Daddy," 1971; "Little Bitty Pretty One," 1972; "Lookin' Through the Windows," 1972; "Corner of the Sky," 1972; "Dancing Machine," 1974; "Forever Came Today," 1975

Jacobs, Dick, "Main Title & Molly-O," 1956; "Petticoats of Portugal," 1956

Jaggerz, "The Rapper," 1970, RIAA 70

James, Etta, "The Wallflower (Dance With Me, Henry)," 1955; "Trust In Me," 1961; "Something's Got a Hold on Me," 1962; "Pushover," 1963; "Tell Mama," 1967

James Gang, "Walk Away," 1970; "It Must Be Love," 1974

James Gang, RIAA Gold Albums, "James Gang Rides Again," 1971; "Live in Concert," 1972; "Thirds," 1972

James, Joni, "How Important Can It Be," 1955; "My Believing Heart," 1955; "You Are My Love," 1955; "There Goes My Heart," 1958; "Little Things Mean a Lot," 1960

James, Sonny, "Young Love," 1956; "First Date, First Kiss, First Love," 1957; "Only the Lonely," 1969; "Empty Arms," 1971

James, Tommy, "Draggin' the Line," 1971

James, Tommy & The Shondells, "Hanky Panky," 1966, RIAA 66; "Say I Am (What I Am)," 1966; "I Think We're Alone Now," 1967; "Mirage," 1967; "Mony, Mony," 1968; "Crimson & Clover," 1968; "Sweet Cherry Wine," 1969; "Crystal Blue Persuasion," 1969; "Ball of Fire," 1969

Jamies, "Summertime, Summertime," 1958; "Summertime, Summertime," 1962

Jan & Arnie, "Jennie Lee," 1958

Jan & Dean, "Baby Talk," 1959; "Heart of Soul," 1961; "Surf City," 1963; "Honolulu Lulu," 1963; "Drag City," 1963; "Dead Man's Curve," 1964; "The Little Old Lady (From Pasadena)," 1964; "Ride the Wild Surf," 1964; "Popsicle," 1966

Jankowski, Horst, "A Walk in the Black Forest," 1961

Jarmels, "Little Bit of Soap," 1961

Jay & The Americans, "She Cried," 1962; "Only in America," 1963; "Come a Little Bit Closer," 1964; "Let's Lock the Door (And Throw Away the Key)," 1964; "Cara Mia," 1965; "Some Enchanted Evening," 1965; "Sunday & Me," 1965; "This Magic Moment," 1969, RIAA 69; "Walkin' in the Rain," 1969

Jay & The Techniques, "Apples, Peaches, Pumpkin Pie," 1967; "Keep The Ball Rollin'," 1967

Jaye, Jerry, "My Girl Josephine," 1967

Jayhawks, "Stranded in the Jungle," 1956

Jaynettes, "Sally, Go 'Round the Roses," 1963

Jefferson, "Baby Take Me in Your Arms," 1969

Jefferson Airplane, "Somebody to Love," 1967; "White Rabbit," 1967

Jefferson Airplane, RIAA Gold Albums, "Surrealistic Pillow," 1967; "Volunteers," 1970; "Crown of Creation," 1970; "The Worst of Jefferson Airplane," 1971; "Bark," 1971; "Long John Silver," 1973

Jefferson Starship, "Miracles," 1975; "With Your Love," 1976

Jefferson Starship, RIAA Gold Albums, "Dragon Fly," 1975; "Red Octopus," 1975; "Spitfire," 1976

Jefferson Starship, RIAA Platinum Album, "Spitfire," 1976

Jeffrey, Joe, Group, "My Pledge of Love," 1969

Jelly Beans, "I Wanna Love Him So Bad," 1964

Jennings, Waylon, & Willie Nelson & Jessie Colter & Tompall Glaser, RIAA Gold Album, "The Outlaws," 1976

Jensen, Kris, "Torture," 1962

Jethro Tull, "Living in the Past," 1972; "Bungle in the Jungle," 1974

Jethro Tull, RIAA Gold Albums, "Benefit," 1970; "Aqua-Lung," 1971; "Thick as a Brick," 1972; "Stand Up," 1972; "Living in the Past," 1972; "A Passion Play," 1973; "War Child," 1974; "Minstrel in the Gallery," 1975; "M. U., The Best of Jethro Tull," 1976

Jigsaw, "Sky High," 1975

Jimenez, Jose, "The Astronaut," 1961

Jive Bombers, "Bad Boy," 1957

Jive Five, "My True Story," 1961; "What Time Is It?" 1962; "I'm a Happy Man," 1965

Jo, Damita, "I'll Save the Last Dance for You," 1960; "I'll Be There," 1961; "If You Go Away," 1966

Joel, Billy, "Piano Man," 1974

Joel, Billy, RIAA Gold Album, "Piano Man," 1975

John, Dr., "Right Place, Wrong Time," 1973; "Such a Night," 1973

John, Elton, "Your Song," 1970; "Friends," 1971; "Levon," 1971; "Rocket Man," 1972; "Crocodile Rock," 1972, RIAA 73; "Daniel," 1973; "Goodbye Yellow Brick Road," 1974, RIAA 74; "Saturday Night Is a Good Night for Fighting," 1974; "Bennie & the Jets," 1974, RIAA 74; "The Bitch Is Back," 1974; "Don't Let the Sun Go Down on Me," 1974, RIAA 74; "Someone Saved My Life Tonight," 1975, RIAA 75; "Lucy in the Sky with Diamonds," 1975, RIAA 75; "Pinball Wizard," 1975; "Philadelphia Freedom," 1975, RIAA 75; "Island Girl," 1975, RIAA 75; "Grow Some Funk of Your Own"/"I Feel Like a Bullet," 1976

John, Elton, RIAA Gold Albums, "Elton John," 1971; "Tumbleweed Connection," 1971; "Friends," 1971; "Madman Across the Water," 1972; "Honky Chateau," 1972; "Don't Shoot Me, I'm Only the Piano Player," 1973; "Goodbye Yellow Brick Road," 1973; "Caribou," 1974; "Greatest Hits," 1974; "Captain Fantastic & the Brown Dirt Cowboy," 1975; "Rock of the Westies," 1975; "Here & There," 1976

John, Elton, & Kiki Dee, "Don't Go Breaking My Heart," 1976, RIAA 76

John, Little Willie, "Fever," 1956; "Talk to Me," 1958; "Sleep," 1960

John, Robert, "If You Don't Want My Love," 1968; "The Lion Sleeps Tonight," 1972, RIAA 72

Johnnie & Joe, "Over the Mountain, Across the Sea," 1957

Johnny & The Hurricanes, "Crossfire," 1959; "Red River Rock," 1959; "Reveille Rock," 1959; "Beatnik Rock," 1960; "Down Yonder," 1960

Johns, Sammy, "Chevy Van," 1975, RIAA 75; "Peas in a Pod," 1976

Johnson, Betty, "I Dreamed," 1956; "The Little Blue Man," 1958; "Dream," 1958

Johnson, Marv, "Come to Me," 1959; "You Got What It Takes," 1959; "I Love the Way You Love," 1960; "Move Two Mountains," 1960

Joiner, Arkansas Jr. High School Band, "National City," 1960

Jon & Robin & The In Crowd, "Do It Again a Little Bit Slower," 1967

Jones, George, "White Lightning," 1959

Jones, Jack, "Lollipops & Roses," 1962; "Wives & Lovers," 1963; "Dear Heart," 1964; "The Race Is On," 1965; "The Impossible Dream," 1966

Jones, Jimmy, "Handy Man," 1960; "Good Timin'," 1960

Jones, Joe, "You Talk Too Much," 1960

Jones, Linda, "Hypnotized," 1967

Jones, Quincy, RIAA Gold Album, "Body Heat," 1974

Jones, Tom, "It's Not Unusual," 1965; "What's New Pussycat," 1965; "Thunderball," 1965; "Green, Green Grass of Home," 1966; "Detroit City," 1967; "Delilah," 1968; "Help Yourself," 1968; "Love Me Tonight," 1969; "I'll Never Fall in Love Again," 1969, RIAA 69; "Without Love (There Is Nothing)," 1969, RIAA 70; "Daughter of Darkness," 1970; "I (Who Have Nothing)," 1970; "I Can't Stop Loving You," 1970; "She's a Lady," 1971, RIAA 71; "Puppet Man"/ "Resurrection Shuffle," 1972

Jones, Tom, RIAA Gold Albums, "Fever Zone," 1969; "Help Yourself,"

1969; "This Is Tom Jones," 1969; "Tom Jones Live!" 1969; "Tom Jones Live at Las Vegas," 1969; "Green Green Grass," 1969; "Tom," 1970; "I (Who Have Nothing)," 1971; "She's a Lady," 1972; "Tom Jones Live at Caesar's Palace," 1972

Joplin, Janis (see Big Brother & Holding Company), "Kozmic Blues," 1969; "Me & Bobby McGee," 1971; "Cry Baby," 1971; "Down On Me," 1972

Joplin, Janis, RIAA Gold Albums, "Cheap Thrills" (with Big Brother & The Holding Company), 1968; "Kozmic Blues," 1969; "Pearl," 1971; "Joplin in Concert," 1972; "Janis Joplin's Greatest Hits," 1975

Jr. Walker & The All-Stars, "How Sweet It Is," 1965; "Shotgun," 1965; "Pucker Up Buttercup," 1966; "What Does It Take to Win Your Love," 1969

Justis, Bill, "Raunchy," 1957

Just Us, "I Can't Grow Peaches on a Cherry Tree," 1966

Kaempfert, Bert, "Wonderland by Night," 1960; "Red Roses for a Blue Lady," 1965; "Three O'Clock in the Morning," 1965

Kaempfert, Bert, RIAA Gold Albums, "Blue Midnight," 1967; "Wonderland By Night," 1969; "Bert Kaempfert's Greatest Hits," 1969

Kalin Twins, "When," 1958; "Forget Me Not," 1958

Kallen, Kitty, "Go on with the Wedding," 1955; "If I Give My Heart to You," 1959; "My Coloring Book," 1962

Kasenetz-Katz Singing Orchestral Circus, "Quick Joey Small (Run, Joey, Run)," 1968

Kay, John, "I'm Movin' On," 1972

Kaye, Sammy, "Charade," 1964

Kayli, Bob, "Everyone Was There," 1958

K.C. & The Sunshine Band, "Get Down Tonight," 1975; "That's the Way I Like It," 1975; "Shake Your Booty," 1976

K-Doe, Ernie, "Mother-In-Law," 1961

Keith, "Ain't Gonna Lie," 1966; "98.6," 1966

Keller, Jerry, "Here Comes Summer," 1959

Kellum, Murry, "Long Tall Texan," 1963

Kelly, Monty, "Summer Set," 1960

Kendricks, Eddie, "Keep on Truckin'," 1973; "Boogie Down," 1974; "Shoe-shine Boy," 1975

Kennedy, John Fitzgerald, RIAA Gold Album, "John Fitzgerald Kennedy Memorial Album," 1964

Kenner, Chris, "I Like It Like That," 1961; "Land of 1000 Dances," 1963

Kenton, Stan, "Mama Sang a Song," 1962

Kiki Dee Band, "I've Got the Music in Me," 1975

Kilgore, Theola, "The Love of My Man," 1963

Kim, Andy, "How'd We Ever Get This Way," 1968; "Shoot'em Up, Baby," 1968; "Rainbow Ride," 1968; "Baby, I Love You," 1969, RIAA 69; "So Good Together," 1969; "Be My Baby," 1970; "Rock Me Gently," 1974, RIAA 74*

Kimberly, Adrian, "Pomp and Circumstance," 1961

King, B. B., "Every Day I Have The Blues," 1955; "Rock Me Baby," 1964; "Paying the Cost to Be the Boss," 1968; "Why I Sing the Blues," 1969; "The Thrill Is Gone," 1969

King, Ben E., "Spanish Harlem," 1961; "Stand By Me," 1961; "Don't Play That Song," 1962; "I (Who Have Nothing)," 1963; "Supernatural Thing," 1975

King, Carole, "It Might as Well Rain until September," 1962; "It's Too Late"/ "I Feel the Earth Move," 1971, RIAA 71; "So Far Away"/"Smackwater Jack," 1971; "Sweet Seasons," 1972; "Been to Canaan," 1972; "You've Got a Friend," 1973; "You Light Up My Life," 1973; "Corazon," 1973; "Nightingale," 1974; "Jazzman," 1975; "Only Love Is Real," 1976

King, Carole, RIAA Gold Albums, "Tapestry," 1971; "Carole King Music," 1971; "Rhymes and Reasons," 1972; "Fantasy," 1973; "Wrap Around Joy," 1974; "Thoroughbred," 1976

King, Claude, "Wolverton Mountain," 1962

King Curtis, "Soul Twist," 1962; "Memphis Soul Stew," 1967

King, Freddy, "Hide Away," 1961

King Harvest, "Dancing in the Moonlight," 1972

King, Jonathan, "Everyone's Gone to Moon," 1965

King Pins, "Ode to Billy Joe," 1967

Kingsmen, "Louie, Louie," 1963; "Money," 1964; "The Jolly Green Giant," 1965

Kingston Trio, "Tom Dooley," 1959, RIAA 59; "Tijuana Jail," 1959; "MTA," 1959; "A Worried Man," 1959; "Where Have all the Flowers Gone," 1962; "Scotch & Soda," 1962; "Greenback Dollar," 1963; "Reverend Mr. Black," 1963; "Desert Pete," 1963

Kingston Trio, RIAA Gold Albums, "Kingston Trio at Large," 1960; "Kingston Trio," 1960; "Here We Go Again," 1960; "From the Hungry i," 1960; "Sold Out," 1961; "String Along," 1962; "The Best of the Kingston Trio," 1964

Kramer, Billy J., "Little Children," 1964; "Bad to Me," 1964; "I'll Keep You Satisfied," 1964; "From a Window," 1964; "Trains and Boats and Planes," 1965

Kristofferson, Kris, "Loving Her Was Easier (Than Anything I'll Ever Do Again)," 1971; "Why Me," 1973, RIAA 73

Kristofferson, Kris, RIAA Gold Albums, "The Silver-Tongued Devil and I," 1972; "Jesus Was a Capricorn," 1973; "Me and Bobby McGee," 1974

Kristofferson, Kris, and Rita Coolidge, RIAA Gold Album, "Kris & Rita, Full Moon," 1975

Kuban, Bob, and The In-Men, "The Cheater," 1966

Kuf-Linx, "So Tough," 1958

LaBelle, "Lady Marmalade," 1975, RIAA 75

LaBelle, RIAA Gold Album, "Nightbirds," 1975

LaBelle, Patti, and The Blue Belles, "I Sold My Heart to the Junkman," 1962; "Down the Aisle," 1963; "You'll Never Walk Alone," 1964

Lady Flash, "Street Singing," 1976

Lai, Francis, "Theme from *Love Story*," 1971

Laine, Frankie, "A Woman in Love," 1955; "Moonlight Gambler," 1956; "Love Is a Golden Ring," 1957; "Making Memories," 1967; "Laura, What's He Got That I Ain't Got," 1967; "You Gave Me a Mountain," 1969

Lance, Major, "The Monkey Time," 1963; "Hey Little Girl," 1963; "Um, Um, Um, Um, Um, Um," 1964; "The Matador," 1964; "Rhythm," 1964

Lanson, Snooky, "It's Almost Tomorrow," 1955

Lanza, Mario, RIAA Gold Albums, "The Student Prince," 1960; "The Great Caruso," 1968

Larks, "The Jerk," 1964

LaRosa, Julius, "Domani," 1955; "Suddenly There's a Valley," 1955; "Lipstick and Candy and Rubber Sole Shoes," 1956

LaSalle, Denise, "Trapped By a Thing Called Love," 1971, RIAA 71

Laurie, Linda, "Ambrose, Part 5," 1959

Lawrence, Eddie, "The Old Philosopher," 1956

Lawrence, Steve, "Party Doll," 1957; "Fraulein," 1957; "Pretty Blue Eyes," 1959; "Footsteps," 1960; "Portrait of My Love," 1961; "Go Away Little Girl," 1962; "Don't Be Afraid, Little Darlin'," 1963; "Poor Little Rich Girl," 1963; "Walking Proud," 1963

Lawrence, Vicki, "The Night the Lights Went Out in Georgia," 1973, RIAA 73

Leaves, "Hey Joe," 1966

Led Zeppelin, "Whole Lotta Love," 1969, RIAA 70; "Stairway to Heaven," LP Cut; "Immigrant Song," 1970; "Black Dog," 1971; "Rock and Roll," 1972

Led Zeppelin, RIAA Gold Albums, "Led Zeppelin," 1969; "Led Zeppelin II," 1970; "Led Zeppelin III," 1971; "House of the Holy," 1973; "Physical Graffiti," 1975; "Presence," 1976

Led Zeppelin, RIAA Platinum Album, "Presence," 1976

Lee, Brenda, "One Step at a Time," 1957; "Dynamite," 1957; "Sweet Nuthin's," 1959; "I'm Sorry"/"That's All You Gotta Do," 1960; "I Want to Be Wanted"/"Just a Little," 1960; "Rockin' Around the Christmas Tree," 1960; "Emotions," 1961; "You Can Depend on Me," 1961; "Dum Dum," 1961; "Fool Number One," 1961; "Break It to Me Gently," 1962; "Everybody Loves Me But You," 1962; "Heart in Hand," 1962; "All Alone Am I," 1962; "Losing You," 1963; "My Whole World Is Falling Down"/"I Wonder," 1963; "The Grass Is Greener," 1963; "As Usual," 1963; "Think," 1964; "Is It True," 1964; "Too Many Rivers," 1965; "Coming on Strong," 1966

Lee, Curtis, "Pretty Little Angel Eyes," 1961

Lee, Dickie, "Patches," 1962; "I Saw Linda Yesterday," 1962; "Laurie (Strange Things Happen)," 1965

Lee, Jackie, "The Duck," 1965

Lee, Leapy, "Little Arrows," 1968

Lee, Michele, "L. David Sloane," 1968

Lee, Peggy, "Mr. Wonderful," 1956; "Fever," 1958; "Hallelujah, I Love Him So," 1959; "Is That All There Is," 1969

LeFevre, Raymond, "The Day the Rains Came," 1958; "Ame Caline (Soul Coaxing)," 1968

Left Banke, "Walk Away Renee," 1966; "Pretty Ballerina," 1967

LeGrand, Michel, "Brian's Song," 1972

Lemon Pipers, "Green Tambourine," 1967, RIAA 68

Lennon, John, "Give Peace A Chance" with Plastic Ono Band, 1969; "Cold Turkey" with Plastic Ono Band, 1969; "Instant Karma (We All Shine On)" with Yoko Ono, 1970, RIAA 70; "Power to the People," with Plastic Ono Band, 1971; "Imagine" with Plastic Ono Band, 1971; "Whatever Gets You Through the Night," 1974; "Stand By Me," 1975; "Number Nine Dream," 1975

Lennon, John, RIAA Gold Albums, "The Plastic Ono Band Live Peace in Toronto," 1970; "Plastic Ono Band," 1971; "Imagine," 1971; "Mind Games," 1973; "Walls and Bridges," 1974

Lennon Sisters with Lawrence Welk, "Tonight You Belong to Me," 1956

Lester, Ketty, "Love Letters," 1962

Lettermen, "The Way You Look Tonight," 1961; "When I Fall in Love," 1961; "Come Back Silly Girl," 1962; "Theme from *A Summer Place*," 1965; "I Only Have Eyes for You," 1966; "Going Out of My Head"/"Can't Take My Eyes Off You," 1967; "Hurt So Bad," 1969

Lettermen, RIAA Gold Albums, "The Lettermen! And Live!" 1969; "Best of the Lettermen," 1969; "Goin' Out of My Head," 1970; "Hurt So Bad," 1970

Lewis, Barbara, "Hello Stranger," 1963; "Puppy Love," 1964; "Baby, I'm Yours," 1965; "Make Me Your Baby," 1965; "Make Me Belong to You," 1966

Lewis, Bobby, "Tossin' and Turnin'," 1961; "One Track Mind," 1961

Lewis, Gary, and The Playboys, "This Diamond Ring," 1965, RIAA 67; "Count Me In," 1965; "Save Your Heart for Me," 1965; "Everybody Loves a Clown," 1965; "She's Just My Style," 1965; "Sure Gonna Miss Her," 1966; "Green Grass," 1966; "My Heart's Symphony," 1966; "Paint Me a Picture," 1966; "Where Will the Words Come From," 1966; "Sealed with Kiss," 1968

Lewis, Gary, and The Playboys, RIAA Gold Album, "Golden Greats," 1969

Lewis, Jerry, "Rock-A-Bye Your Baby with a Dixie Melody," 1956

Lewis, Jerry Lee, "Whole Lotta Shakin' Going On," 1957; "Great Balls of Fire," 1957; "Breathless," 1958; "High School Confidential," 1958; "What'd I Say," 1961; "Me and Bobby McGee," 1971; "Chantilly Lace," 1972

Lewis, Ramsey, "The 'In' Crowd," 1965; "Hang on Sloopy," 1965; "Wade in the Water," 1966

Lewis, Ramsey, RIAA Gold Album, "Sun Goddess," 1975

Lewis, Smiley, "I Hear You Knockin'," 1955

Light, Enoch, RIAA Gold Album, "Persuasive Percussion," 1968

Lightfoot, Gordon, "If You Could Read My Mind," 1970; "Sundown," 1974, RIAA 74; "Carefree Highway," 1974; "Rainy Day People," 1975; "The Wreck of the Edmund Fitzgerald," 1976

Lightfoot, Gordon, RIAA Gold Albums, "If You Could Read My Mind," 1971; "Sundown," 1974

Lighthouse, "One Fine Morning," 1971

Lind, Bob, "Elusive Butterfly," 1966

Linden, Kathy, "Billy," 1958; "Goodbye, Jimmy, Goodbye," 1959

Lindsay, Mark (see Paul Revere and The Raiders), "Arizona," 1969, RIAA 70; "Silver Bird," 1970; "And the Grass Won't Pay No Mind," 1970

Little Anthony and The Imperials, "Tears on My Pillow," 1958; "Shimmy Shimmy Ko-Ko-Bop," 1959; "I'm on the Outside (Looking In)," 1964; "Goin' Out of My Head," 1964; "Hurt So Bad," 1965; "Take

Me Back," 1965; "I Miss You So," 1965; "Out of Sight, Out of Mind," 1969

Little Caesar and The Romans, "Those Oldies but Goodies (Remind Me of You)," 1961

Little Dippers, "Forever," 1960

Little Eva, "Loco-Motion," 1962; "Keep Your Hands Off My Baby," 1962; "Let's Turkey Trot," 1963

Little Joe and The Thrillers, "Peanuts," 1957

Little Milton, "We're Gonna Make It," 1965

Little Richard, "Tutti Frutti," 1955; "Long Tall Sally"/"Slippin' and Slidin'," 1956; "Rip It Up"/"Reddy Teddy," 1956; "The Girl Can't Help It," 1957; "Lucille"/"Send Me Some Lovin'," 1957; "Jenny, Jenny," 1957; "Keep a Knockin'," 1957; "Good Golly, Miss Molly," 1958; "Ooh! My Soul," 1958; "Baby Face," 1958; "Freedom Blues," 1970

Little Sister, "You're the One," 1970

Little Walter, "My Babe," 1955

Little Willie John, "Fever," 1956; "Talk to Me," 1958; "Sleep," 1960

Lobo, "Me and You and a Dog Named Boo," 1971; "I'd Love You to Want Me," 1972, RIAA 72; "Don't Expect Me to Be Your Friend," 1972; "How Can I Tell Her," 1973

Lockin, Hank, "Send Me the Pillow You Dream On," 1958; "Please Help Me, I'm Falling," 1960

Loggins and Messina, "Your Mama Don't Dance," 1972, RIAA 73; "Thinking of You," 1973; "My Music," 1974

Loggins & Messina, RIAA Gold Albums, "Loggins and Messina," 1973; "Sittin' In," 1973; "Full Sail," 1973; "On Stage," 1974; "Mother Lode," 1974; "Native Sons," 1976

Loggins, Dave, "Please Come to Boston," 1974

Lolita, "Sailor," 1960

London, Julie, "Cry Me a River," 1955

London, Laurie, "He's Got the Whole World in His Hands, 1958, RIAA 58

London Symphony Orchestra with Chamber Choir and Friends, RIAA Gold Album, "Tommy," 1972

Long, Shorty, "Here Comes the Judge," 1968

Longet, Claudine, RIAA Gold Album, "Claudine," 1970

Looking Glass, "Brandy (You're a Fine Girl)," 1972, RIAA 72; "Jimmy Loves Mary Ann," 1974

Lopez, Trini, "If I Had a Hammer," 1963; "Kansas City," 1963; "Lemon Tree," 1965

Lopez, Trini, RIAA Gold Album, "Trini Lopez at PJ's," 1965

Los Bravos, "Black Is Black," 1966

Los Indios Tabajaras, "Maria Elena," 1963

Lost Generation, "The Sly, the Slick and the Wicked," 1970

Lou, Bonnie, "Daddy-O," 1955

Loudermilk, John D., "Language of Love," 1961

Love, "My Little Red Book," 1966; "Seven and Seven Is," 1966

Love, Darlene, "(Today I Met) The Boy I'm Gonna Marry," 1963

Love Unlimited Orchestra, "Walking in the Rain with the One I Love," 1972, RIAA 72; "Love's Theme," 1974, RIAA 74; "Satin Soul," 1974; "I Belong to You," 1975

Love Unlimited Orchestra, RIAA Gold Albums, "Under the Influence of Love Unlimited," 1974; "Rhapsody in White," 1974; "White Gold," 1975

Lowe, Jim, "The Green Door," 1956; "Four Walls," 1957

Lovin' Spoonful, "Do You Believe in Magic," 1965; "You Didn't Have To Be So Nice," 1965; "Daydream," 1966; "Did You Ever Have to Make Up Your Mind," 1966; "Summer in the City," 1966, RIAA 66; "Rain on the Roof," 1966; "Nashville Cats," 1966; "Darling Be Home Soon," 1967; "Six O'Clock," 1967; "She Is Still a Mystery," 1967

Lovin' Spoonful, RIAA Gold Album, "The Best of the Lovin' Spoonful," 1967

Luke, Robin, "Susie Darlin'," 1958

Lulu, "Shout," 1964; "To Sir with Love," 1967, RIAA 67; "Best of Both Worlds," 1967; "Oh Me Oh My I'm a Fool for You Baby," 1969

Luman, Bob, "Let's Think About Living," 1960

Lundberg, Victor, "An Open Letter to My Teenage Son," 1967

Lyman, Arthur, "Yellow Bird," 1961

Lymon, Frankie, and The Teenagers, "Why Do Fools Fall in Love," 1956; "I Want You to Be My Girl," 1956; "Goody Goody," 1957

Lynn, Barbara, "You'll Lose a Good Thing," 1962

Lynn, Loretta, RIAA Gold Albums, "Don't Come Home Drinkin'," 1970; "Loretta Lynn's Greatest Hits," 1972

Lynne, Gloria, "I Wish You Love," 1964

Mabley, Moms, "Abraham, Martin and John," 1969

MacDonald, Jeanette, and Nelson Eddy, RIAA Gold Album, "Jeanette Mac-Donald and Nelson Eddy Favorites," 1966

MacGregor, Byron, "Americans," 1974, RIAA 74

Mack, Lonnie, "Memphis," 1963; "Wham!" 1963

MacRae, Gordon, "The Secret," 1958

MacRae, Gordon, RIAA Gold Album, "Oklahoma," 1958

Maddox, Johnny, "Crazy Otto Medley," 1955

Madigan, Betty, "Dance, Everyone, Dance," 1958

Maestro, Johnny, "Model Girl," 1961

Maestro, Johnny, and the Brooklyn Bridge, "The Worst That Could Happen," 1968

Magic Lanterns, "Shame, Shame," 1968

Maharis, George, "Teach Me Tonight," 1962

Main Ingredient, "Everybody Plays the Fool," 1972, RIAA 72; "Just Don't Want to Be Lonely," 1974, RIAA 74

Majors, "A Wonderful Dream," 1962

Makeba, Miriam, "Pata Pata," 1967

Malo, "Suavecito," 1972

Maltby, Richard, "Theme from *The Man With the Golden Arm*," 1956

Mama Cass, "Dream a Little Dream of Me," 1968; "It's Getting Better," 1969; "New World Coming," 1970

Mamas and Papas, "California Dreamin'," 1966, RIAA 66; "Monday, Monday," 1966, RIAA 66; "I Saw Her Again," 1966; "Look Through My Window," 1966; "Words of Love," 1966; "Dancing in the Street," 1966; "Dedicated to the One I Love," 1967; "Creeque Alley," 1967; "Twelve Thirty," 1967; "Glad to Be Unhappy," 1967

Mamas and Papas, RIAA Gold Albums, "If You Can Believe Your Eyes and Ears," 1966; "The Mamas and Papas," 1966; "The Mamas and Papas Deliver," 1967; "Farewell to the First Golden Era," 1968

Manchester, Mellissa, "Midnight Blue," 1975; "Just Too Many People," 1975

Mancini, Henry, "Mr. Lucky," 1960; "Moon River," 1961; "Days of Wine and Roses," 1963; "Charade," 1963; "The Pink Panther Theme," 1964; "Love Theme from *Romeo and Juliet*," 1969, RIAA 69; "Theme from *Love Story*," 1971

Mancini, Henry, RIAA Gold Albums, "Peter Gunn," 1959; "Breakfast at Tiffany's," 1962; "The Pink Panther," 1965; "The Best of Mancini," 1967; "A Warm Shade of Ivory," 1969

Manfred Mann, "Do Wah Diddy Diddy," 1964; "Sha La La," 1964; "Pretty Flamingo," 1966; "Mighty Quinn (Quinn the Eskimo)," 1968

Manhattans, "Kiss and Say Goodbye," 1976, RIAA 76, RIAA Platinum 76; "The Manhattans," RIAA Gold Album, 1976

Manhattan Transfer, "Operator," 1975

Manilow, Barry, "Mandy," 1975, RIAA 75; "Could It Be Magic," 1975; "I

Write the Songs," 1976, RIAA 76; "Trying to Get the Feeling
   Again," 1976

Manilow, Barry, RIAA Gold Albums, "Barry Manilow II," 1975; "Trying to
   Get the Feeling," 1975; "This One's for You," 1976

Mann, Barry, "Who Put the Bomp (In the Bomp, Bomp, Bomp)," 1961

Mann, Carl, "Mona Lisa," 1959

Mann, Gloria, "Teen Age Prayer," 1955

Mann, Herbie, "Memphis Underground," 1969; "Hijack," 1975

Mantovani, "Around the World," 1957; "Main Theme from *Exodus*," 1960

Mantovani, RIAA Gold Albums, "Christmas Carols," 1961; "Theatre Land,"
   1961; "Film Encores, Vol. 1," 1961; "Gems Forever," 1961;
   "Strauss Waltzes," 1961; "Exodus," 1963; "Mantovani's Golden
   Hits," 1970

Manu Dibango, "Soul Makossa," 1973

Marathons, "Peanut Butter," 1961

Marcels, "Blue Moon," 1961; "Heartaches," 1961

March, Little Peggy, "I Will Follow Him," 1963; "I Wish I Were a Princess,"
   1963; "Hello Heartache, Goodbye Love," 1963

Marchan, Bobby, "There's Something on Your Mind," 1960

Maresca, Ernie, "Shout! Shout! (Knock Yourself Out)," 1962

Mark IV, "I Got a Wife," 1959

Marketts, "Surfer's Stomp," "Balboa Blue," 1962; "Out of Limits," 1963;
   " 'Batman' Theme," 1966

Mar-Keys, "Last Night," 1961; "Philly Dog," 1966

Markham, Pigmeat, "Here Comes the Judge," 1968

Marks, Guy, "Loving You Has Made Me Bananas," 1968

Marley, Bob, & The Wailers, "Roots, Rock, Reggae," 1976

Marmalade, "Reflections of My Life," 1970

Marterie, Ralph, "Tricky," 1957; "Shish-Kebab," 1957

Martha and The Vandellas, "Come and Get These Memories," 1963; "Heat
   Wave," 1963; "Quicksand," 1963; "Live Wire," 1964; "In My Lone-
   ly Room," 1964; "Dancing in the Street," 1964; "Nowhere to Run,"
   1965; "You've Been in Love Too Long," 1965; "My Baby Loves
   Me," 1966; "I'm Ready for Love," 1966; "Jimmy Mack," 1967;
   "Love Bug Leave My Heart Alone," 1967; "Honey Chile," 1967

Martin, Bobbi, "Don't Forget I Still Love You," 1964; "For the Love of
   Him," 1970

Martin, Dean, "Memories Are Made of This," 1955; "Innamorata," 1956;
   "Standing on the Corner," 1956; "Return to Me," 1958; "Angel
   Baby," 1958; "Volare," 1958; "Everybody Loves Somebody,"
   1964, RIAA 64; "The Door Is Still Open to My Heart," 1964;
   "You're Nobody Till Somebody Loves You," 1964; "Send Me

The Pillow You Dream On," 1965; "(Remember Me) I'm the One
Who Loves You," 1965; "Houston," 1965; "I Will," 1965; "Some-
where There's a Someone," 1966; "Come Running Back," 1966;
"A Million to One," 1966; "In the Chapel in the Moonlight," 1967;
"Little Ole Wine Drinker, Me," 1967; "In the Misty Moonlight,"
1967

Martin, Dean, RIAA Gold Albums, "Everybody Loves Somebody," 1965;
"The Door Is Still Open to My Heart," 1965; "I'm the One Who
Loves You," 1966; "Dean Martin Sings Again," 1966; "Dream with
Dean," 1968; "Welcome to My World," 1968; "Houston," 1968;
"Somewhere There's a Someone," 1968; "Dean Martin's Christmas
Album," 1968; "Dean Martin's Greatest Hits, Vol. 1," 1969; "Gentle
on My Mind," 1969; "Dean Martin's Greatest Hits, Vol. 2," 1970

Martin, Tony, "Walk Hand in Hand," 1956

Martin, Trade, "That Stranger Used to Be My Girl," 1962

Martin, Vince, and The Tarriers, "Cindy, Oh Cindy," 1956; "Banana Boat
Song," 1956

Martindale, Wink, "Deck of Cards," 1961

Martino, Al, "I Love You Because," 1963; "Painted, Tainted Rose," 1963;
"Living a Lie," 1963; "I Love You More and More Every Day,"
1964; "Tears and Roses," 1964; "Always Together," 1964; "Spanish
Eyes," 1965; "Mary in the Morning," 1967; "Love Theme from *The
Godfather*," 1972; "Volaré," 1976

Martino, Al, RIAA Gold Album, "Spanish Eyes," 1966

Marvelettes, "Please Mr. Postman," 1961; "Twistin' Postman," 1962; "Playboy," 1962; "Beechwood 4-5789," 1962; "Too Many Fish in the
Sea," 1964; "I'll Keep Holding On," 1965; "Don't Mess with Bill,"
1966; "The Hunter Gets Captured by the Game," 1967; "When
You're Young and in Love," 1967; "My Baby Must Be a Magician,"
1967

Masekela, Hugh, "Grazing in the Grass," 1968, RIAA 68

Mashmakan, "As the Years Go By," 1970

Mason, Barbara, "Yes, I'm Ready," 1965; "Sad, Sad Girl," 1965

Mason, Dave, RIAA Gold Albums, "Alone Together," 1974; "Dave Mason,"
1976

Mathis, Johnny, "Wonderful! Wonderful!" 1957; "It's Not for Me to Say,"
1957; "Chances Are"/"The Twelfth of Never," 1957; "Wild Is the
Wind," 1957; "A Certain Smile," 1958; "Call Me," 1958; "Someone," 1959; "Small World," 1959; "Misty," 1959; "Starbright,"
1960; "Maria," 1960; "Gina," 1962; "What Will Mary Say," 1963;
"Every Step of the Way," 1963

Mathis, Johnny, RIAA Gold Albums, "Johnny's Greatest Hits," 1959;
"Heavenly," 1960; "Warm," 1960; "Merry Christmas," 1960; "More

of Johnny's Greatest Hits," 1962; "Faithfully," 1962; "Swing Softly," 1962; "Open Fire, Two Guitars," 1962; "All Time Greatest Hits," 1976

Matthews' Southern Comfort, "Woodstock," 1971

Matys Brothers, "Who Stole the Keeshka?" 1963

Mauriat, Paul, "Love Is Blue," 1968, RIAA 68

Mauriat, Paul, RIAA Gold Album, "Blooming Hits," 1968

Maxwell, Robert, "Shangri-La," 1964

May, Billy, "The Man with the Golden Arm," 1956

Mayfield, Curtis, "(Don't Worry) If There's a Hell Below, We're All Going to Go," 1970; "Freddie's Dead (Theme from *Superfly*)," 1972, RIAA 72; "Superfly," 1972, RIAA 72

Mayfield, Curtis, RIAA Gold Albums, "*Superfly* Original Soundtrack," 1972; "Curtis," 1973; "Back to the World," 1973

McCall, C. W., "Convoy," 1976, RIAA 76

McCall, C. W., RIAA Gold Album, "Black Bear Road," 1976

McCartney, Paul, RIAA Gold Album, "McCartney," 1970

McCartney, Paul and Linda, RIAA Gold Album, "Ram," 1971

McCartney, Paul, & Wings with Linda McCartney, "Another Day"/"Oh Woman Why," 1971; "Uncle Albert"/"Admiral Halsey," 1971, RIAA 71; "Give Ireland Back to the Irish," 1972; "Mary Had a Little Lamb"/ "Little Woman Love," 1972; "Hi, Hi, Hi," 1972; "My Love," 1973, RIAA 73; "Live and Let Die," 1973, RIAA 73; "Band on the Run," 1974, RIAA 74; "Helen Wheels," 1974; "Jet," 1974; "Sally-G," 1975; "Listen to What the Man Said," 1975, RIAA 75; "Letting Go," 1975; "Venus and Mars Rock Show," 1975; "Silly Love Songs," 1976, RIAA 76; "Let 'em In," 1976

McCartney, Paul, and Wings with Linda McCartney, RIAA Gold Albums, "Wildlife," 1972; "Red Rose Speedway," 1973; "Band on the Run," 1973; "Venus and Mars," 1975; "Wings at the Speed of Sound," 1976

McCartney, Paul, and Wings, RIAA Platinum Album, "Wings at the Speed of Sound," 1976

McCormick, Gayle, "It's a Cryin' Shame," 1971

McCoy, Van, and The Soul City Symphony, "The Hustle," 1975, RIAA 75; "Change With the Times," 1975

McCoys, "Hang on Sloopy," 1965; "Fever," 1965; "Come on Let's Go," 1966

McCracklin, Jimmy, "The Walk," 1958

McDaniels, Gene, "A Hundred Pounds of Clay," 1961; "Tower of Strength," 1961; "Chip Chip," 1962; "Point of No Return," 1962

McGovern, Maureen, "The Morning After," 1973, RIAA 73; "We May Never Love Like This Again," 1974

McGriff, Jimmy, "I've Got a Woman," 1962

McGuire, Barry, "Eve of Destruction," 1965

McGuire Sisters, "Sincerely," 1955; "He," 1955; "Picnic," 1956; "Delilah Jones," 1956; "Sugartime," 1957; "May You Always," 1959; "Just For Old Times' Sake," 1961

McKenzie, Scott, "San Francisco (Be Sure to Wear Flowers in Your Hair)," 1967

McLain, Tommy, "Sweet Dreams," 1966

McLean, Don, "American Pie," 1971, RIAA 72; "Vincent"/"Castles in the Air," 1972; "Dreidel," 1972

McLean, Don, RIAA Gold Album, "American Pie," 1972

McLean, Penny, "Lady Bump," 1975

McLean, Phil, "Small Sad Sam," 1961

McNamara, Robin, "Lay a Little Lovin' on Me," 1970

McNeely, Big Jay, "There Is Something on Your Mind," 1959

McPhatter, Clyde, "Seven Days," 1956; "Treasure of Love," 1956; "Without Love (There Is Nothing)," 1957; "Just to Hold My Hand," 1957; "Long Lonely Nights," 1957; "Come What May," 1958; "A Lover's Question," 1958; "Lovey Dovey," 1959; "Ta Ta," 1960; "Lover Please," 1962; "Little Bitty Pretty One," 1962

McRae, George, "Rock Your Baby," 1974; "I Ain't Lyin'," 1975

McRae, Gwen, "Rockin' Chair," 1975

Mead, Sister Janet, "The Lord's Prayer," 1974, RIAA 74

Meader, Vaughn, RIAA Gold Album, "The First Family," 1962

Medley, Bill, "Brown Eyed Woman," 1968

Melanie, "Lay Down (Candles in the Rain)," 1970; "Brand New Key," 1971, RIAA 71; "The Nickel Song," 1972; "Ring the Living Bell," 1972

Melanie, RIAA Gold Albums, "Candles in the Rain," 1971; "Gather Me," 1972

Mellokings, "Tonite, Tonite," 1957

Melvin, Harold, and The Bluenotes, "I Miss You," 1972; "If You Don't Know Me By Now," 1972, RIAA 72; "The Love I Lost," 1973, RIAA 73; "Bad Luck," 1975; "Wake Up Everybody," 1976

Melvin, Harold, and The Bluenotes, RIAA Gold Albums, "To Be True," 1975; Wake Up Everybody," 1976

Mendes, Sergio, and Brasil '66, "Mas Que Nada," 1966; "The Look of Love," 1968; "The Fool on the Hill," 1968; "Scarborough Fair," 1969

Mendes, Sergio, & Brasil '66, RIAA Gold Albums, "Sergio Mendes and Brasil '66," 1967; "Look Around," 1968; "Equinox," 1969; "Fool on the Hill," 1969

Mercy, "Love (Can Make You Happy)," 1969, RIAA 69

Mindbenders, "A Groovy Kind of Love," 1966

Mineo, Sal, "Start Movin'," 1957

Minneapolis Symphony Orchestra, RIAA Gold Album, "1812 Overture," 1963

Miracles, "Shop Around," 1960; "You've Really Got a Hold on Me," 1962; "Mickey's Monkey," 1963; "I Like It Like That," 1964; "OOO Baby Baby," 1965; "The Tracks of My Tears," 1965; "My Girl Has Gone," 1965; "Going to a Go-Go," 1965; "(Come 'Round Here) I'm the One You Need," 1966; "The Love I Saw in You Was Just a Mirage," 1967; "I Second That Emotion," 1967; "If You Can Want," 1968; "Yester Love," 1968; "Special Occasion," 1968; "Baby, Baby Don't Cry," 1969; "Who's Gonna Take the Blame," 1970; "The Tears of a Clown," 1970; "I Don't Blame You at All," 1971; "Sweet Harmony," 1973; "Love Machine," 1975, RIAA 76

Mitchell, Chad, Trio, "Lizzie Borden," 1962; "The Marvelous Toy," 1963

Mitchell, Guy, "Ninety Nine Years (Dead or Alive)," 1956; "Singing the Blues," 1956; "Knee Deep in the Blues," 1957; "Rock-a-Billy," 1957; "Heartaches by the Number," 1959

Mitchell, Joni, "Big Yellow Taxi," 1970; "You Turn Me on, I'm a Radio," 1972; "Help Me," 1974

Mitchell, Joni, RIAA Gold Albums, "Ladies of the Canyon," 1970; "Blue," 1971; "For the Roses," 1972; "Court and Spark," 1974; "Miles of Aisles," 1974; "The Hissing of Summer Lawns," 1975

Mitchell, Willie, "20-75," 1964; "Soul Serenade," 1968

Mitchum, Robert, "The Ballad of Thunder Road," 1958; "The Ballad of Thunder Road," 1962

Moby Grape, "Omaha," 1967

Mocedades, "Eres Tu (Touch the Wind)," 1974

Modugno, Domenico, "Nel Blu Dipinto Di Blu (Volare)," 1958

Mojo Men, "Sit Down, I Think I Love You," 1967

Moments, "Love on a Two-Way Street," 1970, RIAA 70; "Sexy Mama," 1974; "Look At Me (I'm in Love)," 1975

Monkees, "Last Train To Clarksville," 1966, RIAA 66; "I'm a Believer," 1966, RIAA 66; "(I'm Not Your) Steppin' Stone," 1966; "A Little Bit Me, a Little Bit You," 1967, RIAA 67; "The Girl I Knew Somewhere," 1967; "Pleasant Valley Sunday," 1967, RIAA 67; "Words," 1967; "Daydream Believer," 1967, RIAA 67; "Valleri," 1968, RIAA 68; "D. W. Washburn," 1968

Monkees, RIAA Gold Albums, "The Monkees," 1966; "More of the Monkees," 1967; "Headquarters," 1967; "Pisces, Aquarius, Capricorn and Jones Ltd.," 1967; "The Birds, The Bees and The Monkees," 1968

Monotones, "Book of Love," 1958

Monro, Matt, "My Kind of Girl," 1961; "Walk Away," 1964

Monroe, Vaughn, "Black Denim Trousers and Motorcycle Boots," 1955; "In the Middle of the House," 1956

Monte, Lou, "Lazy Mary," 1958; "Pepino, the Italian Mouse," 1963

Montenegro, Hugo, "The Good, the Bad and the Ugly," 1968

Montenegro, Hugo, RIAA Gold Album, "The Good, the Bad and the Ugly," 1969

Montez, Chris, "Let's Dance," 1962; "Call Me," 1966; "The More I See You," 1966; "There Will Never Be Another You," 1966; "Time After Time," 1966

Moody Blues, "Go Now!" 1965; "Tuesday Afternoon (Forever Afternoon)," 1968; "Question," 1970; "The Story in Your Eyes," 1971; "Isn't Life Strange," 1972; "Nights in White Satin," 1972, RIAA 72; "I'm Just a Singer (In a Rock and Roll Band)," 1973

Moody Blues, RIAA Gold Albums, "To Our Children's Children's Children," 1970; "Days of Future Passed," 1970; "On the Threshold of a Dream," 1970; "A Question of Balance," 1970; "In Search of the Lost Chord," 1970; "Every Good Boy Deserves a Favor," 1971; "Seventh Sojourn," 1972; "This Is the Moody Blues," 1974

Moonglows, "Sincerely," 1954-55; "See Saw," 1956; "Ten Commandments of Love," 1958

Moore, Bob, "Mexico," 1961

Moore, Bobby, and The Rhythm Aces, "Searchin' for My Love," 1968

Moore, Jackie, "Precious, Precious," 1971, RIAA 71

Moore, Dorothy, "Misty Blue," 1976

Morgan, Jane, "Fascination" with The Troubadors, 1957; "The Day the Rains Came," 1958

Morgan, Jane, and Roger Williams, "Two Different Worlds," 1956

Morgan, Jaye P., "That's All I Want from You," 1955; "Pepper-Hot Baby," 1955

Mormon Tabernacle Choir, "Battle Hymn of the Republic," 1959

Mormon Tabernacle Choir, RIAA Gold Album, "The Lord's Prayer," 1963

Morrison, Van (see Them), "Brown Eyed Girl," 1967; "Come Running," 1970; "Domino," 1970; "Blue Money," 1971; "Wild Night," 1971

Motherlode, "When I Die," 1969

Motion Picture Original Soundtracks, RIAA Gold Albums, "West Side Story," 1963; "Exodus," 1963; "The Music Man," 1963; "Carousel," 1964; "The King and I," 1964; "My Fair Lady," 1964; "Mary Poppins," 1964; "The Sound of Music," 1965; "Dr. Zhivago," 1966; "Thoroughly Modern Millie," 1967; "A Man and a Woman," 1967; "Dr. Doolittle," 1968; "The Graduate," 1968; "Gigi," 1968; "Camelot," 1968; "The Jungle Book," Walt Disney, 1968; "Funny Girl," 1968; "The Good, the Bad and the Ugly," 1968; "2001: A Space Odyssey,"

236

1969; "How the West Was Won," 1969; "Romeo and Juliet," 1969; "Oliver," 1969; "Easy Rider," 1970; "Midnight Cowboy," 1970; "Woodstock," 1970; "Paint Your Wagon," 1970; "Hendrix and Redding at Monterey" Monterey Pop, 1970; "Love Story," 1971; "Woodstock II," 1971; "Fiddler on the Roof," 1971; "Superfly," 1972; "Dueling Banjos" Soundtrack of *Deliverance*, 1973; "Cabaret," 1973; "Jesus Christ Superstar," 1973; "Jonathan Livingston Seagull," 1973; "American Graffiti," 1973; "The Sting," 1974; "The Way We Were," 1974; "Claudine," 1974; "The Great Gatsby," 1974; "Tommy," 1975; "Funny Lady," 1975

Mott The Hoople, "All the Young Dudes," 1972

Mountain, "Mississippi Queen," 1970

Mountain, RIAA Gold Albums, "Mountain Climbing," 1970; "Nantucket Sleigh Ride," 1971

Mouth and MacNeal, "How Do You Do?" 1972, RIAA 72

Mozart, Mickey, Quintet, "Little Dipper," 1959

Muldaur, Maria, "Midnight at the Oasis," 1974; "I'm a Woman," 1974

Muldaur, Maria, RIAA Gold Album, "Maria Muldaur," 1974

Mungo Jerry, "In the Summertime," 1970, RIAA 70

Murmaids, "Popsicles and Icicles," 1973

Murphey, Michael, "Wildfire," 1975, RIAA 75; "Renegade," 1975

Murphey, Michael, RIAA Gold Album, "Blue Sky, Night Thunder," 1975

Murphy, Walter, and Big Apple Band, "A Fifth of Beethoven," 1976, RIAA 76

Murray, Anne, "Snowbird," 1970, RIAA 70; "Danny's Song," 1973; "What About Me," 1973; "You Won't See Me," 1974; "Love Song," 1974

Murray, Anne, RIAA Gold Album, "Snowbird," 1973

Music Explosion, "Little Bit o' Soul," 1967, RIAA 67

Music Machine, "Talk, Talk," 1966

Myles, Billy, "The Joker," 1957

Mystics, "Hushabye," 1959

Nabors, Jim, RIAA Gold Albums, "Jim Nabors Sings," 1968; "Jim Nabors' Christmas Album," 1970; "The Lord's Prayer," 1974

Napoleon XIV, "They're Coming to Take Me Away, Ha-Haaa!" 1966

Nash, Graham, "Chicago," 1971

Nash, Graham, RIAA Gold Album, "Songs for Beginners," 1971

Nash, Graham, and David Crosby, "Immigration Man," 1972

Nash, Graham, and David Crosby, RIAA Gold Album, "Graham Nash and David Crosby," 1972

Nash, Johnny, "A Very Special Love," 1957; "Hold Me Tight," 1968; "Cupid," 1969; "I Can See Clearly Now," 1972, RIAA 72; "Stir It Up," 1972

Nashville Teens, "Tobacco Road," 1964

Nazareth, "Love Hurts," 1976, RIAA 76

Nazareth, RIAA Gold Album, "Hair of the Dog," 1976

National Lampoon, "Deteriorata," 1972

Neely, Sam, "Loving You Crossed My Mind," 1972

Neighborhood, "Big Yellow Taxi," 1970

Nelson, Ricky, "A Teenager's Romance"/"I'm Walking," 1957; "You're My One and Only Love," 1957; "Bebop Baby," 1957; "Have I Told You Lately That I Love You," 1957; "Stood Up"/"Waitin' in School," 1957; "Believe What I Say"/"My Bucket's Got a Hole in It," 1958; "Poor Little Fool," 1958; "Lonesome Town"/"I Got a Feeling," 1958; "Never Be Anyone Else But You"/"It's Late," 1959; "Sweeter Than You"/"Just a Little Too Much," 1959; "I Wanna Be Loved," 1959; "Young Emotions," 1960; "I'm Not Afraid," 1961; "Travelin' Man"/"Hello Mary Lou," 1961; "A Wonder Like You"/"Everlovin'," 1971; "Young World," 1962; "Teen Age Idol," 1962; "It's Up to You," 1962; "I Got a Woman," 1963; "String Along," 1963; "Fools Rush In," 1963; "For You," 1963; "She Belongs to Me," 1969; "Garden Party," 1972, RIAA 72

Nelson, Sandy, "Teen Beat," 1959; "Let There Be Drums," 1961

Nelson, Terry, "Ballad Hymn of Lt. Calley," 1971, RIAA 71

Nelson, Willie, "Blue Eyes Crying in the Rain," 1975

Nelson, Willie, RIAA Gold Album, "Red Headed Stranger," 1976

Neon Philharmonic, "Morning Girl," 1969

Nero Peter, "Theme from Summer of '42," 1971

Nero, Peter, RIAA Gold Album, "Summer of '42," 1972

Nervous Norvus, "Transfusion," 1956; "Ape Call," 1956

Nesmith, Michael, and The First National Band, "Joanne," 1970

Neville, Arron, "Tell It Like It Is," 1966

Newbeats, "Bread and Butter," 1964; "Everything's Alright," 1964; "Run, Baby, Run," 1965

New Birth, RIAA Gold Album, "It's Been a Long Time," 1974

Newbury, Mickey, "An American Trilogy," 1971

New Christy Minstrels, "This Land Is Your Land," 1962; "Green, Green," 1963; "Saturday Night," 1963; "Today," 1964

New Christy Minstrels, RIAA Gold Album, "Ramblin'," 1964

New Colony Six, "I Will Always Think About You," 1968; "Things I'd Like to Say," 1968

Newhart, Bob, RIAA Gold Albums, "Bob Newhart, Button Down Mind," 1962; "The Button Down Mind Strikes Back," 1967

Newley, Anthony, "What Kind of Fool Am I," 1962

Newman, Thunderclap, "Something in the Air," 1969

New Seekers, "Look What They've Done to My Song, Ma," 1970; "I'd Like to Teach the World to Sing (In Perfect Harmony)," 1971, RIAA 72; "Pinball Wizard"/"See Me, Feel Me," 1973

Newton, Wayne, "Danke Schoen," 1963; "Red Roses for a Blue Lady," 1965; "Dreams of the Everyday Housewife," 1968; "Daddy Don't You Walk So Fast," 1972, RIAA 72; "The Hungry Years," 1976

Newton-John, Olivia, "If Not for You," 1971; "Let Me Be There," 1974, RIAA 74; "If You Love Me (Let Me Know)," 1974, RIAA 74; "I Honestly Love You," 1974, RIAA 74; "Have You Never Been Mellow," 1975, RIAA 75; "Please, Mr. Please," 1975, RIAA 75; "Something Better to Do," 1975; "He Ain't Heavy, He's My Brother,"/ "Let It Shine," 1976; "Come on Over," 1976; "Don't Stop Believin'," 1976

Newton-John, Olivia, RIAA Gold Albums, "If You Love Me, Let Me Know," 1974; "Have You Never Been Mellow," 1975; "Clearly Love," 1975; "Come on Over," 1976; "Don't Stop Believin'," 1976

New Vaudeville Band, "Winchester Cathedral," 1966, RIAA 66

New Vaudeville Band, RIAA Gold Album, "Winchester Cathedral," 1966

New York City, "I'm Doing Fine Now," 1973

Nightingale, Maxine, "Right Back Where We Started From," 1976, RIAA 76

Nilsson, Harry, "Everybody's Talkin'," 1969; "Me and My Arrow," 1971; "Without You," 1971, RIAA 72; "Jump into the Fire," 1972; "Coconut," 1972; "Spaceman," 1972

Nilsson, Harry, RIAA Gold Albums, "Nilsson Schmilsson," 1972; "Son of Schmilsson," 1972

1910 Fruitgum Co., "Simon Says," 1968, RIAA 68; "1, 2, 3, Red Light," 1968, RIAA 68; "Indian Giver," 1969, RIAA 69

Nino and The Ebb Tides, "Juke Box Saturday Night," 1961

Nite-Liters, "K-Jee," 1971

Nitty Gritty Dirt Band, "Buy for Me the Rain," 1967; "Mr. Bojangles," 1970

Nitty Gritty Dirt Band, RIAA Gold Album, "William E. McEuen Presents . . ." 1973

Nitzche, Jack, "The Lonely Surfer," 1963

Noble, Nick, "The Bible Tells Me So," 1955; "To You, My Love," 1956

Noble, Cliff, and Co., "The Horse," 1968, RIAA 68

Noguez, Jacky, "Ciao, Ciao Bambina," 1959

Nutmegs, "Story Untold," 1955
Nugent, Ted, RIAA Gold Album, "Ted Nugent," 1976
Nu Tornados, "Philadelphia, USA," 1958
Nutty Squirrels, "Uh! Oh! Part 2," 1959

Ocean, "Put Your Hand in the Hand," 1971, RIAA 71
Ocean, Billy, "Love Really Hurts Without You," 1976
Ochs, Phil, "Small Circle of Friends," 1967
O'Connor, Carroll, and Jean Stapleton, "Those Were the Days," 1971
O'Dell, Kenny, "Beautiful People," 1967
Ohio Express, "Beg, Borrow and Steal," 1967; "Yummy, Yummy, Yummy,"
    1968, RIAA 68; "Down at Lulu's," 1968; "Chewy Chewy," 1968,
    RIAA 69
Ohio Players, "Funky Worm," 1973; "Skin Tight," 1974, RIAA 74; "Fire,"
    1975, RIAA 75; "Love Roller Coaster," 1976, RIAA 76; "Who'd
    She Coo?" 1976
Ohio Players, RIAA Gold Albums, "Skin Tight," 1974; "Fire," 1974;
    "Honey," 1975; "Contradiction," 1976
O'Jays, "Lonely Drifter," 1963; "Back Stabbers," 1972, RIAA 72; "Love
    Train," 1973, RIAA 73; "Put Your Hands Together," 1974; "For
    the Love of Money," 1974, RIAA 74; "I Love Music," 1976, RIAA
    76; "Livin' for the Weekend," 1976
O'Jays, RIAA Gold Albums, "Back Stabbers," 1973; "Ship Ahoy," 1974;
    "Survival," 1975; "Live in London," 1975; "Family Reunion,"
    1975
O'Kaysions, "Girl Watcher," 1968, RIAA 68
O'Keefe, Danny, "Good Time Charlie's Got the Blues," 1972
Oldfield, Mike, "Tubular Bells," 1974
Oldfield, Mike, RIAA Gold Album, "Tubular Bells," 1974
Oliver, "Good Morning Starshine," 1969; "Jean," 1969, RIAA 69
Olympics, "Western Movies," 1958; "Big Boy Pete," 1960; "Hully Gully
    Baby," 1962
100 Proof, "Somebody's Been Sleeping (In My Bed)," 1970, RIAA 70
Orbison, Roy, "Ooby Dooby," 1956; "Up Town," 1960; "Only the Lonely,"
    1960; "Blue Angel," 1960; "I'm Hurtin'," 1960; "Running Scared,"
    1961; "Crying"/"Candy Man," 1961; "Dream Baby," 1962; "The
    Crowd," 1962; "Leah"/"Workin' for the Man," 1962; "In Dreams,"
    1963; "Falling," 1963; "Mean Woman Blues"/"Blue Bayou," 1963;

"Pretty Paper," 1963; "It's Over," 1964; "Oh, Pretty Woman," 1964, RIAA 64; "Goodnight," 1965

Orbison, Roy, RIAA Gold Album, "Roy Orbison's Greatest Hits," 1966

Original Caste, "One Tin Soldier," 1969

Originals, "Baby, I'm for Real," 1969; "The Bells," 1970

Orlando, Tony (see Tony Orlando and Dawn), "Halfway to Paradise," 1961; "Bless You," 1961

Orlando, Tony, and Dawn, "Candida," 1970, RIAA 70; "Knock Three Times," 1970, RIAA 70; "Tie a Yellow Ribbon," 1973, RIAA 73; "Say, Has Anybody Seen My Sweet Gypsy Rose," 1973, RIAA 73; "Who Is in the Strawberry Patch," 1974; "He Don't Love You," 1975, RIAA 75; "Morning Beautiful," 1975; "You're All I Need," 1975; "Cupid," 1976

Orlando, Tony, and Dawn, RIAA Gold Albums, "Dawn's New Ragtime Follies," 1975; "Tuneweaving," 1975; "Tony Orlando and Dawn's Greatest Hits," 1975

Orleans, "Dance with Me," 1975; "Still the One," 1976

Orlons, "The Wah Watusi," 1962; "Don't Hang Up," 1962; "South Street," 1963; "Not Me," 1963; "Crossfire!" 1963

Ormandy, Eugene, and the Philadelphia Symphony Orchestra, RIAA Gold Albums, "The Glorious Sound of Christmas," 1963; "Handel's *Messiah*, 1963

Orpheus, "Can't Find the Time," 1969

Osmond, Donny, "Sweet and Innocent," 1971, RIAA 71; "Go Away Little Girl," 1971, RIAA 71; "Hey Girl"/"I Knew You When," 1971, RIAA 72; "Puppy Love," 1972, RIAA 72; "Too Young," 1972; "Why"/"Lonely Boy," 1972; "Twelfth of Never," 1973, RIAA 73; "Morning Side of the Mountain," 1975; "C'mon, Marianne," 1976

Osmond, Donny, RIAA Gold Albums, "Donny Osmond Album," 1971; "To You With Love," 1972; "Portrait of Donny," 1972; "Too Young," 1973; "My Best to You," 1973

Osmond, Little Jimmy, "Long Haired Lover from Liverpool," 1972

Osmond, Marie, "Paper Roses," 1973, RIAA 73

Osmond, Marie and Donny, "I'm Leaving It All Up to You," 1974, RIAA 74; "Deep Purple," 1976

Osmond, Marie and Donny, RIAA Gold Album, "I'm Leaving It All Up to You," 1975

Osmonds, "One Bad Apple," 1971, RIAA 71; "Double Lovin'," 1971; "Yo-Yo," 1971, RIAA 71; "Down by the Lazy River," 1972, RIAA 72; "Hold Her Tight," 1972; "Crazy Horse," 1972; "The Proud Ones," 1976

Osmonds, RIAA Gold Albums, "Osmonds," 1971; "Homemade," 1972;

"Phase III," 1972; "The Osmonds Live," 1972; "Crazy Horses," 1973

O'Sullivan, Gilbert, "Alone Again (Naturally)," 1972, RIAA 72; "Clair," 1972, RIAA 73; "Get Down," 1973, RIAA 73

Otis, Johnny, Show, "Willie and the Hand Jive," 1958

Outlaws, "There Goes Another Love Song," 1976

Outlaws, RIAA Gold Album, "The Outlaws," 1976

Outsiders, "Time Won't Let Me," 1966; "Girl in Love," 1966; "Respectable," 1966

Owen, Reg, "Manhattan Spiritual," 1958

Owens, Buck, "Act Naturally," 1963; "Together Again," 1964; "I've Got a Tiger by the Tail," 1965; "Waitin' in the Welfare Line," 1966

Owens, Buck, RIAA Gold Album, "Best of Buck Owens," 1968

Owens, Donnie, "Need You," 1958

Ozark Mountain Daredevils, "Jackie Blue," 1975

Pacific Gas and Electric, "Are You Ready?" 1970

Packers, "Hole in the Wall," 1965

Page, Patti, "Croce Di Oro," 1955; "Go on with the Wedding," 1955; "Allegheny Moon," 1956; "Mama from the Train," 1956; "A Poor Man's Roses," 1957; "Old Cape Cod"/"Wondering," 1957; "I'll Remember Today," 1957; "Belonging to Someone," 1958; "Left Right out of Your Heart," 1958; "Hush, Hush, Sweet Charlotte," 1965

Paper Lace, "The Night Chicago Died," 1974, RIAA 74

Parade, "Sunshine Girl," 1967

Paradons, "Diamonds and Pearls," 1960

Paris Sisters, "I Love How You Love Me," 1961

Parker, Fess, "Ballad of Davy Crockett," 1955; "Wringle Wrangle," 1957

Parker, Robert, "Barefootin'," 1966

Parks, Michael, "Long Lonesome Highway," 1970

Parliament, "(I Wanna) Testify," 1969; "Tear the Roof off the Sucker," 1976

Parliament, RIAA Gold Album, "Mothership Connection," 1976

Parliament, RIAA Platinum Album," Mothership Connection," 1976

Parsons, Bill (see Bobby Bare), "The All-American Boy," 1958

Partridge Family with Shirley Jones and David Cassidy, "I Think I Love You," 1970, RIAA 70; "Doesn't Somebody Want to Be Wanted," 1971, RIAA 71; "I'll Meet You Halfway," 1971; "I Woke Up in Love This

Morning," 1971; "It's One of Those Nights (Yes Love)," 1971;
"Breaking Up Is Hard to Do," 1972; "Looking Through the Eyes of
Love," 1972

Partridge Family with Shirley Jones and David Cassidy, RIAA Gold Albums,
"The Partridge Family Album," 1970; "Up to Date," 1971; "Sound
Magazine," 1971; "A Partridge Family Christmas Card," 1971;
"Partridge Family Shopping Bag," 1972; "The Partridge Family at
Home," 1972

Pastels, "Been So Long," 1959

Pastel Six, "The Cinnamon Cinder," 1962

Patience and Prudence, "Tonight You Belong to Me," 1956; "Gonna Get
Along Without Ya Now," 1956

Patty and The Emblems, "Mixed-Up, Shook-Up Girl," 1964

Paul, Billy, "Me and Mrs. Jones," 1972, RIAA 72

Paul, Billy, RIAA Gold Album, "360 Degrees of Billy Paul," 1973

Paul and Paula, "Hey Paula," 1962, RIAA 63; "Young Lovers," 1963, "First
Quarrel," 1963

Pavone, Rita, "Remember Me," 1964

Payne, Freda, "Band of Gold," 1970, RIAA 70; "Deeper and Deeper," 1970;
"Bring the Boys Home," 1971, RIAA 71

Peaches and Herb, "Let's Fall in Love," 1966; "Close Your Eyes," 1967;
"For Your Love," 1967; "Love Is Strange," 1967

Peanut Butter Conspiracy, "It's a Happening Thing," 1967

Peels, "Juanita Banana," 1966

Penguins, "Earth Angel," 1954-55

People, "I Love You," 1968

People's Choice, "I Likes To Do It," 1971; "Do It Anyway You Wanna,"
1975, RIAA 75

Peppermint Rainbow, "Will You Be Staying After Sunday," 1969

Pericoli, Emilio, "Al Di La," 1962

Perkins, Carl, "Honey Don't," 1956; "Matchbox," 1956; "Blue Suede Shoes,"
1956

Perkins, Tony, "Moonlight Swim," 1957

Persuaders, "Thin Line Between Love and Hate," 1971, RIAA 71

Peter and Gordon, "A World Without Love," 1964; "Nobody I Know,"
1964; "I Don't Want to See You Again," 1964; "I Go to Pieces,"
1965; "True Love Ways," 1965; "To Know You Is to Love You,"
1965; "Woman," 1966; "Lady Godiva," 1966; "Knight in Rusty
Armour," 1966; "Sunday for Tea," 1967

Peter, Paul, and Mary, "Lemon Tree," 1962; "If I Had a Hammer," 1962;
"Puff the Magic Dragon," 1963; "Blowin' in the Wind," 1963;

Platt, Eddie, "Tequila," 1958

Platters, "Only You," 1955; "The Great Pretender," 1955; "(You've Got)
The Magic Touch," 1956; "My Prayer"/"Heaven on Earth," 1956;
"You'll Never Never Know"/"It Isn't Right," 1956; "On My Word
of Honor"/"One in a Million," 1956; "I'm Sorry"/"He's Mine,"
1957; "My Dream," 1957; "Twilight Time," 1958; "Smoke Gets in
Your Eyes," 1958; "Enchanted," 1959; "Harbor Lights," 1960;
"Red Sails in the Sunset," 1960; "To Each His Own," 1960; "If I
Didn't Care," 1961; "I'll Never Smile Again," 1961; "I Love You
1000 Times," 1966; "With This Ring," 1967

Platters, RIAA Gold Albums, "Encore, Golden Hits," 1961; "More Encores
of Golden Hits," 1965

Playmates, "Jo-Ann," 1958; "Don't Go Home," 1958; "Beep Beep," 1958;
"What Is Love?" 1959

Poco, "Keep on Tryin'," 1975

Poets, "She Blew a Good Thing," 1966

Poni-Tails, "Born Too Late," 1958

Pointer Sisters, "Yes We Can Can," 1973; "Fairy Tale," 1974

Pointer Sisters, RIAA Gold Albums, "Pointer Sisters," 1974; "That's a
Plenty," 1974

Poppy Family, "Which Way You Goin' Billy?" 1970, RIAA 70; "That's
Where I Went Wrong," 1970

Posey, Sandy, "Born a Woman," 1966; "Single Girl," 1966; "I Take It Back,"
1967

Post, Mike, "The Rockford Files," 1975; "Manhattan Spiritual," 1975

Pourcel, Franck, "Only You," 1959

Powell, Jane, "True Love," 1956

Powers, Joey, "Midnight Mary," 1963

Pozo-Seco Singers, "Time," 1966; "I Can Make It With You," 1966

Prado, Perez, "Cherry Pink and Apple Blossom White," 1955; "Patricia,"
1958, RIAA 58

Prelude, "After the Gold Rush," 1974

Premiers, "Farmer John," 1964

Presidents, "5-10-15-20 (25-30 Years of Love)," 1970

Presley, Elvis, "Heartbreak Hotel"/"I Was the One," 1956; "I Want You, I
Need You, I Love You"/"My Baby Left Me," 1956; "Don't Be
Cruel"/"Hound Dog," 1956; "Love Me Tender"/"Anyway You
Want Me (That's How I Will Be)," 1956; "Too Much"/"Playing
For Keeps," 1957; "All Shook Up"/"That's When Your Heartaches
Begin," 1957; "(Let Me Be Your) Teddy Bear"/"Loving You,"
1957; "Jailhouse Rock"/"Treat Me Nice," 1957; "Don't"/"I Beg of
You," 1958; "Wear My Ring Around Your Neck"/"Doncha' Think

It's Time," 1958; "Hard Headed Woman"/"Don't Ask Me Why,"
1958, RIAA 58; "One Night"/"I Got Stung," 1958; "(Now and
Then There's) A Fool Such as I"/"I Need Your Love Tonight,"
1959; "A Big Hunk o' Love"/"My Wish Came True," 1959; "Stuck
on You"/"Fame and Fortune," 1960; "It's Now or Never"/"A Mess
of Blues," 1960; "Are You Lonesome Tonight?"/"I Gotta Know,"
1960; "Surrender," 1961; "I Feel So Bad"/"Wild in the Country,"
1971; "(Marie's the Name) His Latest Flame"/"Little Sister," 1961;
"Can't Help Falling in Love"/"Rock-a-Hula Baby," 1962, RIAA 62;
"Good Luck Charm," 1962; "She's Not You"/"Just Tell Her Jim
Said Hello," 1962; "Return to Sender," 1962; "One Broken Heart
for Sale," 1963; "(You're The) Devil in Disguise," 1963; "Bossa
Nova Baby," 1963; "Kissin' Cousins," 1964; "It Hurts Me," 1964;
"What'd I Say"/"Viva Las Vegas," 1964; "Such a Night," 1964;
"Ask Me"/"Ain't That Loving You Baby," 1964; "Do the Clam,"
1965; "(Such An) Easy Question"/"It Feels So Right," 1965;
"I'm Yours," 1965; "Tell Me Why," 1966; "Frankie and Johnny"/
"Please Don't Stop Loving Me," 1966; "Love Letters," 1966; "Big
Boss Man," 1967; "Guitar Man," 1968; "US Male," 1968; "If I Can
Dream," 1968; "In the Ghetto," 1969, RIAA 69; "Clean Up Your
Own Back Yard," 1969; "Suspicious Minds," 1969, RIAA 69;
"Don't Cry Daddy"/"Rubberneckin'," 1970, RIAA 70; "Kentucky
Rain," 1970; "The Wonder of You"/"Mama Liked the Roses," 1970;
"You Don't Have to Say You Love Me"/"Patch It Up," 1970; "I
Really Don't Want to Know"/"There Goes My Everything," 1970;
"Burning Love," 1972, RIAA 72; "Separate Ways," 1972; "My
Boy," 1974; "Hurt," 1976

Presley, Elvis, RIAA Gold Albums, "Elvis," 1960; "Elvis Golden Records,"
1961; "Blue Hawaii," 1961; "GI Blues," 1963; "Elvis Christmas Album," 1963; "Girls, Girls, Girls," 1963; "Elvis Presley," 1966; "Elvis' Gold Records, Vol. 2," 1966; "Elvis' Golden Records, Vol. 3,"
1966; "How Great Thou Art," 1968; "Loving You," 1968; "His
Hand in Mine," 1969; "Elvis' TV Special," 1969; "From Vegas to
Memphis," 1969; "From Elvis in Memphis," 1970; "On Stage, February, 1970," 1970; "Elvis Recorded at Madison Square Garden,"
1972; "World Wide 50 Gold Award Hits, Vol. 1," 1973; "Elvis—
Aloha from Hawaii Via Satellite," 1973; "Elvis—That's the Way It
Is," 1973; "Elvis—A Legendary Performer, Vol. 1," 1975

Preston, Billy, "Outa-Space," 1972, RIAA 72; "Space Race," 1973, RIAA
73; "Will It Go Round in Circles," 1973, RIAA 73; "Nothing from
Nothing," 1974, RIAA 74

Preston, Johnny, "Running Bear," 1959; "Cradle of Love," 1960; "Feel So
Fine," 1960

Previn, Andre, and David Rose, "Like Young," 1959

Price, Alan, Set, "I Put a Spell on You," 1966; "Hi Lili, Hi Lo," 1966; "The House That Jack Built," 1967

Price, Lloyd, "Just Because," 1957; "Stagger Lee," 1958; "Where Were You (On Our Wedding Day)," 1959; "Personality," 1959; "I'm Gonna Get Married," 1959; "Come into My Heart," 1959; "Lady Luck," 1960; "Question," 1960; "Misty," 1963

Price, Ray, "Crazy Arms," 1956; "City Lights," 1958; "Danny Boy," 1967; "For the Good Times," 1970; "I Won't Mention It Again," 1971

Price, Ray, RIAA Gold Album, "For the Good Times," 1971

Pride, Charley, "Kiss an Angel Good Mornin'," 1971, RIAA 72

Pride, Charley, RIAA Gold Albums, "The Best of Charley Pride," 1970; "Charley Pride's 10th Album," 1971; "Just Plain Charley," 1971; "Charley Pride in Person," 1971; "Charley Pride Sings Heart Songs," 1972; "The Best of Charley Pride," 1972; "The Sensational Charley Pride," 1973; "From Me to You," 1973; "The Country Way," 1973; "Do You Think to Pray," 1975; "(Country) Charley Pride," 1975

Prima, Louis, and Keely Smith, "That Old Black Magic," 1958; "I've Got You Under My Skin," 1959

Proby, P. J., "I Apologize," 1965; "Niki Hoeky," 1967

Procol Harum, "A Whiter Shade of Pale," 1967; "Conquistador," 1972

Procol Harum, RIAA Gold Album, "Procol Harum with Edmonton Symphony Orchestra," 1972

Pruett, Jeanne, "Satin Sheets," 1973

Pryor, Richard, RIAA Gold Album, "Is It Something I Said?" 1975

Prysock, Red, "Hand Clappin'," 1955

Puckett, Gary, and The Union Gap, "Woman, Woman," 1967; "Young Girl," 1968; "Lady Willpower," 1968; "Over You," 1968; "Don't Give in to Him," 1969; "This Girl Is a Woman Now," 1969

Puckett, Gary, and The Union Gap, RIAA Gold Albums, "Young Girl," 1969; "Gary Puckett and The Union Gap's Greatest," 1971

Pure Prairie League, "Amie," 1975

Pure Prairie League, RIAA Gold Album, "Bustin' Out," 1976

Purify, James and Bobby, "I'm Your Puppet," 1966; "Shake a Tail Feather," 1967; "Let Love Come Between Us," 1967; "I'm Your Puppet," 1976

Pursell, Bill, "Our Winter Love," 1963

Pyramids, "Penetration," 1964

Quaker City Boys, "Teasin'," 1958

Queen, "Killer Queen," 1975; "Bohemian Rhapsody," 1976, RIAA 76; "You're My Best Friend," 1976

Queen, RIAA Gold Albums, "Sheer Heart Attack," 1975; "A Night at the Opera," 1976

Question Mark and The Mysterians, "96 Tears," 1966, RIAA 66

Quin-Tones, "Down the Aisle of Love," 1958

Raindrops, "The Kind of Boy You Can't Forget," 1963

Rainwater, Marvin, "Gonna Find Me a Bluebird," 1957

Ralke, Don, "77 Sunset Strip," 1959

Ramrods, "(Ghost) Riders in the Sky," 1961

Ran-Dells, "Martian Hop," 1963

Randolph, Boots, "Yakety Sax," 1963

Randolph, Boots, RIAA Gold Albums, "Yakety Sax," 1967; "Boots with Strings," 1969

Randy and The Rainbows, "Denise," 1963

Rare Earth, "Get Ready," 1970; "(I Know) I'm Losing You," 1970; "Born to Wander," 1970; "I Just Want to Celebrate," 1971; "Hey Big Brother," 1971

Rascals, "Good Lovin'," 1966, RIAA 67; "You Better Run," 1966; "I've Been Lonely Too Long," 1967; "Groovin'," 1967; "How Can I Be Sure," 1967; "It's Wonderful," 1967; "A Beautiful Morning," 1967, RIAA 68; "A Ray of Hope," 1968; "Carry Me Back," 1969

Rascals, RIAA Gold Albums, "Groovin'," 1968; "Collections," 1968; "The Young Rascals," 1968; "Time Peace, The Rascals' Greatest Hits," 1968; "Freedom Suite," 1969

Rasperries, "Go All the Way," 1972, RIAA 72; "I Wanna Be with You," 1972

Rawls, Lou, "Love Is a Hurtin' Thing," 1966; "Dead End Street," 1967; Your Good Thing (Is About to End)," 1969; "A Natural Man," 1971; "You'll Never Find Another Love Like Mine," 1976, RIAA 76

Rawls, Lou, RIAA Gold Albums, "Lou Rawls Live!" 1967; "All Things in Time," 1976

Ray, Diane, "Please Don't Talk to the Lifeguard," 1963

Ray, James, "If You Gotta Make a Fool of Somebody," 1961

Ray, Johnnie, "Just Walking in the Rain," 1956; "You Don't Owe Me a

Thing," 1957; "Look Homeward, Angel," 1957; "Yes, Tonight, Josephine," 1957

Rayburn, Margie, "I'm Available," 1957; "Freight Train," 1957

Rays, "Silhouettes"/"Daddy Cool," 1957

Rebels, "Wild Weekend," 1962

Redbone, "The Witch Queen of New Orleans," 1971; "Come and Get Your Love," 1974, RIAA 74

Redding, Otis, "Mr. Pitiful," 1965; "I've Been Loving You Too Long," 1965; "Respect," 1965; "Satisfaction," 1966; "Fa-Fa-Fa-Fa-Fa-Fa," 1966; "Try a Little Tenderness," 1967; "(Sittin' On) The Dock of the Bay," 1968, RIAA 68; "The Happy Song (Dum-Dum)," 1968; "Papa's Got a Brand New Bag," 1968

Redding, Otis, and Carla Thomas, "Tramp," 1967

Reddy, Helen, "I Don't Know How to Love Him," 1971; "I Am Woman," 1972, RIAA 72; "Delta Dawn," 1973, RIAA 73; "Peaceful," 1973; "Leave Me Alone (Ruby Red Dress)," 1974, RIAA 74; "You and Me Against the World," 1974; "Bluebird," 1974; "Angie Baby," 1975, RIAA 75; "Ain't No Way to Treat a Lady," 1975; "Emotion," 1975; "Somewhere in the Night," 1976; "I Can't Hear You No More," 1976

Reddy, Helen, RIAA Gold Albums, "I Am Woman," 1973; "Long Hard Climb," 1973; "Love Song for Jeffrey," 1974; "I Don't Know How to Love Him," 1974; "Free and Easy," 1974; "Helen Reddy's Greatest Hits," 1975; "No Way to Treat a Lady," 1976; "Music, Music," 1976

Redeye, "Games," 1970

Reed, Jerry, "Amos Moses," 1971, RIAA 71; "When You're Hot, You're Hot," 1971

Reed, Jimmy, "You Don't Have to Go," 1955; "Honest I Do," 1957; "Baby What You Want Me to Do," 1960; "Big Boss Man," 1961; "Bright Lights Big City," 1961

Reese, Della, "And That Reminds Me," 1957; "Don't You Know," 1959; "Not One Minute More," 1959

Reeves, Jim, "Four Walls," 1957; "He'll Have to Go," 1960; "I'm Gettin' Better," 1960; "Am I Losing You," 1960; "Distant Drums," 1966

Reeves, Jim, RIAA Gold Albums, "The Best of Jim Reeves," 1966; "Distant Drums," 1968

Reflections, "(Just Like) Romeo and Juliet," 1964

Regents, "Barbara-Ann," 1961

Renay, Diane, "Navy Blue," 1964; "Kiss Me Sailor," 1964

Rene and Rene, "Lo Mucho Que Te Quiero," 1968

Reunion, "Life Is a Rock (But the Radio Rolled Me)," 1975

Revere, Paul, and The Raiders, "Steppin' Out," 1965; "Just Like Me," 1965; "Kicks," 1966; "Hungry," 1966; "The Great Airplane Strike," 1966; "Good Thing," 1966; "Ups and Downs," 1967; "Him or Me, What's It Gonna Be?" 1967; "I Had a Dream," 1967; "Too Much Talk," 1968; "Don't Take It So Hard," 1968; "Mr. Sun, Mr. Moon," 1969; "Let Me," 1969; "Indian Reservation," 1971, RIAA 71; "Birds of a Feather," 1971

Revere, Paul, and The Raiders, RIAA Gold Albums, "Just Like Us," 1967; "Midnight Ride," 1967; "Spirit of '67," 1967; "Paul Revere and The Raiders' Greatest," 1967

Renolds, Debbie, "Tammy," 1957; "Am I That Easy to Forget," 1960

Reynolds, Jody, "Endless Sleep," 1958

Reynolds, Lawrence, "Jesus Is a Soul Man," 1969

Rhinoceros, "Apricot Brandy," 1969

Rhodes, Emitt, "Fresh as a Daisy," 1971

Rhythm, Heritage, "Theme from 'SWAT'," 1976, RIAA 76; "Theme from 'Barretta'," 1976

Rich, Charlie, "Lonely Weekends," 1960; "Mohair Sam," 1965; "Behind Closed Doors," 1973, RIAA 73; "Most Beautiful Girl," 1973, RIAA 73; "A Very Special Love Song," 1973; "Everytime You Touch Me," 1975; "Since I Fell for You," 1976; "America, the Beautiful," 1976

Rich, Charlie, RIAA Gold Albums, "Behind Closed Doors," 1973; "Very Special Love Songs," 1974; "There Won't Be Anymore," 1974

Richard, Cliff, "Living Doll," 1959; "Theme for a Dream," 1961; "It's All in the Game," 1963; "Blue Turns to Grey," 1964; "Devil Woman," 1976

Riddle, Nelson, "Lisbon Antigua," 1955; "Port Au Prince," 1956; " 'Route 66' Theme," 1962

Righteous Brothers, "Little Latin Lupe Lu," 1963; "You've Lost That Lovin' Feeling," 1964; "Just Once in My Life," 1965; "Unchained Melody," 1965; "Ebb Tide," 1965; "(You're My) Soul and Inspiration," 1966, RIAA 66; "He," 1966; "Rock and Roll Heaven," 1974

Righteous Brothers, RIAA Gold Albums, "Soul and Inspiration," 1966; "The Righteous Brothers' Greatest Hits," 1969

Riley, Jeannie C., "Harper Valley PTA," 1968

Rinky-Dinks, "Early in the Morning," 1958

Rios, Augie, "Donde Esta Santa Claus?" 1958

Rios, Miguel, "A Song of Joy," 1970

Rip Chords, "Gone," 1963; "Hey Little Cobra," 1964; "Three Window Coupe," 1964

Riperton, Minnie, "Lovin' You," 1975, RIAA 75

Riperton, Minnie, RIAA Gold Album, "Perfect Angel," 1975

Ritchie Family, "Brazil," 1975; "The Best Disco in Town," 1976

Ritter, Tex, "The Wayward Wind," 1956; "I Dreamed of a Hillbilly Heaven," 1961

Rivers, Johnny, "Memphis," 1964; "Maybelline," 1964; "Mountain of Love," 1964; "Midnight Special," 1965; "Seventh Son," 1965; "Where Have All the Flowers Gone," 1965; "Secret Agent Man," 1966; "(I Washed My Hands In) Muddy Water," 1966; "Poor Side of Town," 1966; "Baby I Need Your Lovin'," 1967; "The Tracks of My Tears," 1967; "Summer Rain," 1967; "Rockin' Pneumonia, Boogie Woogie Flu," 1973, RIAA 73; "Help Me Rhonda," 1975

Rivers, Johnny, RIAA Gold Albums, "Realization," 1969; "A Touch of Gold, Vol. 2," 1975; "Johnny Rivers' Golden Hits," 1975

Rivieras, "California Sun," 1964

Rivingtons, "Papa-Oom-Mow-Mow," 1962

Robbins, Marty, "Singing the Blues," 1956; "A White Sport Coat (And a Pink Carnation)," 1957; "The Story of My Life," 1957; "She Was Only Seventeen," 1958; "The Hanging Tree," 1959; "El Paso," 1959; "Big Iron," 1960; "Ballad of the Alamo," 1960; "Don't Worry," 1961; "Devil Woman," 1962; "Ruby Ann," 1962; "My Woman, My Woman, My Wife," 1970; "El Paso City," 1976

Robbins, Marty, RIAA Gold Album, "Gunfire Ballads and Trail Songs," 1965

Robert and Johnny, "We Belong Together," 1958

Roberts, Austin, "Something's Wrong with Me," 1972

Robertson, Don, "The Happy Whistler," 1956

Robic, Ivo, "Morgen," 1959

Robinson, Floyd, "Makin' Love," 1959

Robinson, Smokey, (See The Miracles), "Baby That's Back'atcha," 1975; "The Agony and the Ecstasy," 1975

Robinson, Vickie Sue, "Turn the Beat Around," 1976

Rochell and The Candles, "Once Upon a Time," 1961

Rock-A-Teens, "Woo-Hoo," 1959

Rockin Rebels, "Wild Weekend," 1963

Rocky Fellers, "Killer Joe," 1963

Rodgers and Hammerstein, RIAA Gold Album, "South Pacific," 1959

Rodgers, Eileen, "Miracle of Love," 1956; "Treasure of Your Love," 1958

Rodgers, Jimmie, "Honeycomb," 1957; "Kisses Sweeter Than Wine," 1957; "Oh-Oh, I'm Falling in Love Again," 1958; "Secretly," 1958; "Are You Really Mine," 1958; "Bimbombey," 1958; "(TLC) Tender Love and Care," 1960; "Waltzing Matilda," 1960; "The World I Used to Know," 1964; "It's Over," 1966

Roe, Tommy, "Sheila," 1962, RIAA 69; "Everybody," 1963; "Sweet Pea,"

Wave"/"Love Is a Rose," 1975; "Tracks of My Tears," 1976; "That'll Be the Day," 1976

Ronstadt, Linda, RIAA Gold Albums, "Heart Like a Wheel," 1975; "Don't Cry Now," 1975; "Prisoner in Disguise," 1975; "Hasten Down the Wind," 1976

Rooftop Singers, "Walk Right In," 1963; "Tom Cat," 1963

Roommates, "Glory of Love," 1961

Rose, David, "The Stripper," 1962

Rose, David, RIAA Gold Album, "The Stripper and Other Fun Songs," 1969

Rose Garden, "Next Plane to London," 1967

Rosie and The Originals, "Angel Baby," 1960

Ross, Diana, "Reach Out and Touch (Somebody's Hand)," 1970; "Ain't No Mountain High Enough," 1970; "Remember Me," 1970; "Reach Out I'll Be There," 1971; "Touch Me in the Morning," 1973; "No Matter What Sign," 1973; "Last Time I Saw Him," 1974; "Theme from *Mahogany*," 1975, RIAA 76; "Love Hangover," 1976, RIAA 76; "One Love in My Lifetime," 1976

Ross, Jack, "Cinderella," 1962

Ross, Jackie, "Selfish One," 1964

Ross, Spencer, "Tracy's Theme," 1960

Routers, "Let's Go," 1962

Rover Boys, "Graduation Day," 1956

Roxy Music, "Love Is the Drug," 1976

Royal, Billy Joe, "Down in the Boondocks," 1965; "I Knew You When," 1965; "Cherry Hill Park," 1969

Royal Guardsmen, "Snoopy vs. the Red Baron," 1966, RIAA 67; "The Return of the Red Baron," 1967

Royal Scots Dragoon Guard, Pipes and Drums and Band of the, "Amazing Grace," 1972

Royal Teens, "Short Shorts," 1958; "Believe Me," 1959

Royaltones, "Poor Boy," 1958

Ruby and The Romantics, "Our Day Will Come," 1963; "My Summer Love," 1963; "Hey There Lonely Boy," 1963; "Young Wings Can Fly," 1963

Rubys, "You, I," 1969

Ruffin, David, "My Whole World Ended (The Moment You Left Me)," 1969

Ruffin, Jimmy, "What Becomes of the Broken Hearted," 1966; "I've Passed This Way Before," 1966; "Gonna Give Her All the Love I've Got," 1967

Rufus (featuring Chaka Kahn), "Tell Me Something Good," 1974, RIAA 74;

"Once You Get Started," 1974; "Sweet Thing," 1976; "Dance With Me," 1976

Rufus, featuring Chaka Kahn, RIAA Gold Albums, "Rags to Rufus," 1974; "Rufusized," 1974; "Rufus, Featuring Chaka Kahn," 1976; "Sweet Thing," 1976

Rundgren, Todd, "We Gotta Get You a Woman (Leroy, Boy)," 1970; "I Saw the Light," 1972; "Hello It's Me," 1974; "Good Vibrations," 1976

Rundgren, Todd, RIAA Gold Album, "Something, Anything?" 1975

Runt (see Todd Rundgren)

Rush, Merrilee, and The Turnabouts, "Angel of the Morning," 1968

Rush, Tom, "Who Do You Love," 1971

Russell, Bobby, "1432 Franklin Pike Circle Hero," 1968; "Saturday Morning Confusion," 1971

Russell, Leon, "Tight Rope," 1972; "Lady Blue," 1975

Russell, Leon, RIAA Gold Albums, "Leon Russell and The Shelter People," 1972; "Carney," 1972; "Leon Live," 1973; "Will o' the Wisp," 1976

Ryan, Charlie, and The Timberline Riders, "Hot Rod Lincoln," 1960

Rydell, Bobby, "Kissin' Time," 1959; "We Got Love," 1959; "Wild One," 1960; "Little Bitty Girl," 1960; "Swingin' School"/"Ding-a-Ling," 1960; "Volare," 1960; "Sway," 1960; "Good Time Baby," 1961; "That Old Black Magic," 1961; "The Fish," 1961; "I Wanna Thank You," 1961; "I've Got Bonnie," 1962; "I'll Never Dance Again," 1962; "The Cha-Cha-Cha," 1962; "Butterfly Baby," 1963; "Wildwood Days," 1963; "Forget Him," 1963; "Sway (Disco Version)," 1976

Rydell, Bobby, and Chubby Checker, "Jingle Bell Rock," 1961

Ryder, John and Anne, "I Still Believe in Tomorrow," 1969

Ryder, Mitch and The Detroit Wheels, "Jenny Take a Ride!" 1965; "Little Latin Lupe Lu," 1966; "Devil with a Blue Dress on and Good Golly Miss Molly," 1966; "Sock It to Me, Baby!" 1967; "Too Many Fish in the Sea"/"Three Little Fishes," 1967

Sadler, Sgt. Barry, "The Ballad of the Green Berets," 1966, RIAA 66
Sadler, Sgt. Barry, RIAA Gold Album, "Ballad of the Green Berets," 1966
Safaris, "Image of a Girl," 1960
Sailcat, "Motorcycle Mama," 1972
St. Peters, Crispian, "The Pied Piper," 1966
Sakamoto, Kyu, "Sukiyaki," 1963

Salsoul Orchestra, "Tangerine," 1975

Sam and Dave, "Hold On! I'm a Comin'," 1966; "Soul Man," 1967, RIAA 67; "I Thank You," 1968

Sami Jo, "Tell Me a Lie," 1974

Sam The Sham and The Pharaohs, "Wooly Bully," 1965, RIAA 65; "Ju Ju Hand," 1965; "Lil' Red Riding Hood," 1966, RIAA 66; "The Hair on My Chinny Chin Chin," 1966; "How Do You Catch a Girl," 1966

Sandpebbles, "Love Power," 1967

Sandpipers, "Guantanamera," 1966; "Come Saturday Morning," 1969

Sandpipers, RIAA Gold Album, "Guantanamera," 1968

Sands, Evie, "Any Way That You Want Me," 1969

Sands, Jodie, "With All My Heart," 1957

Sands, Tommy, "Teen-Age Crush," 1957; "Goin' Steady," 1957

San Remo Golden Strings, "Hungry for Love," 1965

San Sebastian Strings, RIAA Gold Album, "The Sea," 1968

Santamaria, Mongo, "Watermelon Man," 1963

Santana, "Evil Ways," 1970; "Black Magic Woman," 1970; "Oye Como Va," 1971; "Everybody's Everything," 1971

Santana, RIAA Gold Albums, "Santana," 1969; "Abraxas," 1970; "Santana," 1971; "Caravanserai," 1972; "Welcome," 1973; "Santana's Greatest Hits," 1974; "Amigos," 1976

Santana, Carlos, and Buddy Miles, RIAA Gold Album, "Carlos Santana and Buddy Miles," 1972

Santana, Carlos, and John McLaughlin, RIAA Gold Album, "Love Devotion Surrender," 1973

Santo and Johnny, "Sleep Walk," 1959; "Tear Drop," 1959

Sayer, Leo, "Long Tall Glasses," 1975

Sapphires, "Who Do You Love," 1964

Scaggs, Boz, "It's Over," 1976; "Lowdown," 1976

Scaggs, Boz, RIAA Gold Album, "Silk Degrees," 1976

Scaggs, Boz, RIAA Platinum Album, "Silk Degrees," 1976

Scott, Bobby, "Chain Gang," 1955

Scott, Freddy, "Hey Girl," 1963; "Are You Lonely for Me," 1969

Scott, Jack, "My True Love," 1958; "Leroy," 1958; "With Your Love," 1958; "Goodbye Baby," 1958; "What in the World's Come Over You," 1960; "Burning Bridges," 1960

Scott, Linda, "I've Told Every Little Star," 1961; "Don't Bet Money Honey," 1961; "I Don't Know Why," 1961

Scott, Peggy, and Jo Jo Benson, "Lover's Holiday," 1968; "Pickin' Wild Mountain Berries," 1968; "Soulshake," 1969

Seals and Crofts, "Summer Breeze," 1972; "Hummingbird," 1973; "Diamond Girl," 1973; "I'll Play for You," 1975; "Get Closer," 1976

Seals & Crofts, RIAA Gold Albums, "Summer Breeze," 1972; "Diamond Girl," 1973; "Unborn Child," 1974; "I'll Play For You," 1975; "Seals and Crofts Greatest Hits," 1975; "Get Closer," 1976

Searchers, "Needles and Pins," 1964; "Don't Throw Your Love Away," 1964; "Love Potion Number Nine," 1964; "Bumble Bee," 1965; "What Have They Done to the Rain," 1965

Sebastion, John, "Welcome Back," 1976, RIAA 76

Secrets, "The Boy Next Door," 1963

Sedaka, Neil, "The Diary," 1958; "Oh! Carol," 1959; "Stairway to Heaven," 1960; "You Mean Everything to Me," 1960; "Run Samson Run," 1960; "Calendar Girl," 1960; "Little Devil," 1971; "Happy Birthday, Sweet Sixteen," 1961; "Breaking Up Is Hard to Do," 1962; "Next Door to an Angel," 1962; "Alice in Wonderland," 1963; "Let's Go Steady Again," 1963; "Laughter in the Rain," 1975; "That's When the Music Takes Me," 1975; "The Immigrant," 1975; "Bad Blood," 1975, RIAA 75; "Breaking Up Is Hard to Do," 1976; "Love in the Shadows," 1976; "Steppin' Out," 1976; "You Gotta Make Your Own Sunshine," 1976

Sedaka, Neil, RIAA Gold Albums, "Sedaka's Back," 1975; "The Hungry Years," 1975

Seeds, "Pushin' Too Hard," 1966

Seekers, "I'll Never Find Another You," 1965; "A World of Our Own," 1965; "Georgy Girl," 1967, RIAA 67

Seger, Bob, System, "Ramblin' Gamblin' Man," 1969

Senator Bobby, "Wild Thing," 1967

Sensations, "Music, Music, Music," 1961; "Let Me In," 1962

Serendipity Singers, "Don't Let the Rain Come Down," 1964; "Crooked Little Man," 1964

Seville, David, "Armen's Theme," 1956; "Witch Doctor," 1958; "The Bird on My Head," 1958

Shades of Blue, "Oh How Happy," 1966

Shadows, "Apache," 1961

Shadows of Knight, "Gloria," 1966

Sha Na Na, "(Just Like) Romeo and Juliet," 1975

Sha Na Na, RIAA Gold Album, "Golden Age of Rock and Roll," 1973

Shangri-Las, "Remember (Walkin' in the Sand)," 1964; "Leader of the Pack," 1964; "Give Him a Great Big Kiss," 1964; "Give Us Your Blessings," 1965; "I Can Never Go Home Anymore," 1965

Shannon, "Abergavenny," 1969

Shannon, Del, "Runaway," 1961; "Hats Off to Larry," 1961; "So Long

Baby," 1961; "Little Town Flirt," 1962; "Handy Man," 1964; "Keep Searchin'," 1964

Sharp, Dee Dee, "Mashed Potato Time," 1962; "Gravy," 1962; "Ride!" 1962; "Do the Bird," 1963

Sharpe, Ray, "Linda Lu," 1959

Shaw, George, "No Arms Can Ever Hold You," 1955

Shaw, Robert, Chorale, RIAA Gold Album, "Christmas Hymns and Carols," 1964

Shaw, Sandie, "Girl Don't Come," 1965

Shells, "Baby Oh Baby," 1960

Shep and The Limelites, "Daddy's Home," 1961

Shepherd Sisters, "Alone," 1957

Sherman, Allan, "Hello Mudduh, Hello Fadduh!" 1963

Sherman, Allan, RIAA Gold Album, "My Son, the Folk Singer," 1962

Sherman, Bobby, "Little Woman," 1969, RIAA 69; "La La La (If I Had You)," 1970, RIAA 70; "Easy Come, Easy Go," 1970, RIAA 70; "Hey, Mister Sun," 1970; "Julie, Do Ya Love Me," 1970, RIAA 70; "Cried Like a Baby," 1971; "The Drum," 1971

Sherman, Bobby, RIAA Gold Albums, "Bobby Sherman," 1970; "Here Comes Bobby," 1970; "With Love, Bobby," 1970

Shields, "You Cheated," 1958

Shirelles, "I Met Him on a Sunday," 1958; "Dedicated to the One I Love," 1959; "Tonight's the Night," 1960; "Will You Love Me Tomorrow," 1960; "Dedicated to the One I Love," 1961; "Mama Said," 1961; "Big John," 1961; "Baby It's You," 1961; "Soldier Boy," 1962; "Welcome Home Baby," 1962; "Everybody Loves a Lover," 1962; "Foolish Little Girl," 1963; "Don't Say Goodnight and Mean Good-bye," 1963

Shirley and Company, "Shame, Shame, Shame," 1974

Shirley and Lee, "Feel So Good," 1955; "Let the Good Times Roll," 1956; "I Feel Good," 1956

Shocking Blue, "Venus," 1969, RIAA 70

Shondell, Troy, "This Time," 1961

Shore, Dinah, "Love and Marriage," 1955; "Chantez, Chantez," 1957

Showmen, "It Will Stand," 1961

Sigler, Bunny, "Let the Good Times Roll and Feel So Good," 1967

Silhouettes, "Get a Job," 1958

Silkie, "You've Got to Hide Your Love Away," 1965

Silver, "Wham Bam," 1976

Silver Convention, "Fly Robin Fly," 1975, RIAA 75; "Get Up and Boogie," 1976, RIAA 76

Silver Convention, RIAA Gold Album, "Save Me," 1975

Simeone, Harry, Chorale, "The Little Drummer Boy," 1958

Simeone, Harry, Chorale, RIAA Gold Album, "Drummer Boy," 1969

Simmons, Jumpin' Gene, "Haunted House," 1964

Simon and Garfunkel, "The Sounds of Silence," 1965, RIAA 66; "Homeward
    Bound," 1966; "I Am a Rock," 1966; "The Dangling Conversation,"
    1966; "A Hazy Shade of Winter," 1966; "At the Zoo," 1967; "Fakin'
    It," 1967; "Scarborough Fair," 1968; "Mrs. Robinson," 1968, RIAA
    68; "The Boxer," 1969; "Bridge Over Troubled Water," 1970, RIAA
    70; "Cecelia," 1970; "My Little Town," 1975

Simon and Garfunkel, RIAA Gold Albums, "Parsley, Sage, Rosemary, and
    Thyme," 1967; "Sounds of Silence," 1967; "Bookends," 1968;
    Wednesday Morning 3 A.M.," 1969; "Bridge Over Troubled Water,"
    1970; "Simon and Garfunkel's Greatest Hits," 1972

Simon, Carly, "That's the Way I've Always Heard It Should Be," 1971;
    "Anticipation," 1971; "You're So Vain," 1972

Simon, Carly, RIAA Gold Albums, "No Secrets," 1972; "Anticipation,"
    1973; "Hot Cakes," 1974; "The Best of Carly Simon," 1975

Simon, Carly, and James Taylor, "Mockingbird," 1974

Simon, Joe, "(You Keep Me) Hangin' On," 1968; "The Chokin' Kind," 1969,
    RIAA 69; "Drowning in the Sea of Love," 1972, RIAA 72; "Power
    of Love," 1972, RIAA 72; "Get Down, Get Down," 1975

Simon, Paul, "Mother and Child Reunion," 1972; "Me and Julio Down by
    the Schoolyard," 1972; "Kodachrome," 1973; "Love Me Like a
    Rock," 1973, RIAA 73; "Gone at Last," 1975; "50 Ways To Leave
    Your Lover," 1976, RIAA 76; "Still Crazy After All These Years,"
    1976

Simon, Paul, RIAA Gold Albums, "Paul Simon," 1972; "There Goes Rhymin'
    Simon," 1973; "Live Rhymin'," 1974; "Still Crazy After All These
    Years," 1975

Simone, Nina, "I Loves You, Porgy," 1959

Sinatra, Frank, "Love and Marriage," 1955; "The Tender Trap," 1955; "How
    Little We Know," 1956; "Can I Steal a Little Love," 1957; "All
    The Way," 1957; "Witchcraft," 1958; "High Hopes," 1959; "Talk
    to Me," 1959; "Ol' MacDonald," 1960; "Pocketful of Miracles,"
    1961; "Softly, As I Leave You," 1964; "It Was a Very Good Year,"
    1965; "Strangers in the Night," 1966; "Summer Wind," 1966;
    "That's Life," 1966; "The World We Know," 1967; "Cycles," 1968;
    "Hey! Jealous Love," 1956; "My Way," 1969; "I Believe I'm Gonna
    Love Ya," 1975

Sinatra, Frank, RIAA Gold Albums, "Come Dance with Me," 1961; "Frank
    Sinatra Sings for Only the Lonely," 1962; "Nice 'n' Easy," 1962;
    "Songs for Swinging Lovers," 1962; "This Is Sinatra," 1962;

258

"Sinatra's Sinatra," 1965; "September of My Years,"1966; "A Man and His Music," 1966; "Strangers in the Night," 1966; "That's Life," 1967; "Sinatra at the Sands," 1967; "Cycles," 1969; "My Way," 1970; "Frank Sinatra's Greatest Hits," 1970

Sinatra, Nancy, "These Boots Are Made for Walkin'," 1966, RIAA 66; "How Does That Grab You, Darlin'?" 1966; "Sugar Town," 1966; "Love Eyes," 1967; "Lightning's Girl," 1967

Sinatra, Nancy, RIAA Gold Album, "Boots," 1966

Sinatra, Nancy, and Dean Martin, "Things," 1967

Sinatra, Nancy and Frank, "Somethin' Stupid," 1967, RIAA 67

Sinatra, Nancy, and Lee Hazlewood, "Summer Wine," 1967; "Jackson," 1967; "Lady Bird," 1967; "Some Velvet Morning," 1968

Sinatra, Nancy, and Lee Hazlewood, RIAA Gold Album, "Nancy and Lee," 1970

Singing Nun (Soeur Sourire), "Dominique," 1963

Singing Nun (Soeur Sourire), RIAA Gold Album, "Singing Nun," 1963

Sir Douglas Quintet, "She's About a Mover," 1965; "The Rains Came," 1966; "Mendocino," 1969

Six Teens, "A Casual Look," 1956

Skelton, Red, "The Pledge of Allegiance," 1969

Skip and Flip, "It Was I," 1959; "Cherry Pie," 1960

Skylark, "Wildflower," 1973

Skyliners, "Since I Don't Have You," 1959; "This I Swear," 1959; "Pennies from Heaven," 1960

Skynyrd, Lynyrd, "Sweet Home Alabama," 1974; "Free Bird," 1974

Skynyrd, Lynyrd, RIAA Gold Albums, "Second Helping," 1974; "Pronounced Leh-nard Skin-nerd," 1974; "Nuthin' Fancy," 1975

Sledge, Percy, "When a Man Loves a Woman," 1966, RIAA 66; "Warm and Tender Love," 1966; "It Tears Me Up," 1966; "Take Time to Know Her," 1968

Sly and The Family Stone, "Dance to the Music," 1968; "Everyday People," 1968, RIAA 69; "Stand!" 1969; "Hot Fun in the Summertime," 1969; "Thank You"/"Everybody Is a Star," 1970, RIAA 70; "I Want to Take You Higher," 1970; "Family Affair," 1971, RIAA 71; "Runnin' Away," 1972; "If You Want Me to Stay," 1973, RIAA 73

Sly and The Family Stone, RIAA Gold Albums, "Stand!" 1969; "Sly and The Family Stone's Greatest Hits," 1970; "There's a Riot Goin' On," 1971; "Fresh," 1973; "Small Talk," 1974

Small Faces, "Itchycoo Park," 1967

Small, Millie, "My Boy Lollipop," 1964

Smith, "Baby It's You," 1969

Smith, Huey (Piano), and The Clowns, "Rocking Pneumonia and the Boogie Woogie Flu," 1957; "Don't You Just Know It," 1958

Smith, Hurricane, "Oh, Baby, What Would You Say?" 1972

Smith, Jimmy, "Walk on the Wild Side," 1962

Smith, O. C., "The Son of Hickory Holler's Tramp," 1968; "Little Green Apples," 1968, RIAA 68; "Daddy's Little Man," 1969

Smith, Ray, "Rockin' Little Angel," 1960

Smith, Sammi, "Help Me Make It Through the Night," 1971, RIAA 71

Smith, Somethin', and The Redheads, "In a Shanty in Old Shanty Town," 1956

Smith, Verdelle, "Tar and Cement," 1966

Smith, Whistling Jack, "I Was Kaiser Bill's Batman," 1967

Smothers Brothers, RIAA Gold Albums, "Think Ethnic," 1966; "The Two Sides of the Smothers Brothers," 1967; "Purple Onion," 1968

Snow, Hank, "I've Been Everywhere," 1962; "Ninety Miles an Hour," 1963

Snow, Phoebe, "Poetry Man," 1975

Snow, Phoebe, RIAA Gold Albums, "Phoebe Snow," 1975; "Second Childhood," 1976

Sommers, Joanie, "Johnny Get Angry," 1962

Sonny, "Laugh at Me," 1965

Sonny and Cher, "I Got You Babe," 1965, RIAA 66; "Baby Don't Go," 1965; "Just You," 1965; "But You're Mine," 1965; "Little Man," 1966; "The Beat Goes On," 1967; "All I Ever Need Is You," 1971; "A Cowboy's Work Is Never Done," 1972

Sonny and Cher, RIAA Gold Albums, "Look At Us," 1965; "All I Ever Need Is You," 1972; "Sonny and Cher Live," 1972

Sopwith Camel, "Hello, Hello," 1967

Soul, Jimmy, "Twistin' Matilda," 1962; "If You Wanna Be Happy," 1963

Soul Survivors, "Expressway to Your Heart," 1967

Sounds Orchestral, "Cast Your Fate to the Wind," 1965

South, Joe, "Games People Play," 1969; "Don't It Make You Want to Go Home," 1969; "Walk a Mile in My Shoes," 1970

Souther, Hillman and Furay, RIAA Gold Album, "The Souther, Hillman, Furay Band," 1974

Spaniels, "Goodnight, Sweetheart, Goodnight," 1954-55

Spanky and Our Gang, "Sunday Will Never Be the Same," 1967; "Making Every Minute Count," 1967; "Lazy Day," 1967; "Sunday Mornin'," 1968; "Like to Get to Know You," 1968; "Give a Damn," 1968

Sparkletones with Joe Bennett, "Black Slacks," 1957

Spencer Davis Group, "Keep on Running," 1966; "Somebody Help Me," 1966; "Gimme Some Lovin'," 1967; "I'm a Man," 1967

Spinners, "That's What Girls Are Made For," 1961; "It's a Shame," 1970; "I'll Be Around"/"How Could I Let You Get Away," 1972, RIAA 72; "Could It Be I'm Falling in Love," 1972, RIAA 73; "One of a Kind Love Affair," 1973, RIAA 73; "Then Came You," 1975, RIAA 75; "Mighty Love," 1975; "They Just Can't Stop It (Games People Play)," 1975; "The Rubberband Man," 1976

Spinners, RIAA Gold Albums, "Spinners," 1973; "Mighty Love," 1974; "New and Improved," 1974; "Pick of the Litter," 1975

Spiral Staircase, "More Today Than Yesterday," 1969

Spirit, "I Got a Line on You," 1969

Spirit, RIAA Gold Album, "Twelve Dreams of Dr. Sardonicus," 1976

Springfield, Dusty, "I Only Want to Be with You," 1964; "Wishin' and Hopin'," 1964; "You Don't Have to Say You Love Me," 1966; "All I See Is You," 1967; "The Look of Love," 1967; "Son of a Preacher Man," 1968; "A Brand New Me," 1969; "Silly, Silly Fool," 1970

Springfield, Rick, "Speak to the Sky," 1972

Springfields, "Silver Threads and Golden Needles," 1962

Springsteen, Bruce, "Born to Run," 1975; "10th Avenue Freezeout," 1976

Springsteen, Bruce, RIAA Gold Album, "Born to Run," 1975

Stafford, Jim, "Spiders and Snakes," 1974, RIAA 74; "My Girl Bill," 1974; "Wildwood Weed," 1974; "I Got Stoned and Missed It," 1975

Stafford, Jo, "Suddenly There's a Valley," 1955; "It's Almost Tomorrow," 1955

Stafford, Terry, "Suspicion," 1964

Stampeders, "Sweet City Woman," 1971; "Hit the Road, Jack," 1976

Stampley, Joe, "Soul Song," 1973

Standells, "Dirty Water," 1966

Staple Singers, "Heavy Makes You Happy (Sha-Na-Boom Boom)," 1971; "Respect Yourself," 1971; "I'll Take You There," 1972; "If You're Ready (Come Go with Me)," 1973, RIAA 73; "Let's Do It Again," 1975, RIAA 75

Stapleton, Cyril, "The Children's Marching Song," 1959

Starbuck, "Moonlight Feels Right," 1976

Starland Vocal Band, "Afternoon Delight," 1976, RIAA 76

Starr, Edwin, "Agent Double-O Soul," 1965; "Twenty-Five Miles," 1969; "War," 1970; "Stop the War Now," 1970

Starr, Kay, "Rock and Roll Waltz," 1955

Starr, Randy, "After School," 1957

Starr, Ringo, "It Don't Come Easy," 1971, RIAA 71; "Back Off Boogaloo," 1972; "Photograph," 1973, RIAA 73; "You're Sixteen," 1974,

RIAA 74; "Oh My, My!" 1974; "No No Song," 1975; "Only You," 1975; "A Dose of Rock 'n' Roll," 1976

Starr, Ringo, RIAA Gold Albums, "Ringo," 1973; "Goodnight Vienna," 1974

Statler Brother, "Flowers on the Wall," 1965

Staton, Candi, "Stand by Your Man," 1970; "Young Hearts Fun Free," 1976

Status Quo, "Pictures of Matchstick Men," 1968

Stealer's Wheel, "Stuck in the Middle with You," 1973

Steam, "Na Na Hey Hey Kiss Him Goodbye," 1969, RIAA 69

Steely Dan, "Do It Again," 1972; "Reelin' in the Years," 1973; "Rikki, Don't Lose That Number," 1974

Steely Dan, RIAA Gold Albums, "Can't Buy a Thrill," 1973; "Pretzel Logic," 1974; "Katy Lied," 1975; "Royal Scam," 1976

Steppenwolf, "Born to Be Wild," 1968, RIAA 68; "Magic Carpet Ride," 1969, RIAA 69; "Rock Me," 1969; "Monster," 1969

Steppenwolf, RIAA Gold Albums, "Steppenwolf," 1968; "Steppenwolf the 2nd," 1969; "Monster," 1970; "Live Steppenwolf," 1970; "Steppenwolf 7," 1971; "Steppenwolf Gold," 1971

Stereos, "I Really Love You," 1961

Steve and Eydie (Steve Lawrence and Eydie Gorme), "I Want to Stay Here," 1963

Stevens, Cat, "Wild World," 1971; "Moon Shadow," 1971; "Peace Train," 1971; "Morning Has Broken," 1972; "Sitting," 1972; "Another Saturday Night," 1974; "Oh Very Young," 1974; "Ban-Apple Gas," 1976

Stevens, Cat, RIAA Gold Albums, "Tea for Tillerman," 1971; "Teaser and the Firecat," 1971; "Catch Bull at Four," 1972; "Foreigner," 1973; "Buddha and the Chocolate Box," 1974; "Cat Stevens Greatest Hits," 1975; "Numbers," 1976; "Mona Bone Jakon," 1976

Stevens, Connie, "Sixteen Reasons," 1960

Stevens, Doobie, "Pink Shoe Laces," 1959

Stevens, Ray, "Jeremiah Peabody's Poly Unsaturated Quick Dissolving Fast Acting Pleasant Tasting Green and Purple Pills," 1961; "Harry, the Hairy Ape," 1963; "Mr. Businessman," 1968; "Gitarzan," 1969, RIAA 69; "Along Came Jones," 1969; "Everything Is Beautiful," 1970, RIAA 70; "America, Communicate with Me," 1970; "The Streak," 1974, RIAA 74; "Misty," 1975

Stevenson, B. W., "My Maria," 1973

Stewart, Billy, "I Do Love You," 1965; "Sitting in the Park," 1965; "Summertime," 1966; "Secret Love," 1966

Stewart, Rod, "Maggie May"/"Reason to Believe," 1971, RIAA 71; "(I Know) I'm Losing You," 1971; "Handbags and Gladrags," 1972; "You Wear It Well," 1972; "Twistin' the Night Away," 1973; "Pinball Wizard," 1973

Styx, "Lady," 1975; "Lorelei," 1976

Styx, RIAA Gold Album, "Styx II," 1975

Sugarloaf, "Green-Eyed Lady," 1970

Summer, Donna, "Love to Love You Baby," 1975, RIAA 76; "Could It Be Magic," 1976; "Try Me, I Know We Can Make It," 1976

Summer, Donna, RIAA Gold Albums, "Love to Love You Baby," 1976; "Love Trilogy," 1976

Sunny and The Sunglows, "Talk to Me," 1963

Sunshine Company, "Happy," 1967

Supremes, "When the Lovelight Starts Shining Through His Eyes," 1963; "Where Did Our Love Go," 1964; "Baby Love," 1964; "Come See About Me," 1964; "Stop! In the Name of Love," 1965; "Back in My Arms Again," 1965; "Nothing but Heartaches," 1965; "I Hear a Symphony," 1965; "My World Is Empty Without You," 1966; "Love Is Like an Itching in My Heart," 1966; "You Can't Hurry Love," 1966; "You Keep Me Hangin' On," 1966; "Love Is Here and Now You're Gone," 1967; "The Happening," 1967; "Reflections," 1967; "In and Out of Love," 1967; "Forever Came Today," 1968; "Love Child," 1968; "I'm Livin' in Shame," 1969; "The Composer," 1969; "No Matter What Sign You Are," 1969; "Someday We'll Be Together," 1969; "Up the Ladder to the Roof," 1970; "Stoned Love," 1970; "Nathan Jones," 1971; "Floy Joy," 1972; "Automatically Sunshine," 1972; "I'm Gonna Let My Heart Do the Walking," 1976

Supremes and Four Tops, "River Deep, Mountain High," 1970

Supremes (Diana Ross) and The Temptations, "I'm Gonna Make You Love Me," 1968; "I'll Try Something New," 1969

Surfaris, "Wipe Out," 1963; "Surfer Joe," 1963; "Wipe Out," 1966

Swann, Bettye, "Make Me Yours," 1967

Swan, Billy, "I Can Help," 1974, RIAA 74

Sweet, "Little Willy," 1973; "Ballroom Blitz," 1975; "Fox on the Run," 1975, RIAA 76; "Action," 1976

Sweet, RIAA Gold Album, "Desolation Boulevard," 1976

Sweet Inspirations, "Sweet Inspiration," 1968

Sweet Sensations, "Sad Sweet Dreamer," 1975

Swinging Blue Jeans, "Hippy, Hippy Shake," 1964

Swinging Medallions, "Double Shot (of My Baby's Love)," 1966

Sylvers, "Boogie Fever," 1976, RIAA 76; "Cotton Candy," 1976

Sylvia, "Pillow Talk," 1973

Syms, Sylvia, "I Could Have Danced All Night," 1956

Syndicate of Sound, "Little Girl," 1966

Tams, "What Kind of Fool (Do You Think I Am)," 1963; "Hey, Girl, Don't Bother Me," 1964

Tanega, Norma, "Walkin' My Cat Named Dog," 1966

Tarriers, "Cindy Oh Cindy," 1956; "Banana Boat Song," 1956

Taylor, Bobby, and The Vancouvers, "Does Your Mama Know About Me?" 1968

Taylor, James, "Fire and Rain," 1970; "Carolina in My Mind," 1970; "You've Got a Friend," 1971; "Long Ago and Far Away," 1971; "Don't Let Me Be Lonely Tonight," 1972; "How Sweet It Is," 1975; "Shower the People," 1976

Taylor, James, RIAA Gold Albums, "Sweet Baby James," 1970; "You've Got a Friend," 1971; "One Man Dog," 1972; "Gorilla," 1975

Taylor, James, and Carly Simon, "Mockingbird," 1974, RIAA 74

Taylor, Johnny, "Who's Making Love," 1968, RIAA 68; "Take Care of Your Homework," 1969; "Testify (I Wanna)," 1969; "Steal Away," 1970; "Jody's Got Your Girl," 1971; "I Believe in You," 1973, RIAA 73; "Disco Lady," 1976, RIAA 76, RIAA Platinum 76; "Somebody's Gettin' It," 1976

Taylor, Johnny, RIAA Gold Album, "Eargasm," 1976

Taylor, Little Johnny, "Part Time Love," 1963

Taylor, R. Dean, "Indiana Wants Me," 1970

Tavares, "Remember What I Told You to Forget," 1975; "It Only Takes a Minute," 1975; "Heaven Must Be Missing an Angel," 1976, RIAA 76

T-Bones, "No Matter What Shape (Your Stomach's In)," 1965

Techniques, "Hey! Little Girl," 1957

Teddy Bears, "To Know Him, Is to Love Him," 1958

Teegarden and Van Winkle, "God, Love, and Rock and Roll," 1970

Teen Queens, "Eddie My Love," 1956

Tee Set, "Ma Belle Amie," 1970

Television Soundtracks, RIAA Gold Albums, "Sesame Street," 1970; "All in the Family," 1971; "Here's Johnny (Magic Moments of the Tonight Show)," 1974

Tempo, Nino, and April Stevens, "Deep Purple," 1963; "Whispering," 1963; "Stardust," 1964; "All Strung Out," 1966

Tempos, "See You in September," 1959

Temptations, "The Way You Do the Things You Do," 1964; "Girl (Why You Wanna Make Me Blue)," 1964; "My Girl," 1965; "It's Growing," 1965; "Since I Lost My Baby," 1965; "My Baby," 1965; "Get Ready," 1966; "Ain't Too Proud to Beg," 1966; "Beauty Is Only Skin Deep," 1966; "(I Know) I'm Losing You," 1966; "All I Need," 1967; "You're My Everything," 1967; "(Loneliness Made Me Realize) It's You That I Need," 1967; "I Wish It Would Rain," 1968;

265

"I Could Never Love Another (After Loving You)," 1968; "Cloud Nine," 1968; "Run Away Child, Running Wild," 1969; "Don't Let the Joneses Get You Down," 1969; "I Can't Get Next to You," 1969; "Psychedelic Shack," 1970; "Ball of Confusion," 1970; "Just My Imagination (Running Away with Me)," 1971; "Superstar (Remember How You Got Where You Are)," 1971; "Papa Was a Rollin' Stone," 1972; "Shakey Ground," 1975; "Happy," 1975; "Glasshouse," 1975

10 cc, "I'm Not in Love," 1975

Ten Years After, RIAA Gold Album, "A Space in Time," 1971

Tex, Joe, "Hold on to What You Got," 1964; "I Want To (Do Everything for You)," 1965; "A Sweet Woman Like You," 1965; "S.Y.S.L.J.F.M. (The Letter Song)," 1966; "Show Me," 1967; "Skinny Legs and All," 1968, RIAA 68; "I Gotcha," 1972, RIAA 72

Them, "Gloria," 1965; "Here Comes the Night," 1965; "Mystic Eyes," 1965

Thin Lizzy, "The Boys Are Back in Town," 1976

Think, "Once You Understand," 1971

Thomas, B. J., "I'm So Lonesome I Could Cry," 1966; "Mama," 1966; "Billy and Sue," 1966; "The Eyes of a New York Woman," 1968; "Hooked on a Feeling," 1969, RIAA 69; "Raindrops Keep Fallin' on My Head," 1969, RIAA 69; "I Just Can't Help Believing," 1970; "Most of All," 1970; "No Love at All," 1971; "Rock and Roll Lullaby," 1972; "Another Somebody Done Somebody Wrong Song," 1975, RIAA 75

Thomas, B. J., RIAA Gold Album, "Raindrops Keep Fallin' on My Head," 1970

Thomas, Carla, "Gee Whiz (Look at His Eyes)," 1961; "B-A-B-Y," 1966

Thomas, Carla, and Otis Redding, "Tramp," 1967

Thomas, Irma, "Wish Someone Would Care," 1964

Thomas, Rufus, "The Dog," 1963; "Walking the Dog," 1963; "Do the Funky Chicken," 1970; "(Do the) Push and Pull, Part 1," 1970; "The Breakdown," 1971

Thomas, Timmy, "Why Can't We Live Together," 1972

Thompson, Sue, "Sad Movies (Make Me Cry)," 1961; "Norman," 1961; "James (Hold the Ladder Steady)," 1962; "Paper Tiger," 1965

Three Degrees, "Maybe," 1970; "When Will I See You Again," 1974, RIAA 74

Three Dog Night, "Try a Little Tenderness," 1969; "One," 1969, RIAA 69; "Easy to Be Hard," 1969; "Eli's Coming," 1969; "Celebrate," 1970; "Mama Told Me (Not to Come)," 1970, RIAA 70; "Out in the Country," 1970; "One Man Band," 1970; "Joy to the World," 1971, RIAA 71; "Liar," 1971; "An Old Fashioned Love Song," 1971, RIAA 71; "Never Been to Spain," 1971; "The Family of Man," 1972; "Black and White," 1972, RIAA 72; "Pieces of April," 1972;

"Shambala," 1973, RIAA 73; "The Show Must Go On," RIAA 74; "Till the World Ends," 1975

Three Dog Night, RIAA Gold Albums, "Three Dog Night," 1969; "Suitable for Framing," 1969; "Captured Live at the Forum," 1970; "It Ain't Easy," 1970; "Naturally," 1971; "Golden Biscuits," 1971; "Harmony," 1971; "Seven Separate Fools," 1972; "Around the World with Three Dog Night," 1973; "Cyan," 1973; "Hard Labor," 1974; "Joy to the World, Their Greatest Hits," 1975

Thunder, Johnny, "Loop De Loop," 1962

Tillotson, Johnny, "True True Happiness," 1959; "Poetry in Motion," 1960; "Jimmy's Girl," 1961; "Without Love," 1961; "Dreamy Eyes," 1961; "It Keeps Right on a-Hurtin'," 1962; "Send Me the Pillow You Dream On," 1962; "I Can't Help It (If I'm Still in Love with You)," 1962; "Out of My Mind," 1963; "You Can Never Stop Me Loving You," 1963; "Talk Back Trembling Lips," 1963

Tin Tin, "Toast and Marmalade for Tea," 1971

Tiny Tim, "Tiptoe Thru' the Tulips with Me," 1968

Todd, Art and Dotty, "Chanson D'Amour," 1958

Todd, Nick, "Plaything," 1957

Tokens, "The Lion Sleeps Tonight," 1961, RIAA 62; "I Hear Trumpets Blow," 1966; "Portrait of My Love," 1967

Tom and Jerry, "Hey, Schoolgirl," 1957

Toms, Gary, Empire, "7-6-5-4-3-2-1 (Blow Your Whistle)," 1975

Toney, Oscar, Jr., "For Your Precious Love," 1967

Torme, Mel, "Comin' Home Baby," 1962

Tornadoes, "Telstar," 1962

Torok, Mitchell, "Pledge of Love," 1957; "Caribbean," 1959

Tower of Power, "You're Still a Young Man," 1972; "So Very Hard to Go," 1973

Townsend, Ed, "For Your Love," 1958

Toys, "A Lover's Concerto," 1965, RIAA 65; "Attack," 1965

Trade Winds, "New York's a Lonely Town," 1965

Traffic, RIAA Gold Albums, "John Barleycorn Must Die," 1970; "Low Spark Of High Heeled Boys," 1972; "Shoot Out at the Fantasy Factory," 1973; "When the Eagle Flies," 1974

Trammps, "That's Where the Happy People Go," 1976

Trashmen, "Surfin' Bird," 1963

Travis and Bob, "Tell Him No," 1959

Travolta, John, "Let Her In," 1976

Tremeloes, "Here Comes My Baby," 1967; "Silence Is Golden," 1967

T. Rex, "Bang a Gong (Get It On)," 1972

Troggs, "Wild Thing," 1966; "With a Girl Like You," 1966; "Love Is All Around," 1968

Trower, Robin, RIAA Gold Album, "Bridge of Sighs," 1974

Troy, Doris, "Just One Look," 1963

Tucker, Marshall, Band, "Fire on the Mountain," 1976

Tucker, Marshall, Band, RIAA Gold Albums, "The Marshall Tucker Band," 1975; "Where We All Belong," 1975; "Searchin' for a Rainbow," 1976

Tucker, Tanya, "Lizzie and the Rainman," 1975

Tucker, Tommy, "Hi-Heel Sneakers," 1964

Tune Rockers, "The Green Mosquito," 1958

Tune Weavers, "Happy, Happy Birthday, Baby," 1957

Turbans, "When You Dance," 1955

Turner, Ike and Tina, "A Fool in Love," 1960; "It's Gonna Work Out Fine," 1961; "Poor Fool," 1961; "I Want to Take You Higher," 1970; "Proud Mary," 1971, RIAA 71; "Nutbush City Limits," 1972

Turner, Ike and Tina, RIAA Gold Album, "What You Hear Is What You Get," 1972

Turner, Jesse Lee, "Little Space Girl," 1959

Turner, Joe, "Corrina, Corrina," 1956

Turner, Sammy, "Lavender Blue," 1959; "Always," 1959

Turner, Spyder, "Stand By Me," 1966

Turtles, "It Ain't Me Babe," 1965; "Let Me Be," 1965; "You Baby," 1966; "Happy Together," 1967, RIAA 67; "She'd Rather Be with Me," 1967; "You Know What I Mean," 1967; "She's My Girl," 1967; "Elenore," 1968; "You Showed Me," 1969

Turtles, RIAA Gold Album, "Turtles' Greatest Hits," 1968

Twitty, Conway, "It's Only Make Believe," 1958; "The Story of My Love," 1959; "Mona Lisa," 1959; "Danny Boy," 1959; "Lonely Blueboy," 1960; "What Am I Living For," 1960; "Is a Blue Bird Blue?" 1960; "C'est Si Bon," 1961; "You've Never Been This Far Before," 1973

Twitty, Conway, RIAA Gold Album, "You've Never Been This Far Before," 1976

Tyler, Frankie (Frankie Valli), "I Go Ape," 1973

Tymes, "So Much in Love," 1963; "Wonderful! Wonderful!" 1963; "Somewhere," 1963; "People," 1968; "You Little Trustmaker," 1975

Underground Sunshine, "Birthday," 1969

Undisputed Truth, "Smiling Faces Sometimes," 1971

Unifics, "Court of Love," 1968

Unit Four Plus Two, "Concrete and Clay," 1965

Upchurch, Philip, Combo, "You Can't Sit Down, Part 2," 1961

Uriah Heep, "Easy Livin'," 1972

Uriah Heep, RIAA Gold Albums, "Demons and Wizards," 1972; "The Magician's Birthday," 1973; "Uriah Heep Live," 1973; "Sweet Freedom," 1974

Vale, Jerry, "Innamorata," 1956; "You Don't Know Me," 1956; "Have You Looked Into Your Heart," 1964

Valens, Ritchie, "Come On, Let's Go," 1958; "Donna," 1958; "La Bamba," 1959

Valino, Joe, "Garden of Eden," 1959

Valjean, "Theme from 'Ben Casey'," 1962

Valli, Frankie, "(You're Gonna) Hurt Yourself," 1966; "Can't Take My Eyes Off You," 1967, RIAA 67; "I Make a Fool of Myself," 1967; "To Give (The Reason I Live)," 1967; "My Eyes Adored You," 1975, RIAA 75; "Our Day Will Come," 1975; "Fallen Angel," 1976

Valli, June, "The Wedding," 1958

Van Cliburn, RIAA Gold Album, "Tchiakovsky Concerto," 1961

Van Dyke, Leroy, "Auctioneer," 1956; "Walk on By," 1961

Vanilla Fudge, "You Keep Me Hangin' On," 1968

Vanilla Fudge, RIAA Gold Album, "Vanilla Fudge," 1968

Vanity Fare, "Early in the Morning," 1969; "Hitchin' a Ride," 1970

Vaughan, Sarah, "Whatever Lola Wants," 1955; "C'Est La Vie," 1955; "Mr. Wonderful," 1956; "Broken-Hearted Melody," 1959

Vaughn, Billy, "Melody of Love," 1955; "The Shifting Whispering Sands," 1955; "When the White Lilacs Bloom Again," 1956; "Sail Along Silvery Moon," 1957; "Raunchy," 1957; "La Paloma," 1958; "Look for a Star," 1960; "A Swingin' Safari," 1962

Vaughn, Billy, RIAA Gold Albums, "Sail Along Silvery Moon," 1962; "Theme from *A Summer Place*," 1962; "Blue Hawaii," 1962; "Golden Instrumentals," 1969

Vee, Bobby, "Devil or Angel," 1960; "Rubber Ball," 1960; "Stayin' In," 1961; "Take Good Care of My Baby," 1961; "Run to Him," 1961; "Please Don't Ask About Barbara," 1962; "Sharing You," 1962; "Punish Her," 1962; "The Night Has a Thousand Eyes," 1962; "Charms," 1963; "Come Back When You Grow Up," 1967, RIAA 67; "My Girl"/"Hey Girl (Medley)," 1968

269

Velvets, "Tonight (Could Be the Night)," 1961

Ventures, "Walk, Don't Run," 1960; "Perfidia," 1960; "Ram-Bunk-Shush," 1961; "Walk, Don't Run '64," 1964; "Slaughter on Tenth Avenue," 1964; "Hawaii Five-O," 1969

Ventures, RIAA Gold Albums, "Golden Greats," 1970; "The Ventures Play Telstar, Lonely Bull and Others," 1970; "Hawaii Five-O," 1971

Vera, Billy, "With Pen in Hand," 1968

Verne, Larry, "Mr. Custer," 1960

Vibrations, "The Watusi," 1961; "My Girl Sloopy," 1964

Village Stompers, "Washington Square," 1963

Vincent, Gene, "Be-Bop-A-Lula," 1956; "Lotta Lovin'," 1957

Vinton, Bobby, "Roses Are Red," 1962, RIAA 62; "Rain, Rain Go Away," 1962; "Over the Mountain (Across the Sea)," 1963; "Blue on Blue," 1963; "Blue Velvet," 1963; "There! I've Said It Again," 1963; "My Heart Belongs to Only You," 1964; "Tell Me Why," 1964; "Clinging Vine," 1964; "Mr. Lonely," 1964; "Long Lonely Night," 1965; "L-O-N-E-L-Y," 1965; "Satin Pillows," 1965; "Coming Home Soldier," 1966; "Please Love Me Forever," 1967; "Just as Much as Ever," 1967; "Halfway to Paradise," 1968; "I Love How You Love Me," 1968, RIAA 68; "Every Day of My Life," 1972; "Sealed with a Kiss," 1972; "My Melody of Love," 1974, RIAA 74; "Beer Barrel Polka," 1975; "Save Your Kisses for Me," 1976

Vinton, Bobby, RIAA Gold Albums, "Bobby Vinton's Greatest Hits," 1966; "Melodies of Love," 1974

Virtues, "Guitar Boogie Shuffle," 1959

Viscounts, "Harlem Nocturne," 1960

Vito and The Salutations, "Unchained Melody," 1963

Vogues, "You're the One," 1965; "Five O'Clock World," 1965; "Magic Town," 1966; "The Land of Milk and Honey," 1966; "Turn Around, Look at Me," 1968; "My Special Angel," 1968; "Till," 1968

Volumes, "I Love You," 1962

Wade, Adam, "Take Good Care of Her," 1961; "The Writing on the Wall," 1961; "As If I Don't Know You," 1961

Wadsworth Mansion, "Sweet Mary," 1970

Wailers, "Tall Cool One," 1959

Wainright III, Loudon, "Dead Skunk in the Middle of the Road," 1973

Wakeman, Rick, RIAA Gold Albums, "Journey to the Centre of the Earth," 1974; "The Six Wives of Henry VIII," 1975

Washington, Dinah, "What a Diff'rence a Day Makes," 1959; "Unforgettable," 1959; "This Bitter Earth," 1960; "Love Walked In," 1960; "September in the Rain," 1961; "Where Are You," 1962

Watts, Noble "Thin Man," "Hard Times (The Slop)," 1975

Watts 103rd Street Rhythm Band with Charles Wright, "Do Your Thing," 1969; "Love Land," 1970; "Express Yourself," 1970

Wattstax (Various Artists), RIAA Gold Album, "Wattstax, The Living Word," 1973

Wayne, Thomas, "Tragedy," 1959

Weatherly, Jim, "Need to Be," 1974

Weber, Joan, "Let Me Go, Lover," 1954-55

We Five, "You Were on My Mind," 1965; "Let's Get Together," 1965

Weissberg, Eric, and Steve Mandell, "Dueling Banjos," 1973, RIAA 73

Welch, Lenny, "Since I Fell for You," 1963; "Ebb Tide," 1964; "Breaking Up Is Hard to Do," 1970

Welk, Lawrence, "Moritat (A Theme from *The Three Penny Opera),*" 1956; "Last Date," 1960; "Calcutta," 1961, RIAA 61

Welk, Lawrence, RIAA Gold Albums, "Calcutta Album," 1961; "Winchester Cathedral," 1967

Wells, Mary, "The One Who Really Loves You," 1961; "You Beat Me to the Punch," 1962; "Two Lovers," 1962; "Laughing Boy," 1963; "You Lost the Sweetest Boy," 1963; "What's Easy for Two Is So Hard for One," 1963; "My Guy," 1964

Wesley, Fred, and The J.B.'s, "Doing It to Death," 1973, RIAA 73

Weston, Kim (see Marvin Gaye and Kim Weston), "Take Me in Your Arms," 1965

Wet Willie, "Keep on Smilin'," 1974

Wheeler, Billy Edd, "Ode to the Little Brown Shack Out Back," 1965

Whitcomb, Ian, "You Turn Me On," 1965

White, Barry, "I'm Gonna Love You Just a Little More," 1973, RIAA 73; "Never, Never Gonna Give You Up," 1974, RIAA 74; "Can't Get Enough of Your Love, Babe," 1974, RIAA 74; "You're the First, the Last, My Everything," 1974, RIAA 74

White, Barry, RIAA Gold Albums, "I've Got So Much to Give," 1973; "Stone Gone," 1974; "Can't Get Enough," 1974; "Just Another Way to Say I Love You," 1975; "Barry White's Greatest Hits," 1976

White, Tony Joe, "Polk Salad Annie," 1969

White Plains, "My Baby Loves Lovin'," 1970

Whiting, Margaret, "The Wheel of Hurt," 1966

Whittaker, Roger, "The Last Farewell," 1975; "Durham Town," 1976

Who, "My Generation," 1966; "Happy Jack," 1967; "I Can See for Miles,"

1967; "Magic Bus," 1968; "Pinball Wizard," 1969; "I'm Free,"
1969; "Summertime Blues," 1970; "See Me, Feel Me," 1970; "Won't
Get Fooled Again," 1971; "Behind Blue Eyes," 1971; "Join Together," 1972; "Squeeze Box," 1976

Who, RIAA Gold Albums, "Tommy," 1969; "Live at Leeds," 1970; "Who's
Next," 1971; "Meaty, Beaty, Big, and Bouncy," 1972; "Quadro-
phenia," 1973; "Odds and Sods," 1974; "The Who By Numbers,"
1975

Wild Cherry, "Play That Funky Music," 1976

Wild Cherry, RIAA Gold Album, "Wild Cherry," 1976

Williams, Andy, "Canadian Sunset," 1956; "Baby Doll," 1956; "Butterfly,"
1957; "I Like Your Kind of Love," 1957; "Lips of Wine," 1957;
"Are You Sincere," 1958; "Promise Me, Love," 1958; "The Hawai-
ian Wedding Song," 1959; "Lonely Street," 1959; "The Village of
St. Bernadette," 1959; "The Bilbao Song," 1961; "Can't Get Used
to Losing You"/"Days of Wine and Roses," 1963; "A Fool Never
Learns," 1964; "On the Street Where You Live," 1964; "Dear
Heart," 1964; "Music to Watch Girls By," 1967; "Happy Heart,"
1969; "(Where Do I Begin) Love Story," 1971; "Love Theme from
The Godfather," 1972

Williams, Andy, RIAA Gold Albums, "Days of Wine and Roses," 1963;
"Moon River and Other Great Movie Themes," 1963; "The Wonder-
ful World of Andy Williams," 1964; "Andy Williams Christmas Al-
bum," 1964; "Call Me Irresponsible," 1964; "Dear Heart," 1965;
"Great Songs from *My Fair Lady*," 1965; "The Shadow of Your
Smile," 1966; "Born Free," 1967; "Love, Andy," 1968; "Merry
Christmas," 1968; "Honey," 1968; "Happy Heart," 1969; "Get
Together," 1970; "Love Story," 1971; "Andy Williams' Greatest
Hits," 1971; "Love Theme from *The Godfather*," 1972

Williams, Billy, "I'm Gonna Sit Right Down and Write Myself a Letter,"
1957

Williams, Danny, "White on White," 1964

Williams, Hank, RIAA Gold Albums, "Hank Williams' Greatest Hits," 1969;
"Your Cheatin' Heart," 1969

Williams, Larry, "Short Fat Fannie," 1957; "Bony Moronie," 1957

Williams, Mason, "Classical Gas," 1968

Williams, Maurice, and The Zodiacs, "Stay," 1960

Williams, Otis, and His Charms, "Ivory Tower," 1956

Williams, Roger, "Autumn Leaves," 1955; "Almost Paradise," 1957; "Till,"
1957; "Near You," 1958; "Born Free," 1966

Williams, Roger, RIAA Gold Albums, "Till," 1967; "Songs of the Fabulous
Fifties, Vol. 1," 1967; "Songs of the Fabulous Fifties, Vol. 2,"

1967; "I Was Made to Love Her," 1967; "I'm Wondering," 1967; "Shoo-Be-Doo-Be-Doo-Da-Day," 1968; "For Once in My Life," 1968; "My Cherie Amour," 1969; "Yester-Me, Yester-You, Yester-day," 1969; "Never Had a Dream Come True," 1970; "Signed, Sealed, Delivered, I'm Yours," 1970; "Heaven Help Us All," 1970; "We Can Work It Out," 1971; "If You Really Love Me," 1971; "Superstition," 1972; "Higher Ground," 1972; "Livin' for the City," 1973; "Don't Worry 'Bout a Thing," 1973; "You Haven't Done Nothin'," 1974; "Boogie on Reggae Woman," 1974

Wood, Brenton, "The Oogum Boogum Stog," 1967; "Gimme Little Sign," 1967; "Baby You Got It," 1967

Wooley, Sheb, "The Purple People Eater," 1958

Worth, Marion, "Shake Me I Rattle (Squeeze Me I Cry)," 1962

Wray, Link, and His Ray Men, "Rumble," 1958; "Raw-Hide," 1959

Wright, Betty, "Girls Can't Do What the Guys Do," 1968; "Clean Up Woman," 1971, RIAA 71

Wright, Gary, "Dream Weaver," 1976, RIAA 76; "Love Is Alive," 1976

Wright, Gary, RIAA Gold Album, "The Dream Weaver," 1976

Wynette, Tammy, "D-I-V-O-R-C-E," 1968; "Stand By Your Man," 1968

Wynette, Tammy, RIAA Gold Album, "Tammy's Greatest Hits," 1970

Yarbrough, Glenn, "Baby the Rain Must Fall," 1965

Yardbirds, "For Your Love," 1965; "Heart Full of Soul," 1965; "I'm a Man," 1965; "Shapes of Things," 1966; "Over Under Sideways Down," 1966; "Happenings Ten Years Time Ago," 1966

Yellow Balloon, "Yellow Balloon," 1967

Yes, "Roundabout," 1972

Yes, RIAA Gold Albums, "Fragile," 1972; "Close to the Edge," 1972; "Yessongs," 1973; "The Yes Album," 1973; "Tales from Topo-graphic Oceans," 1974; "Relayer," 1974

Young, Barry, "One Has My Name," 1965

Youngbloods, "Get Together," 1969, RIAA 69

Young, Faron, "Hello Walls," 1961

Young-Holt Unlimited, "Soulful Strut," 1969, RIAA 69

Young, Kathy, and The Innocents, "A Thousand Stars," 1960; "Happy Birth-day Blues," 1961

Young, John Paul, "Yesterday's Hero," 1976

Young, Neil, "Heart of Gold," 1972, RIAA 72; "Old Man," 1972; "Only Love Can Break Your Heart," 1972

Young, Neil, RIAA Gold Albums, "After the Gold Rush," 1970; "Harvest," 1972; "Time Fades Away," 1973; "On the Beach," 1974

Young, Neil, and Crazy Horse, RIAA Gold Album, "Everybody Knows This Is Nowhere," 1970

Young Rascals (see Rascals)

Young, Victor, "Around the World," 1957

Yuro, Timi, "Hurt," 1961; "I Apologize," 1961; "What's a Matter Baby," 1962; "Make the World Go Away," 1963

Zacharias, Helmut, "When the White Lilacs Bloom Again," 1956

Zacherle, John (The "Cool Ghoul"), "Dinner with Drac," 1958

Zager & Evans, "In the Year 2525," 1969, RIAA 69

Zappa, Frank, RIAA Gold Album, "Apostrophe," 1976

Zentner, Si, "Up a Lazy River," 1961

Zombies, "She's Not There," 1964; "Tell Her No," 1965; "Time of the Season," 1969, RIAA 69

Z. Z. Top, "Tush," 1975

Z. Z. Top, RIAA Gold Albums, "Tres Hombres," 1974; "Fandango," 1975

276